SOCIAL
MOVEMENTS
AND
POLITICAL
POWER

SOCIAL MOVEMENTS AND POLITICAL POWER

Emerging Forms of Radicalism in the West

CARL BOGGS

Temple University Press Philadelphia

Temple University Press, Philadelphia 19122

Copyright © 1986 by Temple University. All rights reserved

Published 1986

Printed in the United States of America

The paper used in this publication meets the minimum

requirements of American National Standard for

Information Sciences—Permanence of Paper for Printed

Library Materials,

ANSI Z39.48-1984

Library of Congress Cataloging-in-Publication Data

Boggs, Carl.

Social movements and political power.

Includes index.

1. Radicalism—Europe.   2. Radicalism—United

States.   3. Social movements—Europe.   4. Social

movements—United States.   I. Title.

HN380.Z9R33   1986   303.4′84   86-6045

ISBN 0-87722-447-1 (alk. paper)

For Michele Prichard

CONTENTS

PREFACE

The inspiration for this book grew out of a discussion with Carla Ravaioli, an Italian independent left-wing senator and feminist author, at a restaurant in Rome in November 1982. Ravaioli, a longtime political activist and ex-member of the Italian Communist party (PCI), suggested that I write a book on new forms of social struggle that, in her opinion, were reshaping the terrain of political conflict in the West while also undermining many familiar and cherished Marxist premises. As someone committed to a vision of radical social and cultural change that the major leftist parties had failed to pursue—and who felt strongly about the primacy of local activism and grassroots democracy—she had become progressively disillusioned with conventional politics yet hopeful that revitalized popular movements would, in the not-too-distant future, generate fresh alternatives. Although scholarly and journalistic treatments of the new social movements had already appeared in Western Europe and the United States, Ravaioli argued that the topic might be usefully approached from a somewhat different angle, from the viewpoint of a writer who, like herself, was attached to Marxist politics but who had become more and more uneasy with its restrictive categories of thought and action. Having just finished a book on the political thought of Antonio Gramsci and the development of Western Marxism, I had returned to Italy for the purpose of further pursuing my earlier work on the Italian left and the Communist party in particular. So I was initially hesitant to follow Ravaioli's sound advice, whatever the logic of her observations or the intensity of my own concern with those issues surrounding the proliferation of the new movements. The appearance of this book, rather than yet another volume on Italian Marxism or Communism, attests to her persuasiveness.

The more deeply I became involved in this project, the more I was aware of a definite continuity from my previous work, which on the whole centered on a Gramscian preoccupation with elaborating the conceptual basis of a new radicalism, and the present effort. For what the Gramscian theory of a counterhegemonic politics, the radical critique of Eurocommunism, and the problematic of the new movements all share is the idea of an emergent post-Marxist paradigm applicable to the conditions of advanced industrial society. This reflection on Gramsci will strike many readers as questionable, given Gramsci's long association with the PCI, his involvement in the Comintern, and his abiding commitment to Marxism as both philosophy and politics. What seems equally compelling, however, is the distinctly "critical" or "Western" character of Gramsci's Marxism which, particularly in his later work, stressed the concerns of ideology, culture, and politics and represents a marked shift away from the thematic of political economy. From this viewpoint, a reading of the *Prison Notebooks* might suggest the glimpses of a post-Marxist discourse struggling to free itself from traditional categories—though Gramsci clearly was not in a position to articulate it as such. As for Eurocommunism (notably in Italy), its obvious slide toward a moderate social-democratic reformism despite organizational residues of Leninism and a symbolic attachment to revolutionary ideology reveals once again the failure of even a reconstituted Marxism to produce a viable transformative strategy in the West. For a number of reasons that I spell out in this study, the fate of Marxist parties in the developed countries has been one of two political extremes, either isolation or assimilation. In this context, the new social forces that first appeared on a mass scale in the 1960s can be viewed as the initial expression of a (potential) radical-democratic or post-Marxist alternative.

Posed in this fashion, the question immediately arises as to what is explicitly "new" or novel about contemporary forms of conflict. It might be argued that there is little real originality in the popular struggles concerning peace, the environment, feminism, direct democracy, and the quality of urban life that emphasizes uniquely "postmaterialist" themes and goals; after all, precursors of such phenomena go back to the middle of the nineteenth century and even earlier. And this is true enough. Still, the novelty of the current movements lies not so much in the discovery of new values and goals as in the historical convergence of economic conditions, social forces, and political expressions within which they are located. Put more directly, the new movements embody a range of diverse and popular forms of revolt over issues that seem endemic to the phase of mature industrial development: economic stagnation, ecological disequilibrium, militarism and nuclear politics, bureaucracy. It is this confluence of objective circumstances and subjective responses, historical opportunities and ideological themes, global crises and popular movements that promises to fundamentally alter the terrain of theoretical discourse and political action. It is precisely this set of conditions that infuses post-Marxist radicalism with historical meaning and potential.

This is not to suggest that a post-Marxist politics is today an accomplished reality, or even that the discourse itself possesses, in the 1980s, the kind of coherence that has typified Marxism or even liberalism during the past century. On the contrary, as I argue in the following pages, a post-Marxist paradigm is *emergent* insofar as its development is partial, limited, and fragmentary, its theoretical basis is weak, and its efforts to achieve strategic articulation are embryonic (and often futile). This predicament, which is natural enough given the unformed and fluid character of the new movements, makes its way into the very title of this book—that is, it corresponds to the ongoing dialectic between the thrust of social movements and the imperatives of political power. The reality is that a radical-democratic insurgency cannot be given practical substance without the leverage made possible by control over state institutions (however remolded). At the same time, the very process of winning and administering power imposes its own dilemmas and constraints. The new movements, as we shall see, have given rise to different strategies for confronting such dilemmas and constraints, and these strategies, too, have been largely partial and even contradictory, to the extent, in some instances, of closing off rather than enlarging space for the diffusion of local movements.

In view of the restrictions imposed by any choice of political strategy, and taking into account the rightward shift of political consensus in many advanced societies, one is tempted to approach this situation with a jaundiced eye: the new movements are in decline, the system has overcome its legitimation crisis, and the new oppositional forms have simply failed to achieve their objectives. Such a judgment, however, would be very shortsighted, even granted its empirical validity. In the broad historical scheme of things, the new movements are still in their infancy whereas, at the same time, the pervasive crises that help to account for them do not seem about to disappear. It is thus likely that the ideological content of the movements, even where their constituencies may not be in perpetual motion, will remain a focus of politics in one form or another well into the future. Harmony, equilibrium, and stability will probably not be enduring features of the global system. To speak of an "irreversible decline" or "death" of the new movements strictly on the basis of brief periods of inertia, therefore, seems quite misleading and ahistorical. What seems most obvious is that, although the old paradigm of oppositional politics is waning, a new one has yet to fully emerge (or at least achieve hegemony on the left). Whether a new, post-Marxist alternative reaches this status will ultimately depend upon a mixture of intellectual, cultural, political, and even global factors that cannot be accurately predicted by even the most sophisticated techniques of social science analysis. This book seeks only to chart various tendencies at work that, under the proper mix of circumstances, could furnish the essence of a lively transformative political culture. There is no assumption of unilinear patterns of development or universal agencies of social progress. My purpose is to identify and analyze the nature of emergent social forces and political formations, not to offer a formula for their success.

It follows that even if we can demonstrate a profound rightward shift in either policies or popular consciousness, this does not short-circuit theoretical efforts to understand oppositional forces as historical phenomena. Relatively brief ideological shifts, especially those linked to changes in electoral fortunes, tend to be cyclical; the presumed triumph of conservatism might well be more short-lived than is commonly supposed. Despite widespread gloom and pessimism on the left, there is little to indicate that we have reached an end to history. Further, the extent of the rightward trajectory itself (though undeniably real) might be far more limited than most observers contend. Even in those countries where conservatism seems to reign, new forms of mass-based opposition have come to the fore and remain very much alive. Thus, the England of Margaret Thatcher has experienced, in the militant and prolonged miners' strike, the most explosive labor struggles of any country in the postwar period; the West Germany of Helmut Kohl has witnessed the continuation of broad citizens' initiatives and the rise of the Greens; and the United States of Ronald Reagan has seen the emergence of a rainbow coalition of popular movements that, though enfeebled after 1984, is likely to remain a powerful force in grassroots politics. Elsewhere, Socialist parties have won or retained power in nearly a dozen Western European countries while, in the Third World, progressive struggles have intensified in Central America, Haiti, Chile, South Africa, the Philippines, and South Korea. The point is not that worldwide revolution is on the horizon, but that the theme of a global right-wing insurgency in the 1980s—with its frequent corollary that the left has been defeated—is often dramatically exaggerated. Popular movements are, by their very nature, typically in a state of transition or even disarray, but they are scarcely historical relics no longer deserving of serious analysis.

My aim is to explore the historical meaning of the new social movements, notably in relation to their strategic potential as it intersects with the sphere of state power. Chapter 2 lays out the material and political conditions that have shaped these movements, presents a typology of movements, identifies the main constituent elements of a new radicalism, and scrutinizes its implications for the Marxist tradition. In the next three chapters I analyze the strategic channeling of the new movements into political formations that compete for power in widely divergent geographical areas: Eurosocialism in the Mediterranean, the new populism in the United States, the Green alternative in West Germany. These strategic models are ideal types insofar as they do not correspond perfectly to new-movement themes and constituencies or to a well-delineated post-Marxist paradigm. On the contrary, an underlying motif of this book is the intractible conflict between the rhythm and energy of the new movements and the political efforts to give them strategic efficacy. Nor do they exhaust every conceivable post-Marxist possibility, although quite clearly the variants I have chosen to study are the only ones to secure a real electoral or political presence in the West. And of course these types overlap considerably in both their ideological thematic and their geographical location, so that there is no intent to suggest, for example, that Green politics is necessarily confined to northern Europe or that certain of its features cannot be found in Eurosocialism and the new populism.

Yet to the degree that each strategy does possess a logic and history (and potential) of its own, the framework I have constructed is not derived from an arbitrary set of criteria. Each alternative confronts a range of opportunities and choices, as well as dilemmas and contradictions, unique to its own setting; each internalizes features of a distinct political culture or national tradition that it seeks to redefine in post-Marxist terms. Although it would be absurd to postulate any universal model, surely the cumulative experiences (positive and negative) of the three strategic options will contribute to a further theorization of radical-democratic politics for the industrialized countries.

The selection of these three examples makes further sense from the standpoint of my own intellectual concerns and personal history. A focus on Eurosocialism can be understood as the continuation of my previous work in the area of southern European politics and my familiarity, since the 1960s, with the Mediterranean left. My fascination with the new populism can be explained in part by my having lived for the past eight years in Santa Monica, California, where progressives guided by this outlook were able to establish their first municipal stronghold, affording me an intimate vantage point from which to observe the concrete workings of this strategy. And my interest in Green politics has been reinforced by a familiarity with West German society that comes from a two-year residency there and several subsequent visits. In each case my own involvements were complemented by interviews and discussions with activists and knowledgeable observers. The vitality of popular movements in each of these areas has made the task of arriving at generalizations grounded in comparative analysis all the easier.

Of course, comparisons of this sort cannot always be established with ease, given immense cultural, political, and geographical variations from one country to another. In what sense are France, Italy, Spain, Greece, West Germany, and the United State comparable? The answer is that few rigorous conclusions applicable to all of these societies are likely to be sustained. Here, as elsewhere, cross-national statements have to be qualified so that contextual differences can be incorporated into the analysis. Still, the industrialized setting of Western Europe and North America does present a range of common challenges, problems, and restraints that, taken together, allow for a cross-national treatment of movements, ideologies, the state, and strategic options that, after all, are not infinite in their variety. Just as there is (within limits) a certain universal logic to capitalist development or bureaucratic integration, there are identifiable patterns of social conflict throughout the industrialized world—all the more so in a period of tightening international economic pressures. In any event, a comparative study of movements and parties must inevitably concentrate on both contrasts and similarities.

This project might never have been completed without the generous contributions of those who offered criticisms and suggestions, provided research guidance and contacts, assisted in preparation of the manuscript, and lent their personal support. The very multiplicity of social movements, conceptual themes, and geographical locales that entered into this study—a reflection perhaps of aims that were grandiose—has made such contributions indispensable. I have chosen to tap the knowledge, experience, and insights of people from disparate points in the ideological spectrum, from liberals to anarchists, from orthodox Marxists to democratic socialists, from populists to Trotskyists—without, I hope, losing sight of my own line of argument. Indeed, my ideas have typically been sharpened or refined, and in some cases significantly recast, in the aftermath of vigorous discussions with colleagues, students, political observers, and friends, during many visits to Europe and a year's stay in Canada.

The chapter on Eurosocialism benefited from interviews and conversations with, or manuscript reviews from, Piero Cammarano, Fernando Claudin, Jim Cohen, Isidre Molas, Leo Panitch, James Petras, Iannis Pissimissus, Larry Portis, José Rodriguez-Ibañez, Daniel Singer, Michalis Spourdolakis, and Henri Weber. I am particularly indebted to Mark Kesselman for his always incisive and constructive responses to my work and his support over several years of correspondence.

The chapter on the new populism, which began with an earlier article I wrote for *Theory and Society* in 1981, owes much to the contributions of John Friedmann, Mark Kann, Laurie Lieberman, Jeff Lustig, Karin Palley, Stephanie Pincetl, Frances Fox Piven, David Smith, and Don Villarejo.

Perhaps more than for any other part of this book, work on the Greens necessarily relied upon the inputs of many people, including Rudolf Bahro, Margaret Fitzsimmons, Gunter Frankenberg, Phil Hill, Joaquim Hirsch, Gary Hudson, Otto Kallscheuer, Dieter Lange, Carl Lankowski, Margit Mayer, Wolf-Dieter Narr, Roland Roth, Christine Schröter, and Roland Vogt. Above all, I wish to thank Marty Bennett for his warm encouragement and for his painstaking critiques of this and other sections of the manuscript.

Among those who contributed in some way to my general understanding of popular movements, social change, and political strategy— or who were kind enough to review various parts or all of the manuscript—I wish to thank Pete Ayrton, Murray Bookchin, Tom Cahill, Robert Leventer, Karen Lucas, Stan Weir, the Saint Louis *Theory and Society* group, Peter Marris, Peter Olney, Dimitri Roussopoulos, Tom Shapiro, and Susan Weissman. I am especially indebted to David Langille, whose contagious enthusiasm for this book helped sustain my sometimes waning energies through 1984–85; he perhaps more than anyone shared my commitment to the vision that emerges here, and he was a constant source of references and ideas. I am grateful to Franz

Baumann, Else Brock, Scott Krier, and Helmut Rez for their help in research and manuscript preparation. Many ideas that found their way into this volume were first encountered in two seminars I conducted on the theories of social movements—one in urban planning at UCLA in spring 1984 and the other in political science at Carleton University in Ottawa in spring 1985, where student participation was quite lively. Among the Carleton students I particularly wish to thank are Peter Bleyer, Ernie Keenes, Bruce Tate, and May Yee. Finally, without the personal encouragement of Christine Covert, Janet Francendese of Temple University Press, Katherine Kovacs, Ray Pratt, Clare Spark, and especially Michele Prichard, this endeavor would have been far less than what it is.

SOCIAL
MOVEMENTS
AND
POLITICAL
POWER

1

THE NEW GLOBAL
CONTEXT OF
SOCIAL MOVEMENTS

This book explores the dynamics of modern social movements, their origins, historical setting, ideologies, internal development, popular constituencies, and, above all, their political trajectories. Throughout the advanced industrial world a rather novel historical conjuncture has given rise, over the past two decades, to literally thousands of local movements bearing almost every conceivable description and enlisting the participation of millions of people: neighborhood groups, environmentalists, women and gays, peace and anti-intervention activists, youth and students, the unemployed, and those involved in the urban struggles of minorities, welfare recipients, tenants, squatters, and the generally disenfranchised. On the contemporary landscape of North America and Western Europe such movements constitute the social basis of recurrent mobilizations for progressive change. Insofar as they are the outgrowth of what Alain Touraine calls the "crisis of industrial culture," they can be understood as potentially decisive agents of historical transformation.[1] From this viewpoint social movements of the "new" variety—that is, movements that are not primarily grounded in labor struggles—do not appear as exceptional or dramatic events but lie permanently at the core of a transformed political universe. They are clearly distinct from the momentary or "primitive" upheavals observed during earlier phases of capitalist development. Contemporary social movements are thus hardly marginal expressions of protest but are situated within the unfolding contradictions of a rapidly changing industrial order, as part of the historic attempts to secure genuine democracy, social equality, and peaceful international relations against the imperatives of exploitation and domination.

Although these movements have roots in earlier (even preindustrial) traditions, as possible transformative agencies they have barely emerged from infancy. And even though they have yet to conquer significant bastions of institutional power in any country, they have begun to lay the groundwork for a new paradigm of oppositional discourse. Their success accordingly cannot be easily measured or quantified. Hence, the fact that they have nowhere overturned the status quo should not obscure their historical importance in posing new issues, shaping consciousness, and opening new areas of political discourse. Indeed, many time-honored debates have already been fundamentally recast in both substance and tone—for example, over the meaning of socialism, the tension between reform and revolution, the ways of viewing political strategy, and, ultimately, the value of Marxist theory itself. The new movements (and their theoretical articulations) have amply illuminated the problematic character of inherited intellectual and political belief systems.

These new circumstances are the expression of a disintegrating world capitalist system in which new economic conditions are undermining traditional social and political forces. The proliferation of social movements at the metropolitan core of an extensive global network can be seen as part of a conflict between a declining but still vigorous system of domination and newly emergent forms of opposition. Ruling blocs in the United States, Western Europe, and Japan have naturally tried to reverse impending decline through a variety of ambitious stratagems. These include state and regionally directed modes of capital accumulation, technological restructuring, and (notably in the United States) rekindling of the arms race. The goal appears to be nothing short of a comprehensive commodification and rationalization of the world. From the vantage point of the mid-1980s these efforts seem to have strengthened the power structures of the leading capitalist nations, while mass depoliticization is perhaps more widespread than at any time since the 1950s. Yet the very interests that seek to universalize their control over all spheres of human existence have simultaneously produced counter-tendencies in the form of economic stagnation, ecological crisis, the erosion of pluralist democracy, a decaying bourgeois culture, and, most ominously, the nuclear threat to global survival. Poverty, repression, social violence, and a pervasive sense of alienation are the fate of increasingly large numbers of people subjected to this regimen in societies conventionally regarded as democratic and affluent.

Of course, depoliticization is typical of a cultural milieu in which cynicism and withdrawal—not to mention the more destructive realities of alcoholism, drug addiction, mental illness, and suicide—are widespread. But the multiple and far-reaching structures of domination in the West have at the same time generated collective forms of resistance, embodied mainly in the new social movements that have flourished largely outside the established political system. In their most mature expression, these movements constitute counterhegemonic struggles in the Gramscian sense to the degree they can lead to an alternative ideological framework that subverts the dominant patterns of thought and action, that challenges myths surrounding the vulnerability of the status quo. Surely the undeniable fact that the new movements initially appeared on the periphery of the political system does not by itself call into question their radical meaning or potential.

Still, it would be foolish to pretend that such movements are free of the contradictions and ambiguities endemic to the social world itself. The very forces and conditions that permeate the structures of domination also shape the nature of resistance and revolt. Social change occurs through a long, uneven historical process that is governed by no linear or lawlike patterns. Even if it could be shown that successive popular mobilizations since the 1960s have established the basis of a subversive political culture, their structural presence is still partial, fragmented, and dispersed—all the more so, given the tide of conservatism sweeping many of the advanced countries in the 1980s. The obstacles to further expansion are many. Probably the most intractable roadblock concerns the capacity of these mobilizations to achieve a generalized (and effective) political impact. It is precisely this—the struggle for a political translation of the new movements—that motivates and gives definition to this study.

Liberalism, which in one guise or another has shaped the European and American political tradition for more than two centuries, today stands far removed from the orbit of the new movements. A hegemonic ideology well into the postwar period, liberalism has since the 1960s steadily disintegrated in the wake of the Vietnam defeat, the new left, economic stagnation, expansion of the authoritarian state, and cold-war mobilization. By the 1980s it had degenerated into a corporate liberalism, the main function of which is to legitimate an outmoded power structure.

This historical reality runs counter to the long-standing claims of the American pluralist heritage. After all, the liberalism of Locke, Jefferson, Bentham, and J. S. Mill had celebrated the virtues of open debate, individual freedom, pluralism, and democratic participation. Tocqueville saw in the liberal political culture of nineteenth-century America a truly civic spirit and sense of involvement that corresponded to a unique blend of community and freedom. The highly visible flaws of "protective democracy," to use C. B. Macpherson's term,[2] were gradually rectified by the extension of citizenship as new social groups entered the political arena. Over time, minorities, workers, women, and others were eventually able to win basic political rights. In its period of ascendancy, liberalism represented, perhaps more than any other tradition, a secular challenge to the feudal legacy of state religion, an ethic of tolerance and individualism directed against all forms of authoritarian control, and a commitment to personal and social autonomy in opposition to the conformist impulses of both right and left.

But liberalism in practice departed increasingly from this original vision. In the United States, its realization depended in great measure upon a self-regulating market, abundant territorial space and natural resources, dynamic community life, and, later, prospects for seemingly endless material growth. It also required a world order in which American economic interests had more or less unlimited room for maneuver. By the 1960s, however, none of these conditions prevailed any longer, with the result that liberalism was finally transformed into a ritualized belief system barely masking a highly centralized and expansionist corporate system. In economic terms liberalism failed to generate any new priorities that could encourage a shift away from outmoded patterns of production, work, and consumption. Moreover, Keynesian efforts to counteract the severe repercussions of capitalist cyclical decline through state-management techniques only reproduced more of the same—varying mixtures of unemployment, inflation, and instability—alongside a swollen bureaucratic apparatus.[3] Politically, the social and institutional pluralism applauded by liberal theorists collapsed into a rigid corporatist framework of bargaining among competing interest groups. The cherished two-party system atrophied to the point where the parties lost any real capacity to mobilize popular constituencies or carry out imaginative programs. Such closure of the public sphere coincided with the emergence of a depoliticized citizenry that Tocqueville would surely never recognize.[4] At the level of foreign policy, liberalism sought to coexist with an aggressive militarism designed to protect U.S. interests in far-flung areas of the world. Behind the rhetoric of freedom, democracy, and national self-determination it furnished ideological cover for right-wing dictatorships, apartheid in South Africa, military intervention in the Third World, and an unprecedented arms race.[5] Differences between Republicans and Democrats in all of these areas, as the 1984 presidential contest between Ronald Reagan and Walter Mondale reflected once again, were blurred beyond recognition.

In this context liberal ideas inevitably lost their relevance to social change, having become obliterated by an institutionalized corporate-military network that bears no resemblance to classical liberal designs. Liberal states, if such phenomena can be said to exist, are no longer capable of ideological renewal and political innovation. They preside over bureaucratic centers of power, tied to a declining economic order, in which the historical tension between capitalism and democracy has been weighted decisively in favor of the former, thereby laying the basis for something akin to state capitalism. Thus liberalism, whatever its claims, is now compromised by a state system with ever-shrinking ideological boundaries at a time when popular movements are striving to broaden those boundaries. The two forces—liberalism and the new movements—occupy polar extremes.

The antagonism between Marxism and social movements is of a different sort, although the larger political consequences are in fact quite similar. Of course, the crucial ideological difference is that Marxism presents itself as a revolutionary theory appropriate to the transition from capitalism to socialism—a theory that, from its inception, clearly sided with those class forces opposed to the dominant order. Much like liberalism, it embraced a secular, modernizing ethos tied to the process of industrialization. The problem was that Marxism contained two rather disparate and contradictory strains: a commitment to popular self-activity as the basis of social transformation, and a rationalizing impulse that gave primacy to a Jacobin-style political mobilization from above. Over time, the guiding practice of Marxist parties and states resolved this tension in the latter direction, epitomized by the centralizing dynamics of Leninism, the Bolshevik Revolution, Soviet state socialism, and virtually the entire subsequent Communist tradition. The other political variant of early Marxism, European Social Democracy, assumed a less vanguardist character but still shared many of the same statist and bureaucratic premises; indeed, Lenin's emphasis

on the dominant role of Marxist intellectuals as bearers of scientific
theory was consistent with the outlook Karl Kautsky brought to German social democracy at the turn of the century. It is perhaps worth
observing here that Robert Michels' famous analysis of oligarchical
tendencies as the natural outgrowth of internal party processes—tendencies conspicuously at odds with proclaimed SPD goals—were in
many ways consonant with the party's theoretical premises.

Although Leninist parties typically rode to power on the crest of
broad insurgent movements, the relationship between the party organization and local struggles has commonly been tense if not hostile. Once
in power, the Bolsheviks in Russia quickly moved to subordinate all
popular organs—soviets, factory committees, trade unions—to the imperatives of party control. The left opposition, including the postrevo-
lutionary anarchist rebellions, was either dismantled or repressed by
military force. This conflicted pattern recurred in the 1930s when the
Spanish Communists mobilized to crush a broad-based anarchist movement, in May 1968 when the French Communists made every effort to
disrupt the mass revolt of new leftists and workers, and more recently
when the political distance between Marxist formations and the new
movements has widened despite momentary points of convergence. As
for social democracy, its evolution since the 1920s has been steadily
rightward; in postwar Western Europe it has given rise to parties of
capitalist rationalization where in power and parties of loyal opposition
where out of power. Social Democrats have been the main heirs of left
Keynesianism and an expanded welfare state—at least until the recent
phase of austerity—which today is equally remote from Marxism and
the new movements, and which is absorbed into the very logic of capitalist development.[6]

If Marxist theory has lost a good deal of its critical and radical thrust
because of its assimilation into official party or state doctrines, its growing legitimation within institutions of higher education poses a different
range of dilemmas. Insofar as the struggle for recognition and acceptance pushed academic Marxists toward the professional norms of the
university, the theory itself has taken on many of the characteristics of
established, mainstream currents within the various disciplines: profes-
sionalism, positivism, and even the archenemy functionalism. Marxism, in this setting, readily degenerates into a conventional ideology,
emptied of political content. To the extent this is so, Marxist scholar-
ship in the universities—like the depoliticized forms of scientific and

official Marxism—maintains a certain self-conscious aloofness from the realm of the social movements.[7]

This state of affairs is hardly accidental, for it has become increasingly obvious that the new movements have posed important questions concerning bureaucracy, the family, feminism, culture, the ecological crisis, the arms race, and racism that Marxism has failed to confront adequately, for numerous reasons. Such movements have further implicitly called into question the entire productivist framework of Marxism, including its primacy of the industrial working class. This predicament, I would argue, is not simply a function of historical contingency, of a need to "reconstruct" the theory to meet new conditions. It is rooted in the basic assumptions of Marxism, as we shall see in the next chapter. The notion that the theoretical limitations and inner contradictions of Marxism can somehow be resolved without disturbing the old paradigm is no longer so commonly defended by leftists in the advanced countries. Sartre's injunction that "Marxism remains the philosophy of our historical epoch" draws an increasingly skeptical response.

A look at the prospects of social transformation in the West, therefore, indicates that the very concepts of socialism, revolution, and emancipation seem to demand a fundamental rethinking that the diverse Marxisms (whether Soviet, Maoist, Western, critical, or structuralist) have never inspired. Only a systematically *post*-Marxist theory, grounded in the rhythm and flow of modern social movements, can stimulate a full reconceptualization of the revolutionary process.[8] In a relatively brief span the new movements have stirred intense debate over the relationship between economic crisis and political change, the viability of mass insurrection, the role of labor, the definition of democracy, and the significance of personal and cultural factors in creating a new society. They have demolished the myth of a unified, all-encompassing movement (or party) with cohesive organization, leadership, strategy, and tactics. They have challenged the premise of a determinant historical motion of events and processes leading, for example, to the familiar linear transition from capitalism to socialism. Perhaps most important, they have held out a range of novel and compelling visions of the future, inspired by the themes of feminism, recovery of community, ecological renewal, and participatory democracy, while rejecting the facile connection between industrial development and human liberation. As André Gorz writes, "Growth-oriented capitalism is dead. Growth-oriented socialism, which closely resembles it, reflects a distorted image of our past, not of our future. Marxism, although irreplaceable as an instrument of analysis, has lost its prophetic value."[9]

Radical alternatives to both liberalism and Marxism have appeared from time to time during roughly the past century, most notably anarchism, syndicalism, and council communism. Their ideological content, however disparate, was generally consistent with the logic of local struggles and movements. Each stood opposed to the narrow conception of revolution in Marx and pressed for a broad redefinition of politics that would take into account all structures of domination. They envisioned a qualitatively new political culture based upon mutual aid, workplace solidarity, community, and direct democracy, goals much closer to Rousseau than to Marx and Engels. And even as they glorified the moment of civil insurrection, they nonetheless rebelled against the primacy of a revolutionary party (or party-state) on the assumption that party hegemony was likely to reproduce new types of hierarchy. From a radical viewpoint, Marxism (and to a greater extent, Leninism) failed to encourage those democratic forms of culture and authority needed to sustain autonomous movements. But if radicalism offered a persuasive critique of Marxism, it too failed in this respect, for altogether different reasons. As I have argued elsewhere, the actual history of anarchism and councilism between the wars was one of defeat, either through overwhelming repression (Russia, Spain), absorption into the established party and trade-union structures (Germany), or internal collapse resulting from localist dispersion (Italy).[10] After the 1930s these traditions lived on in a few European countries (Italy, Spain, France) only as distant utopian images obscured by the twin legacies of Leninism and social democracy, and, of course, by fascism.

Yet only a generation later a new phase of radicalism quite distinct from its antecedents made deep inroads into the political culture of the industrialized West. May 1968 in France and the Hot Autumn (1969) of mass struggles in Italy can be viewed as the most dramatic expression of new-left politics, which reintroduced the familiar themes of workers' control, self-management, and recovery of community. And there were some fresh departures: a diffuse sense of cultural revolt anchored in the youth and student movements, the birth of environmentalism, the beginnings of feminism. On a global level the new left was united in its opposition to U.S. intervention in Vietnam and its solidarity with Third World liberation struggles. Strategically, its commitments echoed those of earlier radical movements—to build an oppositional presence largely outside the corporatist party and trade-union structures (including those nominally Marxist or socialist). It represented an assault on authoritarianism in all spheres of life, with an emphasis on "dual power" centered more on local than national arenas of action. Never a homogeneous force, the new left grew out of a proliferation of small groups, local committees, communes, and so forth. In Western Europe it gathered strength from multiple constituencies around a mélange of different and often bizarre ideologies, including populism, anarchism, neo-Marxism, situationism, Trotskyism, and Maoism. (In the United States the gulf between new-left ideologies and Marxism was more pronounced, given the weakness of the Marxist tradition and the disintegration of the Communist party by the late 1950s.) The romanticized attachment to a "new politics" was therefore necessarily partial and uneven.

By the mid-1970s what had become known in Europe as the extra-parliamentary opposition went into severe decline, its adherents disillusioned with the absence of concrete revolutionary prospects in a situation filled with high expectations and exhausted by the unrealistic demands of collective action often tied to the pressures of intimate, small-group participation. The majority of new-left activists chose to withdraw from politics because of personal, work, or career interests; others entered the Communist or Socialist parties; and a small minority, concluding that the new left was never a serious political vehicle, opted for terrorist organizations like the Red Brigades in Italy, the Baader-Meinhof group in West Germany, and ETA (a Basque separatist group) in Spain. By 1976, with Eurocommunism in full swing and with the Vietnam war over, the new left in both Western Europe and the United States was clearly an historical phenomenon, a thing of the past.

After the eclipse of new-left politics, radical tendencies were kept alive (though perhaps in diluted form) during the subsequent decade by the new social movements. These movements derived momentum from the failure of party systems to confront or resolve problems that were already visible in the 1960s: the downturn of global capitalism, a resurgent militarism, ecological destruction, the growth of the bureaucratic state, and social divisions over race and sex. If this phase lacked the passion, novelty, and fetishism of direct action of the new left, it was still able to generate the kind of durable community-based presence that had eluded previous activists. New institutions were built by environmentalists, tenants, peace activists, consumer advocates, women, gays, and civil rights workers. Many journals, newspapers, and research institutes reflecting this broad range of concerns appeared.

At the same time, these movements did not evolve in any ideologically coherent direction; the very diversity of modern popular struggles can be said to constitute an important part of their essence. Indeed, the explicitly radical component of new movements—for example, the social ecologists, the left wing of the peace movements, the radical feminists, and some anarchist-styled neighborhood groups—constitutes only a small minority. A preponderant number of activists and supporters belong to issue-oriented liberal reform movements or protest organizations that have no explicit antisystem political agenda. Others identify with subcultural communities (gays, squatters) to the extent that they hope to create an autonomous space apart from the dominant institutions and values.[11] It is possible to find socialist currents of varying types and strengths in most of the new movements, and in southern Europe this has been a salient factor in the growth of Eurosocialism since the late 1970s. In the United States, however, the general pattern has been one of cleavage between popular movements and a marginalized socialist tradition.[12] In every locale new-movement activity has contributed to the sporadic expression of novel political formations— the Ecologists in France and England, the Radicals in Italy, the Greens in West Germany and Holland, the Citizens party and the Campaign for Economic Democracy in the United States. Given the peculiar ebb and flow of social movements, their natural tendency toward localism and spontaneism, and their inevitable fragility, their main organizational concern is how to preserve continuity and stability. Movements come and go, disappear and reappear in new forms, and move from one location to another. However, as I shall argue in the following chapters, contemporary popular movements of the sort analyzed here are established social phenomena. More than that, they can be seen as major protagonists of historical change in the West. Yet it is no simple matter to arrive at conclusive generalizations regarding their future political evolution. Whether they can sustain ideological and organizational vitality, and whether they can emerge as vehicles of historical transformation, remains problematic. As we shall see, the possibilities of absorption, repression, and internal disintegration are always present.

A persistent difficulty with radical alternatives throughout the twentieth century, extending from anarchism through council communism, the new left, and the new movements, is a seemingly inherent flight from politics. This has often taken the form of a simple assertion of civil society over the state, movements over party, the "social" realm over the "political." In a positive vein, this obsession with a recovery of grassroots democracy has often energized local communities and broadened the scope of politics—at least where it poses, even for brief periods, a clear relationship between everyday life and collective interaction. But its failure to confront the issue of power has in the end only weakened, rather than empowered, those social forces capable of subverting the status quo. This impasse helps to explain the disintegration of the new left, and it threatens to immobilize the new movements as well. Confined largely to their own social immediacy, local movements are likely to become hopelessly dispersed and politically impotent, whatever their levels of popular support and militancy.

This is not merely a question of whether local movements should enter electoral politics, or become involved in other areas of the political system, since a purist abstentionism is advocated by only a fringe minority in any movement. The problem goes much deeper: how is it possible to transform the state apparatus, revitalize the public sphere, and create new forms of authority so that fundamental change can be initiated, consistent with the radical potential of the new movements? In peace organizations, for example, the absence of a comprehensive strategy permits vacillation between two often ineffectual extremes— between the media-defined mass demonstrations, peace camps, marches, and isolated acts of violence, on the one hand, and the kind of furtive appeals to political leaders to mend their suicidal ways, on the other.[13]

Nor is the escape from politics in this sense just a matter of the presumed irrationality or utopianism of movement leaders, although such inclinations do exist to varying degrees. Rarely do popular expressions of revolt develop according to a linear, neatly structured pattern. Some critics have attacked the new movements for their apparent antimodernist strains, their "narcissistic" preoccupation with immediate gratification, and their glorification of the spiritual realm.[14] Where this critique is valid, the movements can be readily dismissed as amounting to little more than a romantic withdrawal from bourgeois society, a false escape from those modes of domination that are being condemned. Either the ends are unrealizable, or the means selected to achieve generally praiseworthy ends are said to be hopelessly inadequate. Leaving aside the exaggerated nature of such arguments, the problem of extreme subjectivism is undeniably a real one. At the same time, allowing for a slight twist of semantics, one can plausibly insist that, without such emphases (on daily life, recovery of community, free cultural expression, the merger of the personal and public), new social movements would never have become such expansive forces within civil society. There is a positive and regenerative side to the subjective dimension that the critics have missed.

Yet this critique cannot be taken too lightly, since the persistence of deep antimodern and romanticist impulses is clearly related to a kind of antipolitics that blocks articulation of a coherent political strategy that could lend shape to the myriad of rather loosely defined grassroots, regional, and national struggles. (The West German Greens, as I suggest in Chapter 5, constitute perhaps a first systematic effort in this direction.) The ongoing conflict between prefigurative (value-oriented) and instrumental (power-oriented) dimensions of popular movements has all too often been resolved in favor of the prefigurative,[15] with typically fatal results. The "left" presence within some of the movements (above all, the ecologists) is commonly linked to a neo-anarchism with its utopian vision of the future, its unrelenting critique of bourgeois society, and its holistic commitment to social change. But its strong appeals are undermined by a shallow conception of history—by a romantic attachment to a mythic (often preindustrial) past that coexists with an urgent desire for immediate and total overthrow of the power structure. Lost in this outlook is an understanding of the transition from present to future as a complex process, and with it any insightful approach to politics and political strategy. The ferment associated with the new movements has explosive implications for the industrialized countries, but implications do not suggest a particular mode of action.

The new movements have already forced a rethinking of many conventional leftist premises. For example, the very idea of a single model of socialist transformation now seems anachronistic. Here, as in other areas of discourse, there seems to be a fresh start in the direction of new concepts, analyses, and visions; and it is in this direction that the outlines of a post-Marxist radicalism can be detected. In this spirit Touraine counsels that "it is by studying social movements that one becomes able to construct a new image of society."[16] Still, to unravel the logic of these movements is not enough; it is necessary to situate them in an explicit (and reconstructed) political context without losing sight of their novel and innovative character.

But new conditions and new forms of activity have been slow to generate new theory. The organized left is still on the whole tied to past commitments and visions, seemingly fearful of conceptual changes that might disturb old paradigms. Entrenched theoretical frameworks eventually become a repository of myths and illusions, while political opportunities slip by. Communist and Socialist parties, along with some groupings of the radical left, cling to faded symbols that often cloak a social and cultural conservatism as the organizations try to maintain an equilibrium with their environment. Wedded to the realities of an earlier period, their loss of political imagination has become nearly total. Thus the Marxist left still subscribes to the faded promise of technological solutions for a complex array of human problems and to a program of expanded accumulation and economic growth, as if the new phase of ecological restraints and global economic restructuring were someone's distant fantasy. The preference is for simple formulas appropriate to past stages of capitalist development, for a single theory of history that explains every facet of social change. Mostly there is a belief that Marxism, whatever its imperfections, must retain its status as an all-embracing body of theory. Thus, even rather bold attempts to "reconstitute" the theory run into a dead end of obsolete promises and concepts. Along these lines Murray Bookchin observes that "theoretical critique has been notable for its absence of radical reconstruction. Neither the latter generation of 'critical theorists' nor their opponents as reflected by the new formalizations of Marxism have given substance to their visions of freedom and practice." [17]

It follows that if a post-Marxist theory is to emerge on a foundation of new social movements, its categories will correspondingly have to be postmaterialist. After all, advanced capitalism is governed by the imperatives of continuously expanding production and consumption—a dialectic shared by Marxism and liberalism alike, the main difference being that Marxism stresses the quality of material life and social relations to a greater degree. Neither ideology, however, has articulated a persuasive critique of industrialism as a system based upon multiple forms of domination and an institutionalized framework of coercion, waste, and destruction. Neither of them offers complex insights into the problems of bureaucratization, militarism, cultural stagnation, and social atomization that accompany the productivist model of development. Each accepts the one-dimensionality of a growth ethic in which the mechanisms of resource allocation are viewed independently of their broader ecological and social–psychological context.[18] Here again, the popular movements reflect above all a breakdown of economistic formulas with their facile assumption that social progress stems from the constant expansion of productive forces.

Of course, a productivist theory does reflect certain realities of capitalist development and thus furnishes a methodology that can be useful for analyzing the system in its present form. Surely even a post-Marxist schema will have to incorporate an understanding of the economy and class forces into its conceptual structure. It would be absurd to think that the global crisis—or even a postindustrial issue such as environmental decay—can be grasped without an analysis of the crucial (and sometimes decisive) material factors at work. The point here, however, is that a strictly productivist focus always remains trapped within the present and cannot provide transcendent categories of theory and practice. The transition from a bourgeois order to a new type of society, shaped as it must be by a *counter*hegemonic logic, requires a holistic framework: the hierarchy of issues, themes, and priorities will be social, cultural, and political as well as economic. Moreover, one can no longer automatically conclude that global capitalist decline will fit the pattern of a crisis scenario where the system is destroyed by explosive material contradictions. Those contradictions have not disappeared, but the process now appears to be one of progressive stagnation, of deep and gradual structural decline that cannot be attributed to economic indicators alone, rather than of cataclysmic rupture.

The outlines of a post-Marxist approach have been visible in the work of a growing number of social theorists, historians, and political activists at least since the late 1970s. The new movements have given birth to a far-reaching and eclectic, though hardly cohesive, literature that, even though it draws freely on earlier radical currents, suggests a distinct paradigmatic shift away from Marxism as *the* legitimate framework of critical discourse, toward a dialectical theory more sensitive to the transformed historical setting. In actuality, this shift reflects something more: the necessity of multiple paradigms in a situation where the prospects for a single unifying agency (social or political) have vanished. A post-Marxist theory, therefore, can be defined as a critical, dialectical framework that contains a philosophy of praxis that is no longer wedded to the canons of scientific materialism or to the primacy of objective historical forces; a social theory that confronts the reality of multiple and overlapping forms of domination (class, bureaucratic, patriarchal, racial) without reducing that reality to one of its aspects; and a democratic political theory compatible with the ideal of a nonbureaucratic, self-managed society.

Such a departure has many points of origin, follows many paths, and has vast implications for the nature of political conflict in the West.

It can be observed, for instance, in the contributions of those who have shown—at the most general theoretical level—that the historical clash between Marxism and new social movements leads not to the reconstruction of Marxism as a unified theory but instead to its insoluble crisis and, ultimately, to its transcendence. (See, e.g., Stanley Aronowitz, Isaac Balbus, Jean Cohen, Jürgen Habermas.)[19]

It can further be seen in the work of those who argue that the very appearance of the new movements has effectively overturned the Marxian assumption (metaphysical at its base) that the industrial working class is the decisive revolutionary protagonist within capitalist society. (See, e.g., Michael Albert and Robin Hahnel, Zygmunt Baumann, André Gorz, Alain Touraine.)[20]

• who have concluded, on the basis of extensive research, that the complex plurality of these movements inevitably dispels the myth of any privileged or vanguardist subject of social change. (See, e.g., Manuel Castells, Ernesto Laclau and Chantal Mouffe, Touraine.)[21]

• who have analyzed the role of an expanded bureaucratic state in producing novel patterns of popular resistance and opposition in the form of the new movements. (See, e.g., Castells, Joaquim Hirsch.)[22]

• who have shown that local movements exhibit a logic of disruption and confrontation that often challenges the premises of routine institutional politics and centralized organizational forms typical of conventional Marxist strategies. (See, e.g., Frances Fox Piven and Richard Cloward.)[23]

• who identify the new movements as essentially prefigurative formations that resist integration into the instrumental world of administrative influence, interest-group politics, or vanguardist mobilization. (See, e.g., Murray Bookchin, Wini Breines, Richard Gombin, Sheila Rowbotham, Kirkpatrick Sale.)[24]

• who have shown how feminism as a vision of transformed social relations and participatory democratic process is incompatible with (male-style) authoritarian models of organization, leadership, and strategy. (See, e.g., Sara Evans, Kathy Ferguson, Nancy Hartsock, Rowbotham.)[25]

• who stress the degree to which heretofore uncontrolled ecological problems of industrialism reveal the bankruptcy both of capitalist and state-socialist growth-oriented economics. (See, e.g., Rudolf Bahro, Bookchin, Gorz, William Ophuls.)[26]

• who insist that the global dialectic of an escalating arms race and its negation in the form of a rejuvenated peace movement cannot be understood strictly according to the Marxian categories of class forces and imperialism but require additional explanatory variables linked to East-West competition and the rise of permanent war economies. (See, e.g., Bahro, Mary Kaldor, E. P. Thompson.)[27]

• who stress a holistic approach to human concerns like health care, education, and culture, thereby calling attention to qualitative dimensions of social life that push beyond productivist boundaries and reflect issues raised by the new movements. (See, e.g., David Dickson, Hazel Henderson, Ivan Illich, Theodore Roszak.)[28]

If this assemblage of post-Marxist theorists is impressive in its range of contributions—and it is hardly exhaustive—there nonetheless remains a conspicuous lacuna in the area of political strategy, that is, where the social movements begin to intersect with the realm of the state, party systems, interest groups, local governments, and so forth. Most efforts have invariably sidestepped the critical question of how the new movements have entered, or failed to enter, into broad political organizations that seek to win power for the purpose of large-scale societal transformation. Only by exploring these issues, and thereby redirecting the focus upon both state and civil society, can the possibilities of a viable radical politics be fully investigated. An underlying assumption of this book is that the constituent elements of such a politics are already visible throughout the advanced capitalist world, and that they are intelligible in the growth of the new movements. I have identified three general patterns that can be loosely associated with the historical appearance of the new movements: a reconstituted Eurosocialism in Mediterranean Europe (notably France, Spain, and Greece), a new populism in the United States, and a Green tendency in northern Europe. (None of these, however, is confined to a specific geographical region.) Each strategic model, in varying degrees self-consciously post-Marxist, strives to pursue a "third course" between Leninism and social democracy (or between the Soviet and Western capitalist alternatives) and identifies broadly with the historical substance of the new movements (ideological themes, political methods, social constituencies). My task here is to unravel the complex dynamics of each pattern with a critical eye on the variety of potential long-term outcomes.

If my sympathies lie mostly with the radical side of the new movements, I further argue for a theory that incorporates a more dynamic understanding of politics than most post-Marxist currents seem ready to accept. At the same time, I have in mind a concept of politics that is not limited to the institutional sphere of the state, legislative bodies, and party systems, even if it must obviously encompass that sphere. Politics in this sense is viewed as part of a reconceptualized public realm that includes those social, cultural, and psychological aspects of civil society that typically have been the terrain of popular movements, and that are commonly ignored by students of politics. A "new politics" therefore integrates both state and civil society in a manner that allows for a dynamic relationship between the two, between the "political" and "social" realms, parties and movements, institutional activity and grassroots mobilization. This schema rejects the one-dimensionality (either state *or* civil society) that flaws both liberal pluralism, with its emphasis on a rather narrow and formal institutional terrain, and the sometimes wholesale antistatism of new-movement theorists that paves the way either toward a more fortified bureaucratic state or a kind of prefigurative impotence. The problem in both cases stems from an excessively abstract view of social and personal autonomy—whether formal in the liberal definition or cultural and psychological in the neo-anarchist outlook—that blocks establishment of a concrete political mechanism for radical-democratic transformation.

Alongside this set of concerns is yet another critical addendum: the theory and practice of modern social movements would be devoid of historical potential without some kind of organic linkage to working-class struggles. The vision of a post-Marxist or postmaterialist politics does not mean that, simply because economic forces are no longer determinant, class issues can be abandoned entirely. Although large sectors of labor have moved in a corporatist direction, other sectors composed of a much larger proportion of working people (including the growing ranks of unemployed) find themselves more disadvantaged and in many cases more marginalized. And it is these latter constituencies that have often given impetus to the new movements, whatever the clear points of tension between labor politics and social struggles. Moreover, the new movements undeniably have a class base of their own, in both the new middle strata of workers and in the marginalized groupings, and this indicates a sizable overlap of interests and priorities —for example, in the areas of housing, unemployment, occupational health and safety, military spending, social services, and the feminization of poverty. Perhaps the key to any future social transformation in the advanced countries, as I shall elaborate in Chapter 6, depends upon the extent to which a sustained connection between new social movements and working-class struggles—between community and workplace, universal goals and specific material demands—can be theoretically and politically established. Such an historic convergence is inconceivable, however, without the appearance of a new kind of labor movement, and perhaps a redefinition of new-movement initiatives as well.

The ultimate value of a transformative strategy lies in its capacity to liberate such possibilities insofar as it forms not only an immediate locus of action but also supplies a political sense of direction. Strategy thus requires both a coherent understanding of existing social forces and an imaginative projection of human potential. Eurosocialism, the new populism, and the Greens can be seen as original departures along these lines insofar as each combines, in quite diverse ways, the defining characteristics of a post-Marxist (and postliberal) radicalism. Their considerable limits and flaws are to some degree inherent in their very transitional nature, since the movements themselves are relatively novel and, from a political viewpoint, also still fragile and marginal.

2

THE CHANGING UNIVERSE
OF POLITICAL OPPOSITION

There is of course nothing new about the appearance of social movements, radical or otherwise. Modern history offers a rich legacy of many different types of movements, from jacqueries, urban mobs, and millenarian revolts to nationalist, religious, agrarian, and regional forms of populism. These movements follow an unpredictable ebb and flow—a process in which people seek a better world by means of collective action which, with the proper mix of circumstances, can challenge the existing social order. Tangible successes are in fact rare since the conditions for achieving durable change are often lacking: either the historical balance of forces is unfavorable or the subjective elements (ideology, organization, leadership, strategy) are too weakly developed. Yet this is hardly the entire story. If few social movements by themselves have won significant victories, many more have merged with or helped sustain larger movements and parties that managed to conquer state power, as in Russia and China. Movements typically flourish where there are mounting crises of legitimacy, where the old systems of social and authority relations are challenged by broad cultural ferment or social upheaval. Whether these periods of conflict give rise to a radical politics depends upon the capacity of diverse movements to form cohesive social blocs.

Throughout capitalist development, social movements have made an indelible imprint on the political landscape, but they have also run up against the power of large-scale organizations (the state, party systems, interest groups, corporate bureaucracies) that tend to restrict movement autonomy. Local movements have often been absorbed by left-wing organizations or, if absorption proved impossible, have been effectively isolated and marginalized; others have simply been forced into oblivion. In one form or another, then, the antagonism between movements and large-scale formations has been a recurrent feature of industrial society. To some extent this conflict has changed with the transformation of capitalism itself, as political opposition became more and more constricted to the bourgeois public sphere. Thus the model of pluralist democracy that prevailed from the end of World War II into the 1960s was a corporatism built around the Keynesian state and grounded in a social contract among labor, business, and government. This institutionalization of class conflict rested upon a stable interest-group framework in which bargaining and compromise occur within a fixed system of rules and norms. The boundaries of political conflict were more or less those of the pluralist state. If labor insurgency sometimes spilled beyond these boundaries, potentially subversive opposition was generally contained within political limits. Despite enclaves of resistance, the state had effectively triumphed over civil society.

Yet the social contract rested upon an increasingly fragile base, which the new-left rebellions of the 1960s first illuminated. The institutionalized state network in many societies (including the United States, Britain, France, Italy, and to a lesser extent West Germany) faced serious legitimation crises aggravated by several factors: the Vietnam war, the fiscal crisis of the state, resurgent militarism and Third World challenges, and, of course, economic decline. Corporatism persisted, but its "solutions" to the crisis were based upon empty premises—that growth could continue indefinitely, that illusions of democratic participation could be forever reproduced.

The social movements that have appeared since the 1960s constitute a new phenomenon precisely to the extent that they have exploded permanently beyond those old corporatist boundaries. It is not a matter of whether earlier isolated parallels can be located. The important point is that these movements, as emergent broad-based agencies of social change, are situated primarily within civil society rather than the institutional realm of pluralist democracy. Further, the tendency toward *convergence* of some movements (for example, feminism and the peace movement) gives them a radical potential far greater than the sum of particular groups. Even though their capacity to overthrow any power structure is still minimal, they have begun to introduce a new language of critical discourse that departs profoundly from the theory and practice of conventional politics. Hence the popular movements explored in this study can be located within a changing paradigm of social forces and ideological definitions. The new priorities—an end to the arms race and superpower competition, environmental restoration, democratic participation, cultural revolt, new forms of social and sexual relations —are more qualitative and global than previous ones. Themes of this sort permeated earlier populist and anarchist movements, but either they were submerged beneath "larger" objectives or the movements themselves were isolated. Today, these themes are at the forefront of modern social movements. Moreover, to the degree that the radicalism of new movements tends to flow from the deep crisis of industrial society, its roots are generally indigenous and organic, making it naturally resistant to the totalistic ideologies that galvanized the Second and Third Internationals. This proximity to immediate concerns suggests that such movements possess a stronger capacity for what Gramsci called "cultural expansion"; in other words, they are less likely to be assimilated into corporatist hegemony. The evolution of world capitalism has reached a point where popular movements, in one form or another, are bound to flourish since the conditions that brought them into being—the eclipse of the industrial growth model, the threat of nuclear catastrophe, bureaucratization, destruction of the natural habitat, social anomie—cannot be expected to disappear simply through the good intentions of political leaders.

Still, these realities tell us little about the ultimate political meaning of particular movements or groups of movements. The obstacles to a broad politicization are many, including a deeply ingrained sense of powerlessness and the appeal of privatized remedies. But whatever their ultimate trajectory, the new movements will surely loom large in collective struggles for social change in the West. Their complex and fluid nature reflects their own social ambience and sheds light on a newly unfolding universe of political opposition where the lines dividing revolution and reform, civil insurrection and parliamentarism, class and "false" consciousness, state and civil society have been blurred in the altered political setting. I have therefore chosen to begin with a general exploration of those factors most responsible for shaping this changing character of social and political conflict.

THE HISTORICAL CONTEXT

Modern social movements have proliferated in an advanced capitalist environment made congenial by a confluence of developments in the state and party systems, class relations, the global economy, social life, the ecological milieu, and, of course, international politics. If these factors are not uniformly favorable to the growth of movements and differ from country to country, they have predictably led to a crisis of legitimacy that the preferred solutions—a recycled Keynesian welfare state, social democracy, revitalized conservatism—have failed to counter. Efforts to reconsolidate state capitalism have only aggravated basic systemic problems, which are more complex and intractable than either liberal or Marxist theory anticipated.

One such problem is the expansion of centralized state power, which in many countries has meant a gradual tendency toward closure of the bourgeois public sphere. The structural transformation of capitalism— the collapse of market mechanisms giving rise to monopoly control, extensive planning networks, and socialization of production—requires massive state initiative, even where (as in the United States) the myths of free enterprise remain. Whether in the form of coordination, regulation, research and development, fiscal and taxation policies, or welfare services, the corporate state is forced to intervene in order to smooth out the accumulation process and contain the system's disruptive tendencies. It has accomplished this task with varying degrees of success, but even the most mature Keynesian welfare states (for example, Sweden) have faced severe dilemmas in a period of global economic retrenchment. As the state reaches into new areas of social life, its bureaucratic features become more disruptive, its capacity for social control and ideological manipulation more refined. In countries where statist capitalism is most advanced, as in the United States, West Germany, France, and Japan, administrative integration is no longer external to the economy but becomes constitutive of bourgeois society as a whole. The congruence of state and economy, state and civil society is a defining characteristic of modern capitalism.

One outgrowth of statism is the erosion of party systems as agencies of popular mobilization and representation. This truncated pluralism corresponds to what Macpherson calls "equilibrium democracy"[1] based upon restrictive elite competition within a shared normative consensus: bipartisan foreign policy, allegiance to monopoly capital, interest-group bargaining, emphasis on moderate over "extremist" ideologies. Major parties of all labels are submerged into the governmental orbit and take on the character of "quasi-state apparatuses" that blunt social conflict and close off radical alternatives—at least so long as they can retain their mass character.[2] The electorate is courted with broad appeals and diffuse themes ("peace," "economic recovery," "national unity," "leadership renewal"), with expensive media and marketing campaigns that glorify the role of personalities. Critical issues and policy choices are commonly sidestepped or finessed out of existence. As Claus Offe notes, "It is hardly an exaggeration to argue that the party as a political institution has ceased to perform the functions of formulating and securing an agreement on programmatic policy outlines."[3]

Aside from their role in legitimating the corporate state, parties therefore seem to have little ideological identity; their "pragmatism" merely reflects a commitment to institutional stability. This generalization applies as much to mass-based leftist parties (including the Communists) as to right-wing or centrist parties. For example, in Italy since the 1960s the Christian Democrats, Socialists, and Communists—each with a popular electoral base—have exhibited a tendency toward convergence, or *trasformismo*.[4] The American two-party model, in which Democrats and Republicans as moderate catch-all vehicles compete for middle-ground support with hopes of winning a majority, is no longer a novel exception. Even where the multiparty system is preserved, as in Italy and several other Western European countries, convergence simply occurs at the level of parliamentary coalition building rather than electioneering. In all cases, "national" priorities (support for NATO, military spending, desire for trade advantages, patriotic solidarity) tend to overshadow conflict over alternative goals and programs. Party elites uniformly strive to mediate rather than mobilize discrete interests.

The growth of a rationalized state system and the merging of parties effectively disenfranchises broad sectors of the population, especially those already farthest removed from the centers of power. The liberal ideal of democratic participation dissolves into a pluralist social contract uniting governmental, interest-group, and party elites. The absence of real debate and the lack of political competition leave the electorate with very restricted choices, either through electoral campaigns or within national legislative bodies. Elections become critical only insofar as the media presents them as such. Insofar as participation is emptied of substantive meaning, democracy is largely reduced to its formal, procedural dimension.[5] The consequences of such closure are predictable: disaffection from the mass parties, lower voter turnouts, increased mistrust of political leaders, growth in the percentage of "independent" voters (especially in the United States), and, finally, the rise of new social movements.[6]

Interest-group activity, meanwhile, has been characterized by a shift toward corporatism—toward an institutionalized framework of social bargaining involving the state, business, labor, and other organized interests. Corporatism reflects that phase of capitalist development in which the state, through its various departments, agencies, and commissions, mediates social conflict. The governmental apparatus furnishes a mechanism for advancing and legitimating "common goals" since competing groups enter the bargaining arena with a certain public status that confers upon them leverage within a broadly defined ideological (and sometimes programmatic) consensus.[7] According to corporatist norms, no conflict is tolerable that challenges the supreme requirements of capitalist rationalization—economic growth, profit maximization, productivity, and so forth. The fusion of politics and economics around a common decision-making mechanism has often been viewed simply as a concerted effort of capitalist elites to regulate class relations and thereby secure industrial harmony. All of this is true enough, but additional interests and motives must be taken into account: state and military managers who seek consensus on "national" goals, as well as leaders of trade unions and Social Democratic parties who want to strengthen the position of organized labor. Depending upon its particular historical expression, corporatism can put forward many faces, including "liberal" (United States, West Germany), "social democratic" (Sweden, Austria), and "authoritarian" (Japan, late Francoist Spain).[8]

Whatever the specific form of corporatism, its impact on working-class politics—and its consequences for social change in general—turns out to be rather clear. First, the growth of sectoral interest-group politics tied to contractual bargaining tends to fragment labor and undercut its power to act as a unified class.[9] Occupational categories proliferate based on differences of skill, level of organization, relationship to the public sector, role in military production, type of enterprise, geography, and so forth—each category shaped by unique cultural and social factors. This is to say nothing of the racial and gender divisions that permeate the labor force. In a context where the state operates as a bureaucratic unifying force, the disparate elements of class take on an atomized presence instead of the solidary features associated with a collective agency of change. The struggle between wage labor and capital does not occur in terms of deeply articulated interests, ideologies, or political movements. Class consciousness, to the degree that it can be said to exist, moves in precarious ways and in countless different patterns.

At the same time, corporatism encourages ideological moderation and even passivity within its geopolitical sphere of influence. Here the regulation of class conflict actually goes hand-in-hand with the global restructuring of capital. "Fordist" efforts to maximize profits are designed to reduce the work force and impose labor discipline; where effective, they transform workers into commodified objects who can exercise little control over their immediate existence. If powerful trade unions and confederations are integrated into a statist bargaining network, with abundant material and cultural benefits for their members, the working class as a whole can be weakened to the extent it becomes socially fragmented and ideologically pacified. The rationalizing process cannot advance unless unruly social forces yield to the "pragmatic" requirements of technology and bureaucracy.[10] A stable corporatism that rests upon a clearly spelled-out social contract not only domesticates its own popular constituencies but also marginalizes those class forces outside the corporatist consensus (for example, most minority workers, service-sector employees, "guest" workers, the unemployed). For those strata removed from the centers of power, depoliticization often finds expression in privatized lifestyles linked to the culture industry or to various forms of psychological escape.

Moreover, since the corporatist model is held together by a productivist ideology, which stresses that the driving force behind interest-group action is the struggle for material advantage within a growth framework, qualitative issues inevitably get deflected or submerged. Immediate objectives (higher profits, a larger share of the budget, increased wages) automatically take precedence over collective societal interests (environmental preservation, consumer needs, social services), despite obligatory references to the common good. Thus any challenge to the principle of rationalization on ecological grounds will be ruled out by all partners to the social contract because it directly clashes with growth priorities. Questions related to what is produced (tanks, cars, or mass transit systems), rather than how much is produced, are largely ignored even by the trade unions since what matters most is a stable business atmosphere for the present rather than social planning. For example, a conversion program involving transition from military (nonproductive, wasteful) to civilian (socially useful) economic activity is unthinkable within a corporatist arrangement since it poses issues like militarism, foreign intervention, and uses of technology that are extraneous to productivism. Likewise, efforts to combat racism and sexism can achieve at best only limited success since these problems, too, lie on the periphery of corporatism. From this viewpoint, a good deal of organized working-class politics can be understood as reinforcing the logic of corporatist integration.[11]

These tendencies—the decline of party systems and the rise of interest-group corporatism—allow the bureaucratic state and monopoly capital, working in tandem, to penetrate civil society in more comprehensive ways. Setting itself "above" the contending social forces but in reality serving as an integral part of the accumulation process, the state system imposes itself on all aspects of social life. Technocratic imperatives invade not only the workplace but education, housing, health care, cultural consumption, food production, and even neighborhood life. Computer technology enhances the surveillance and control potential of police authorities. The underlying ecological basis of communalism and solidarity is eroded. The power structure assumes an almost "natural" or suprahistorical character, beyond the capacity of people to transform decisively. Its legacy is an atomized mass consciousness that combines elements of passivity, cynicism, and privatism. As Gorz argues, the entire fabric of institutional power is so deeply embedded in the political culture that it matters little what persons or party labels occupy official positions, for the logic of decision making in terms of its real impact on peoples' lives is roughly the same.[12]

It is often forgotten that the systemic impulse toward rationalization stems not only from an obsession with material growth but also from the constant drive for enhanced social control and labor discipline. Elites must regulate all conflict lest it become destabilizing. A technocratic ideology that worships technique and procedure over open, critical discourse serves this very purpose: where such ideology is hegemonic, as in the postwar United States and Western Europe, political opposition faces new and more subtle challenges.

Yet efforts to stave off crisis through development of a more "organized" capitalism have worked only up to a point—that is, only so long as growth could be sustained and popular demands could be confined to corporatist boundaries. Once the economies began to stall and massive social pressures came to the surface (focused on public services,

taxation, the environment, women's and minority issues), the corporatist pattern eroded as systemic conflict became more visible. Philippe
Schmitter observes that "societal corporatism" is but a superstructural
rearrangement of institutions involving "deals among organized privileged minorities" that cannot dissolve the deep structural contradictions
of bourgeois society.[13] The very narrowness of formal mechanisms and
special interests inevitably pushes social conflict outside this arena,
back into civil society, as renewed struggles over "public goods" out-
strip the old limits.[14]

The perpetual endeavor to reconsolidate capitalism by means of
institutional manipulation has therefore produced its own counterten-
dencies. Disenfranchised social groups have contested the instrumental
premises of the social contract; party systems have failed to contain
new challenges; and many trade unions have undergone a dramatic
increase in rank-and-file insurgency (for example, over the issue of
plant closings). As the international position of many Western capitalist economies weakens, following a generation of growth and relative
prosperity, the earlier patterns of structural decline now reappear at a
time when Keynesian countercyclical methods have exhausted their
utility and when global limits to further expansion are more severe.
Moreover, with the eclipse of traditional market relations and the fading
significance of ideologies corresponding to earlier phases of capitalist
development (liberalism, Marxism), the attempt to relegitimate the system on a basis of bureaucratic rationality and technological progress
has failed, paving the way toward legitimation crisis.[15] Such is the historical context of the new social movements.

The experience of the past twenty years or so in the industrialized
world shows that statism, corporatism, and closure of the public sphere
have yet to create a civil society in their own monolithic image. On the
contrary, uniformity of the power structure appears to have generated
its opposite within bourgeois society as a whole: social diversification,
critical ferment, local struggles, widespread alienation from the national
state. Surface ideological homogeneity or "consensus" in most countries
barely conceals an underlying diversity and even polarization.

The reasons for this expanding gulf between the political and the
social realms are numerous. As we have seen, the working class itself is
fragmented through the very logic of corporatism. Equally significant,
strata within the working class have developed in such a way that internal differences are magnified, giving rise to sometimes conflicting

ideological tendencies. It is possible to distinguish at least four broad formations—traditional blue-collar manufacturing, the service sector, the professionals and white-collar workers, and the marginalized (including unemployed)—each with separate (though perhaps overlapping) interests, priorities, and lifestyles. For present purposes it is enough to emphasize that the latter three groupings are growing numerically at the expense of blue-collar labor, with the popular movements finding support largely within the "new middle strata" (service and professional or intellectual workers) and the marginalized. There is, moreover, a trend toward what has been called the "pluralization of social life-worlds": the separation of public and private spheres, the growth of local autonomy, and the dispersion of various centers of life activity such as work, family, community, and culture.[16] This homeless quality of modern social existence is further reinforced by the peculiar spatial fragmentation of urban settings, which reproduces a kind of geographical and social mobility that works against cohesion within and among neighborhoods. Finally, the breakup of traditional unifying ideologies (including religion) has created a legitimation void left unfilled except for an uncertain instrumentalism tied to material growth and administrative stability. Despite the presumably homogenizing and depoliticizing effects of consumerism and the culture industry, the result appears to be more space within civil society for the articulation of multiple and competing systems of belief.

Expanding social and ideological pluralism counters depoliticization and broadens the terrain of local conflict over issues finessed or sidestepped by the national power structure. Thus new-left movements of the 1960s produced a range of counterhegemonic organizations and communities based in grassroots mobilization and which, in the 1970s, were translated into more durable movements, institutions, and, in a few cases, political parties. The statist vision of an administered universe of thought and action has never been realized in any advanced country, despite predictions here and there of impending Orwellian tyranny. As a lively complex of social and cultural relations, civil society has resisted, if only partially, the imposition of centralized economic and political control. Such resistance has meant an ever more antagonistic relationship between state and civil society, between local communities and the corporatist public sphere. The implications of this development seem rather obvious: ties that bind popular constituencies to the old-style instrumentalized politics are loosened, the integrative capacity of the system is damaged, and new fissures within the party system itself begin to appear.

One cannot make sense of these momentous changes without taking into account the global economic decline of capitalism itself. It is sometimes forgotten that, although new social movements express largely postindustrial or qualitative themes, their origins are at one level economic insofar as their historical appearance coincides with the first signs of stagnation in the world capitalist system. Although it is true that the movements do not generally revolve around material struggles narrowly defined, the idea that they are simply expressions of a middle-class, affluent culture is likewise false. The complexity of industrial society suggests that no clear-cut lines of demarcation exist between the economic and the political, social, or cultural realms; at the same time, the movements reproduce that very complexity within their own evolution.

The contemporary decline of capitalism differs from earlier cyclical crises to the degree that it reflects a permanent structural downturn and therefore collapse of a particular model of accumulation. When additional novel factors are introduced into the picture—fiscal crisis of the state, the ecological predicament, "permanent war economy"— it becomes obvious that the new situation is much less amenable to Keynesian intervention. The immediate signs of global crisis are dramatic enough: the virtual end of industrial growth, the decay of the traditional manufacturing sectors, massive fiscal problems and currency instability, the erosion of the welfare state—all occurring in an atmosphere of heightened economic competition between nation-states, of more or less anarchy in the world capitalist system. The concrete and easily visible results of capitalist stagnation have been growing unemployment (10 to 15 percent in most Western European countries), more poverty, declining living standards for most workers, plant closings with their disruption of community and family life, decaying cities, erosion of social services, and a generalized sense of alienation and powerlessness. The era of boundless expansion and prosperity that the United States, West Germany, France, and even Italy anticipated not so long ago has receded further and further from view—even if certain myths linger on. Optimism tied to growth has been replaced by cynicism and insecurity. "Progress" has meant poorer quality housing, education, health care, public transportation, and energy resources.

The current predicament of capitalism is simultaneously structural and global, and therefore cannot be attributed solely to the programs of any specific leader or party; "Reaganomics" in this sense can be viewed more as an effect than cause of the global crisis. The problems are so deep and so closely tied to the downward pull of the world system as to overwhelm the capacity of any single nation-state to reverse them, within the parameters of capitalist development.

A critical ingredient in this downturn is the technological restructuring of capitalism on a global scale, the cornerstone of efforts to revitalize accumulation on a basis of enhanced productivity, capital mobility, and labor discipline. Advanced countries, with the United States in the lead, struggle to overcome stagnation by using the fruits of the scientific-technological revolution to fullest advantage—with some measurable success. The idea is to build upon dynamic new sectors (electronics, computers, nuclear technology, lasers, robotics) that can accelerate the entire productive system while renovating old ones (autos, steel, appliances, textiles, chemicals). Rationalization along these lines depends upon state intervention, planning, and maximum collaboration between business and labor, since without extensive research and development supported by public funds, reduction of labor costs, and relative peace at the workplace, restructuring will run aground. But gains for some multinational corporations and even industrial sectors have not brought the expected benefits to economic systems as a whole. On the contrary, technological innovation has already created more problems and tensions than it has solved. For example, the methods designed to cut labor costs have exacerbated the problem of structural unemployment. And such methods, along with the informational techniques that allow for new increments in capital mobility, have encouraged capital flight from core countries to the periphery, with its abundant sources of cheap labor. Restructuring, furthermore, only worsens international competition among the United States, Japan, and Western Europe since it provokes trade wars, protectionist demands, and monetary instability in the global market. Equally troublesome is the fact that new high-technology sectors (notably, electronics, nuclear energy, and computers) have for various reasons not fulfilled their promises, at least to the extent that hopes for these sectors as a new accelerator have already turned out to be illusory.

Probably the most disruptive effect of technological restructuring, especially in the United States, is the onset of deindustrialization—the massive disinvestment of capital in basic industries and reinvestment in countries where labor and natural resources are plentiful and less expensive. Relocation of capital to such areas (Brazil, South Korea, Taiwan, Malaysia, Thailand) has meant hundreds of plant closings in the United States in the auto, textile, appliance, electronics, and steel industries, with the loss of millions of jobs over the 1970s.[17] In this context, capital mobility serves to boost unemployment, weaken organized labor, and wreak havoc on local communities. A consequent shrinkage of the tax base in many cities and towns has further worsened the urban fiscal crisis and produced despair and pessimism. National and municipal governments face a simultaneous explosion of public demands for services and an erosion of tax monies—the result not only of plant closings but of the famous taxpayers' revolt. The state, as a dispenser of programs and services and as a major employer, emerges more than ever as a focal point of social contradictions and struggles. In order to maintain its legitimacy the state is forced to carry out these programs and services, but it does so less and less effectively as its resources (ideological and material) dwindle.

There is yet another element in the current phase of capitalist decline —the already advanced process of environmental decay—which dramatically calls into question the historic connection between social progress and ceaseless industrialization. Restructuring calls for a propping up of accumulation functions, justified by a growth ethic that favors material growth over social utility within a production system that is designed to exploit finite world resources. In this way capital accumulation devours the very ecological underpinnings of all economic activity: air, water, soil, space, other natural resources.[18] Its destructive legacy is air and water pollution, the spread of toxic chemicals, atmospheric radiation, blighted cities, depleted animal species, and contaminated food. Bloated and wasteful industrial economies have already moved into disequilibrium with nature as the state-corporate system penetrates not only civil society but every recess of the natural environment. This type of ecological imbalance presupposes a vast network of domination (over nature, material resources, and individuals), which in the long run undermines its own infrastructure and therefore its growth potential.[19] Given the near anarchy of global economic relations and the futility of strictly national solutions, there are no planning mechanisms that can reverse this self-perpetuating logic of destruction. Technology, moreover, is at the core of this problem, so that within the present framework of accumulation it cannot offer a way out.[20]

Finally, economic decline stems from still another development unique to the current period—the "permanent war economy." The United States alone spends nearly $300 billion annually to support its vast military infrastructure, or roughly $1 trillion from 1981 through 1984; add to this the rapidly increasing arms expenditures of the NATO countries and Japan, and the total runs to several trillion dollars just since the mid-1970s, with no change in sight. Whatever its ideological rationale, this unprecedented commitment of human, material, and technical resources fuels the nuclear arms race, protects and polices spheres of domination, strengthens domestic class rule, and disseminates (largely for profit) military technology and arms around the world. The result is a perpetual drain on civilian sectors insofar as resources are diverted from socially useful programs to those that are wasteful when they are not actually destructive.[21] The permanent war economy feeds upon anti-Sovietism and the cold war. Its huge bureaucratic-corporate maze of departments and agencies, privileged interests, financial power, and weapons systems makes it a kind of state-within-the-state that lacks real accountability. Interwoven with both the political system and the economy, the military sector functions as the lynchpin of development, with scientific and technological planning shaped more and more by its requirements.[22] Paradoxically, systemic growth seems to depend upon military investment at the very moment the economy as a whole is weakened by such lopsided spending patterns.

This is true precisely because the permanent war economy feeds into those problems associated with capitalist decline: deindustrialization, unemployment, the fiscal crisis, erosion of social services. As is well known, spending for missiles, tanks, planes, and aircraft carriers— even leaving aside outrageous cost overruns that drain public monies— is so technology-intensive that it provides many fewer jobs than would comparable amounts invested in social programs.[23] Moreover, the impasse of the growth economy means that sustained increases in both military and social investment can no longer be expected, so that the decision to augment one (the military) necessitates severe cuts in the other. For these and other reasons the deep crisis tendencies of the system center more and more on the gigantic military–industrial structure, as Reagan's economic policies clearly reveal.

When the focus shifts to the global impact of the arms race, it should be obvious that what E. P. Thompson calls the "accumulating logic of militarism" is not simply a reflex of economic rationality but develops in a specific political context of international power relations and conscious governmental decisions.[24] In this sense the development of a Keynesian military apparatus intersects with the dynamics of global strategic competition between the United States and the Soviet Union, NATO and the Warsaw Pact. As the two massively armed blocs stand in ideological opposition to each other, cold-war antagonism leads to a range of consequences both domestic and international: not only economic decline, but bureaucratization of state power, the threat to human survival, and renewed efforts to repress popular challenges to superpower hegemony within and outside of the bloc system. The resurgence of cold-war politics and militarism since the late 1970s is only the most recent expression of this historical tendency.

The emergence of a powerful "national security" structure requires centralized planning, command hierarchies, technocratic control, and of course secrecy—a labyrinth of functions that gives new meaning to the authoritarian state. As George Konrad observes, the very fact that belligerent states possess nuclear weapons legitimates the efforts of their power structures to impose more rigid forms of social and ideological control upon civil society.[25] Such militarization of politics works against popular dissent since elites may be quick to define any political opposition, especially over issues of foreign policy, as unpatriotic or subversive. Mary Kaldor observes that the "bloc system is a mechanism for controlling diverse and pluralistic tendencies within each bloc and channelling internal dissent into external confrontation."[26]

In the West, cold-war mobilization and military buildups depend upon the maintenance of a liberal-patriotic consensus directed outward, against the Soviet Union and Warsaw Pact countries as implacably hostile enemies. An obvious source of strength for ruling elites, who can justify arms spending, abuses of power, and foreign adventures by manufacturing images of the Soviet "threat," this consensus is incompatible with an authentically democratic politics.[27] With only rare exceptions (for example, the British Labour party), major parties in the advanced countries share the premises of anti-Sovietism and the policies that flow from it; thus, debate on foreign-policy objectives is astonishingly limited. Important military decisions (such as whether, when, where, and how to deploy missiles) are made by a tiny group of military and political managers with at best only token, rubber-stamp legislative approval, at worst in a milieu of total bureaucratic secrecy. These decisions, moreover, very often go against the general direction of public

opinion, as measured in standard surveys.[28] Insofar as entire populations are effectively disenfranchised on foreign-policy issues, the militarized state simply reinforces those general tendencies toward closure
of the public sphere.

But this situation is compounded by yet another, more obvious concern: the threat to human survival posed by the specter of a nuclear
arms race already spiraling out of control. The development of sophisticated weapons systems appears to have its own logic, far removed
from the capacity of popular assemblies to contain or reverse it. The
cycle of strategic threat, response, and counterresponse seemed even
more menacing with the escalation of cold-war tensions in the mid-
1970s. Nuclear "parity" exists in a global framework of tension, suspi-
cion, and constant efforts (mainly by the United States) to achieve
convincing superiority. As Noam Chomsky points out, any geopolitical
region involving potential superpower conflict (such as the Middle
East) could under the right mix of circumstances become the site of a
nuclear confrontation.[29] In the absence of strong countervailing forces,
the logic of militarism can reach the point where political leaders will
have almost complete autonomy to carry out whatever "defense policy"
they choose. One need not fully accept Thompson's thesis of an irrepressible "exterminist" path to believe that an "inertial thrust toward
war" is at least a possibility.[30]

Such a catastrophic future appears all the more likely precisely because virtually every cold-war assumption in the West is so illusory.
Above all, the specter of Soviet incursions into Western Europe or
assault on the United States persists today as nothing more than a
dangerous myth. The undeniable reality is that the Soviet Union is both
economically and technologically well behind the West, and indeed it
has typically found itself following the American lead in the arms race.[31]
What has changed in the present military balance is the Soviet achievement of near parity with the United States in its capacity for nuclear
destruction, and this was partly negated by the deployment beginning
in 1983 of Pershing IIs that can reach Soviet cities in only a few
minutes. Moreover, aside from the issue of relative military strength,
the Soviet leadership is profoundly conservative insofar as it has shown
little inclination toward fostering revolutionary change abroad. Quite
the contrary, although it seeks areas of influence typical of a great
power, its actions have rarely challenged the global status quo. Liberation movements in the Third World normally receive Soviet support

only when they have already achieved success (Cuba, Vietnam, Angola, Nicaragua), and even this support might be understood primarily as a Soviet move to intercept the growth of autonomous centers of revolutionary power.[32]

The cold war (and the various regional "hot" military conflicts that are part of it) operates not so much to contain Soviet "aggression" as to reinforce American hegemony in Western Europe, the Middle East, and parts of the Third World. Since the 1960s this hegemony has come under sustained challenge, beginning with the debacle of Vietnam. This is the historical meaning of Reagan's (and Carter's) efforts to overturn the politics of detente. The United States can utilize its nuclear supremacy as a strategic tool in the interest of the world capitalist system, with the Soviet "enemy" providing a convenient focus.[33] But this tool is not always effective, either in combating liberation struggles or in preserving U.S. competitive advantage vis-à-vis rival capitalist powers like Japan.

At the same time, U.S. efforts to achieve military superiority have created new fissures in the NATO alliance itself. In Western Europe, the old agreements and power relationships established in the aftermath of World War II now seem obsolete and are being challenged by broad sectors of the population that no longer seek refuge in the American military umbrella as a bulwark against the "Soviet threat." The Euromissile deployment ironically only weakened NATO and alienated millions of people from the notion of deterrence through arms buildup. Centrifugal tendencies became visible in dramatic shifts of public opinion and political alignments across the continent, most visibly in West Germany.[34]

This historical convergence of forces, conditions, and developments corresponds to a sharpening (but still controlled) crisis of legitimacy in the industrialized West. The decline of bourgeois hegemony is a long-term process that goes beyond the predicaments of particular governments or leaders. The point is that systemic problems have not been effectively confronted by the ruling party formations, corporate blocs, or Keynesian welfare-state policies. Meanwhile, these problems have been exacerbated by a variety of factors mentioned above, and the capacity of the state apparatus to perform its requisite functions of accumulation, regulation, control, and mediation of interests has started to break down. Growing popular demands upon the state—for more "public goods," for a socialization of services—cannot be fully satisfied

owing to the fiscal crisis and the narrow instrumentalism of the corporatist framework. The result is a legitimation crisis that broadens the
terrain for insurgent social movements, as the appearance of both left
and right populism on a broad scale since the 1960s indicates.

If one reflects upon the past two decades, what seems obvious is a
generalized but still limited breakdown of long-established rules and
norms that have kept intact the multiple forms of domination.[35] As old
patterns of thought and behavior erode, new patterns begin to take
shape as part of a lengthy process that can only be gradual and uneven.
Profound changes in political culture have already inspired popular
struggles over issues concerning the family, gender relations, racism,
education, health care, and bureaucracy. In all of these areas the inherited forms of authority have become less sacrosanct, more open to
question. Despite state-capitalist efforts to domesticate successive waves
of protest and radicalism, this period has witnessed the beginnings of a
novel break with the past.

THE VARIETIES OF POPULAR MOVEMENTS

What are often described as "new" social movements have their origins
in the turbulence of the 1960s and owe much of their growth to the
translation of their insurgent energy into more highly articulated forms
of popular revolt in the 1970s. The new left in Western Europe and
North America converged around a variety of struggles and themes,
and for a brief historical moment formed one huge, amorphous movement: antiwar protests, civil rights and minority activism, the counterculture, environmentalism, the first stirrings of modern feminism. The
unifying catalyst was opposition to American intervention in Vietnam.
During the 1960s popular struggles were characterized by a certain
diffuseness and eclecticism, by a vague sense of collective purpose, by a
lack of organizational identity and strategic orientation. They shared a
"great refusal" to go along with the conventions of bourgeois society
and a romantic yearning for community and a sense of personal identity
that capitalist rationalization had denied or obliterated. They shared a
hostility toward established authority and white middle-class lifestyles
that underpinned it. New-left amorphousness could be detected in the
bizarre mixture of visible ideological influences—from anarchism to

Marxism, from populism to neo-Marxism, from Oriental mysticism to humanistic psychology.

The 1960s produced not only the May Events in France and the Hot Autumn of 1969 in Italy but a wave of rebellions in U.S. cities and on hundreds of university campuses. Its legacy included SDS in West Germany and the United States, scores of radical left groups on the European continent, and, later, the rejuvenation of several deradicalized left-wing parties (notably the Mediterranean Communist parties and French Socialism). There were, moreover, thousands of local organizations, small work groups, projects, institutes, and periodicals that have deeply influenced the political landscape of Western politics. Finally, there was the formation of a new generation of radical and Marxist intellectuals attached mainly (but not exclusively) to expanding systems of higher education.

If a new left known for its massive demonstrations, marches, and rallies, its commitment to a novel assortment of belief systems, and its cultural exhibitionism faded from the scene by the mid-1970s, another new left that gave rise to more durable patterns of political activity evolved along a more cohesive ideological and organizational path. The fact that this phenomenon received considerably less media attention was no real measure of the scope or depth of popular mobilization. The spirit of the new left, if not its precise form, was preserved throughout the 1970s and early 1980s by a proliferation of community-based groups that embodied the interests and values of the earlier period. Most of these groups sooner or later developed into, or merged with, the social movements that are the central concerns of this book. A critical distinction between earlier and later phases, however, lies in the growing differentiation and specificity of these movements. Whereas the 1960s version of radicalism was diffuse and spontaneous, the popular formations of a decade or more later took on a clearer identity, along with a deeper commitment to build new institutions, even if a radical strategic orientation was still absent. And whereas the early new left attached itself to every conceivable borrowed ideology, the later phase was accompanied by a good deal of innovative theorizing grounded in the distinct experiences, challenges, and opportunities presented by advanced industrialism.

The new popular movements can be divided into five general types or patterns: urban social struggles, the environmental or ecology movement, women's and gay liberation, the peace movement, and cultural revolt linked primarily to student and youth activism. With the possible exception of the mobilization against nuclear weapons in the early 1980s, no single catalyst for this phase can be identified; no issue carries the moral urgency of opposition to the Vietnam war. Considerable overlap and convergence among these categories of movements do exist, but each type has its unique set of priorities. And of course there is abundant diversity within each pattern, as we shall see.

It is sometimes forgotten that the most ubiquitous form of opposition since the 1960s has been the urban movement, which reflects the changing nature of social conflict in the major cities of the capitalist world. Not altogether "new," these struggles have grown larger, more visible, and in some cases more convergent. The main protagonists are racial and ethnic minorities, neighborhood activists, tenants and squatters, consumer advocates, and welfare-rights militants. They represent multiple historical tendencies: grassroots resistance to corporate interests and their project of urban restructuring; the rise of what Manuel Castells calls "collective consumption"—the assertion of public goods or social-use values over exchange values;[36] a redefinition of physical and cultural space through the unfolding of alternative forms of community life; a challenge not only to the power structure but to corporatism, machine politics, and traditional political styles. Castells analyzes a broad range of such urban phenomena in various countries, including the Madrid neighborhood-based citizen movements of the 1970s and the integrated and highly politicized Hispanic community in the San Francisco Mission District since the 1960s.[37] In both cases new appropriations of space coincided with the development of community organizations, an immense variety of street activities and celebrations, and a sense of cultural identity that enabled thousands of people to oppose ruling-class designs for urban renewal, with its destructive impact upon autonomous space, local organizational forms, the aesthetic environment, and material well-being.

These examples of embryonic urban revolt, with their commitment to democratic self-management and cultural identity, can be multiplied hundreds of times. A good many of them have been amply discussed and analyzed, including movements of welfare workers and clients in the United States, neighborhood activists in northern Italy, squatters in West Berlin, Turkish immigrants in West Germany, blacks in Britain and the United States, and consumer groups in the United States.[38]

Central to this category of revolt has been the immense variety of racial and ethnic movements that have dominated the urban landscape in many industrialized countries since the 1960s. Increasingly, however, such struggles have spilled far beyond particular communities. They begin to overlap extensively not only with other new-style movements —for example, those concerning housing, social services, peace, and feminism—but also with the more traditional labor movements. For this reason it is rather difficult to classify minority-based struggles neatly within the schema established here. Urban citizens' initiatives, centered mainly outside the point of production, were once considered a typically American phenomenon, but they have been equally visible in Western European countries where rapid industrialization has given rise to much the same kinds of conflict and turbulence. This type of movement has actually grown overall since the 1960s, even if few of them have preserved a militant oppositional politics for long.

The modern version of environmentalism flows out of the youth culture and back-to-the-country trends of the late 1960s. It developed a mass character in response to the ecological damage that is endemic to rampant industrialism and urbanization. Highly diffuse, the environmental movement does not draw from specific constituencies and sometimes adopts the high moral tone of those who feel outraged by the incursions of modern urban civilization. Citizen action groups have organized to fight air and water pollution, toxic wastes, nuclear power, the destruction of natural space (homes, parks, wilderness), threats to occupational health and safety, the contamination of foods, and the killing and mistreatment of animals. Whereas old-style conservationists have typically confined their actions to preserving nature and wildlife (Sierra Club, Audubon Society), more radically oriented ecologists press for total change based upon a Rousseauian vision of organic community (Ecology Action, Friends of the Earth, Greenpeace). What can be defined as ecological radicalism calls for alternative technology, small "human scale" forms of social organization, communitarianism, the elimination of the gulf between urban and rural life, and the restoration of the equilibrium between humans and nature.[39]

The anti-nuclear-power mobilizations that swept Western Europe in the late 1970s and early 1980s were in some ways the prototype of militant environmentalism. They enlisted the participation of hundreds of thousands (mostly youth and students) who built camps, established affinity groups, and often battled police in their efforts to block the installation of costly and dangerous nuclear reactors. Actions generally took place in small towns and rural areas in France, England, West Germany, and the United States. In his analysis of these confrontations, David Elliott writes of the widespread populist distrust of government and corporate technocrats whose goal is to "nuclearize" energy production—a program both economically wasteful and politically antidemocratic.[40] Other smaller but no less militant actions occurred in response to the expansion of the Tokyo and Frankfurt airports, in which local inhabitants sought to preserve their communities against reckless invasion by corporate and military planners. These and other struggles laid the foundations for the emergence of broader political organizations concerned with environmental issues: the Ecologists and Amis de la Terre in France, the Greens in West Germany, the Radical party in Italy, and the various "alliance" groups in the United States (Clamshell, Abalone, Alliance for Survival) along with the Citizens party. Insofar as such formations, too, were part of the generalized revolt against uncontrolled urbanization, their overlap with urban social struggles mentioned above seems natural enough. The more organized expressions of environmentalism have declined since the early 1980s, a result partly of the crisis of the nuclear power industry itself and partly of the siphoning off of energies by the peace movement. Yet it is probably fair to say that ecological sensibilities have spread since the early 1980s and have entered into the collective awareness of other popular movements.[41]

The third pattern of revolt—feminism and the gay movement—has no doubt touched the greatest number of lives, given rise to the broadest forms of participation, and penetrated more deeply into the core of everyday social existence than any of the others. Contemporary feminism (in its liberal, radical, and socialist variants) established a mass presence in the late 1960s and early 1970s, having grown out of women's resentment of male domination within the new left and, in the larger context, out of feminist reawakenings that accompanied the breakdown of postwar social and cultural conservatism. The women's movement was at once an emergent expression of new-left ideology and a transcendence of it. In its early days feminism was preoccupied with the themes of social and sexual relations and with challenging male styles of leadership and work. Devotion to process was inevitably linked to consciousness-raising and to what might be called small-group politics. By the mid-1970s feminist priorities shifted in the direction of specific projects devoted to a range of social problems: rape, wife-battering, health care, abortion, pornography, the family and child care, public services. The struggle to build communities supportive of women's independence typically involved the setting up of new institutions (rape-crisis or health-care centers), periodicals, centers of everyday life (cafés, restaurants, bookstores), and cultural activities (music and film projects). These sought to blend task commitments and organizing efforts with a sensitivity to democratic and collective norms. Not surprisingly, large sections of the feminist movement concentrated their efforts outside the mainstream political structures, closer to local communities and everyday social relations.

The underlying themes of contemporary feminism are the linkage of the personal and political realms, the elimination of sex roles and patriarchal barriers to women's self-activity, the articulation of new political styles, and the struggle for alternative modes of family and social life. In *Beyond the Fragments*, Sheila Rowbotham and her collaborators analyze the political implications of local feminist organizing projects in London. They observe that, given its rather unique and far-reaching experiences with personal politics and democratic process, feminist organizing suggests a basically new model of social transformation that directly challenges the hierarchical bias of both liberal-pluralist and Marxist approaches to political activity.[42]

The United States and England were the birthplace of modern feminism in the late 1960s, but the movement rapidly expanded throughout the advanced capitalist world; women's groups appeared in France, Italy, Spain, West Germany, Holland, and elsewhere. Their diversity was felt in the schools, mass media, city halls, political parties, professional conferences, and of course in the sphere of family and personal relations. In some countries (Italy and Spain) struggles over conventional issues like divorce and abortion have consumed the bulk of energy, but in other countries (the United States and England) there is greater focus on personal relations, group dynamics, and affirmative action. An important terrain for the development of American feminism has been the university, with its abundance of women's studies programs, conferences, seminars, special projects, and courses, all inspired by a generation of feminist scholars who have produced an impressive legacy of books and articles, pamphlets, journals, videos, and films. The very amorphousness of the women's movement is a sign of both strength and weakness—strength insofar as it represents a popular, expansive current, weakness to the extent that its activities are so often fragmented and lacking in strategic focus. Whatever the case, feminism has in fact grown rather dramatically since the late 1960s, in no small measure because of its capacity to transform attitudes about everyday issues, to psychologically activate women in the context of small-group process, and perhaps above all to hold out a plurality of options for personal and collective engagement.

The gay movement shares with feminism a concern for transforming social and sexual relations, but its trajectory has been quite different. Both an outgrowth of bohemian culture in the 1950s and an expression of new-left values, gay liberation became a movement in only a few urban settings (New York, San Francisco, London) during the 1970s. With gay culture now more openly expressive, it was possible for large communities to develop on the basis of a distinct sexual identity, outside the dominant heterosexual lifestyle. In contrast to the women's movement, which seemed to advance in a spontaneous and dispersed fashion, the gay scene took root in large and active subcultures, often with only the most limited political definition. (Lesbianism actually more closely paralleled the feminist pattern, and indeed was an integral part of it.) Gay sensibilities were channeled into new lifestyles based upon aversion to both conventional family life and heterosexual chauvinism; the struggle is not only for a new kind of personal and community life but for the extension of civil rights to all areas of gay life. Other issues were largely secondary. Castells describes the emergence of a bourgeoning gay community in San Francisco (where by 1980 about 25 percent of the electorate was gay) that was able to achieve a semblance of its own free space within which a festive street life, restaurants, taverns, shops, and community centers could flourish.[43]

Perhaps the most visible of the movements, in terms of numbers and media impact, have been the peace mobilizations of the 1980s. There is some continuity from the ban-the-bomb campaigns of the late 1950s through the antiwar struggles of the 1960s to the later huge antinuclear demonstrations. They all shared a certain moral urgency, as well as a rejection of the Realpolitik linked to cold-war ideology. (The anti-intervention groups protesting U.S. involvement in Central America and elsewhere can be seen as a sequel to the new-left phase, but they have generally overlapped little with the peace movement.) In Western Europe and North America resistance to the arms race took the form of massive protests against the 1979 NATO decision to install nearly 500

Pershing II and cruise missiles in West Germany, England, Italy, Holland, and Belgium. These protests reached their peak in 1981–83 when millions of people went into the streets of major European and American cities. Mobilizations attracted 5 million in the fall of 1983 alone, just as NATO was beginning its nuclear "modernization" program. It was a period when hundreds of small disarmament groups and several large umbrella organizations appeared throughout the West. Along with the well-established "peace camps" set up at Greenham Common in England and Comiso in Italy, many smaller and less permanent encampments were set up in West Germany and elsewhere. And the large antinuclear organizations flourished: the Campaign for Nuclear Disarmament (CND) attracted 82,000 members in England by 1983, and a European-wide convention of European Nuclear Disarmament (END) held in West Berlin in May 1983 was attended by more than 3,000 full-time activists.[44] It is too early to say whether this peace consciousness has led to a permanent shift in European political alignments; still, it has clearly been a factor in the resurgence of Mediterranean Socialism, the revitalization of British Labour, and the early successes of the West German Greens.

The initial target of peace actions was the NATO missile deployment, which a majority of Europeans saw as a cold-war provocation that placed their countries at the center of a possible nuclear hurricane. There were also ongoing efforts to secure a nuclear freeze and to establish nuclear-free zones around the world. Given the specter of an uncontrollable arms race, the single and immediate issue of survival— tied to widespread anxieties and fears about war—has galvanized broad strata to an extent greater than any other issue. Yet in going beyond the theme of survival, radical currents within antinuclear organizations arrived at a deeper critique of the permanent war economy and a stronger commitment to dismantling the military structure through the mechanism of social conversion. Within such a framework the struggle for disarmament is organically attached to other concerns: the economic crisis, demand for social services, the environment, democratic participation, feminism, and of course the imperialist presence in the Third World.[45] The women's encampment at Greenham Common perhaps best exemplified this spirit of fusion.[46] From the Western European viewpoint, finally, the peace movement can be understood as the initial phase of a long-term rebellion against postwar U.S. economic, military, and cultural hegemony over the continent.

The fifth type of social movement—encompassing youth revolt, student protests, and countercultural lifestyles—is perhaps most closely associated with the new radicalism of the 1960s. Concentrated in university campuses and towns, it was fueled by the social and cultural breakdown of bourgeois society that meant, above all, disillusionment with conventional lifestyles, bureaucratic regimens, and technocratic education. It linked a generalized sense of political rebellion with "subversive" commitments rooted in Oriental mysticism, communal living, underground art and periodicals, rock music, and a more open sexuality all bound up with the quest for community, grassroots democratic participation, and cultural meaning.[47] Occasionally these movements converged with more familiar leftist concerns such as support for civil rights struggles and opposition to the war in Vietnam; at other times they retreated into insular youth ghettoes or rural hippie communes that emphasized the supremacy of uniquely personal experiences and struggles. The great political episodes of the 1960s—the 1968 May Revolt in France, the 1969 Hot Autumn in Italy, the explosive 1970 upheavals on American college campuses, Peoples' Park in Berkeley— were all essentially youth phenomena, or at least youth-initiated.[48] By the mid-1970s such mobilizations had largely dissipated, except for pockets of rural countercultural settlements in the United States and the persistence of groups like the Provos in Holland and the Metropolitan Indians in Italy. In the late 1970s, however, West Germany experienced a resurgence of youth culture built around the "alternative scene" in cities like West Berlin, Frankfurt, and Hamburg. If this renewal of youth culture harkened back to the peak years of the new left, its appeal was actually broader insofar as it was not simply a youth or student movement but was linked to other tendencies such as the peace movement and the Greens.[49] In various settings, too, punk culture developed as an apparent spinoff from the counterculture, but its adherents (with some exceptions) maintained a studiously antipolitical stance.

The vast ensemble of these popular movements constitutes an historical conjuncture in the development of Western capitalism; their totality adds up to considerably more than their separate parts. They originate on the periphery of the system but they also express some of the fundamental contradictions of modern bourgeois society. They exhibit an unpredictable rhythm, and though they may well be a permanent fixture in the advanced countries, their political translation cannot be easily anticipated.

CONSTITUENT ELEMENTS OF A NEW RADICALISM

What characteristics do the new social movements share? How do they differ from traditional Marxist and labor-based types of left opposition? What are their larger theoretical and political implications?

Perhaps their most striking feature is that they emerge primarily *outside the bourgeois public sphere*—as extra-institutional phenomena rooted in civil society[50]—which is precisely the sense in which they can be understood as social or even prepolitical.[51] They represent a potential break with the bureaucratic state apparatus insofar as they bypass the normal corridors of power (parties, elections, legislative bodies) or at least do not establish a center of gravity there. Historically, they point to a recovery of civil society that has been crushed under the weight of statism and capitalist rationalization. A tension naturally arises between the new movements and those political forces (parties, unions, interest groups) assimilated into the corporate bloc, and this tension carries over to the left opposition itself. Such antagonism varies according to the degree of closure within the power structure. It should therefore come as no surprise that popular movements are strongest in West Germany and the United States, two countries with the most constricted public spheres in the advanced capitalist world.

This peripheral relationship to the bourgeois public sphere is necessarily tied to an expanded conception of politics that incorporates the social life-world of everyday cultural and personal as well as material concerns. The "repoliticization" of civil society from the grassroots involves an ongoing challenge to hegemonic beliefs, values, attitudes, myths—the struggle for a new discursive terrain with distinctive rules and language, with new principles of legitimacy contesting the old ones.[52] The formation of such a new, reconstituted public sphere occurs through the articulation of what Raymond Williams calls an "emergent hegemony."[53] What, from the standpoint of the new movements, constitutes the essence of an emergent hegemony? First, there is at least a partial break with formal democratic mechanisms, a focus on more direct methods of struggle, and a redefinition of power relations so that noninstitutional processes (for example, racial and sexual matters) enter into the public realm. Second, the movements tend toward a more open and participatory style of politics in contrast to the conventional model, with its entrenched hierarchies, manipulative leaders, and limited scope of popular initiative.[54] Further, there is the growth of a subversive political culture that can represent an alternative source of meaning for a multiplicity of local struggles. Thus, Daniel Yankelovich describes the cumulative impact of social movements in the United States that, since the 1960s, have laid the groundwork for a set of "new rules" guiding thought and behavior, corresponding to an historical shift of cultural values away from instrumentalism and materialism toward an ethic of participation, communalism, and self-actualization.[55]

To the extent that popular insurgency has its own logic, new movements build upon polarizing or disruptive tendencies that already exist within capitalist society. A spirit of combat prevails over interest-group consciousness, especially for the more radical elements of the movements. There are in fact two such dimensions of movement activity: one geared to the building of local structures (community organizations, tenants' unions, women's health clinics), the other to direct action in the form of demonstrations, marches, strikes, boycotts, sit-ins, and so forth. Popular mobilization can have rather diverse origins—for example, protests against the dismantling of homes and neighborhoods as part of "urban renewal," civil disobedience over racist policies, and campaigns to reverse the arms race. But rarely is such energy directed toward the actual conquest of institutional power or the representation of specific interests within the state system. New movements are marked by discontinuity, by a pattern of ebb and flow that makes them highly unpredictable, and by a lack of ideological and organizational coherence of the sort associated with traditional leftist parties.[56] Indeed, activists typically view highly structured formulas and normative prescriptions with skepticism and therefore try to avoid being seduced by the "mass-based permanent organization" model that Piven and Cloward argue has inhibited the advance of social movements (notably in the American case).[57] Although direct-action struggles do often encourage a sense of aimlessness or adventurism, their main contribution is to keep alive a collective feeling of political efficacy.

The reluctance to compete for political power in the arena of mass-based parties does not simply reflect the movements' weakness; rather, it stems from a commitment to engage and transform the immediate environment—the household, neighborhood, municipality—as part of a grassroots-based radicalism.[58] This effort to recover a sense of community outside the state-regulated and commodified universe depends upon a systematic reorganization of space to enlarge the realm of (open) public discourse and physical freedom. Such a "new code of space"[59] requires expressive rather than instrumental social relations, consistent with the local, small-scale forms championed by the women's, peace, environmental, and urban struggles. The emergence of community-based feminist networks in London, squatter-occupied territories in West Berlin, gay and Latino neighborhoods in San Francisco, municipal organizations in Madrid, and tenants' movements in many American cities all fit this motif to varying degrees. In these cases the values of community and democracy are inseparably linked—a thematic with antecedents in a Rousseauian preindustrial ideal of face-to-face social relations based upon equality, trust, and reciprocity but which, in the advanced capitalist world, assumes a broader (and perhaps less intimate) sphere of human identity and interaction.[60] A spatial definition of community is needed to sustain counterinstitutions and practices that otherwise can be, and often have been, easily isolated or absorbed into the dominant political culture.[61]

Extending this logic further, popular movements can be seen as reflecting a vital new phase in the historic struggle for democratization. If they do not seek to conquer or overthrow the state or even to win new positions of power within it, they do tend to clash with the imperatives of corporate hegemony in extensive areas of social life.[62] They are subversive precisely insofar as they penetrate the boundaries of pluralist democracy without at the same time gravitating toward the "mass-based permanent organization" model. Both systems of power—pluralism and bureaucratic centralism—duplicate the political division of labor between institutional elites and atomized masses. Within pluralism, moreover, the classical ideal of democratic participation is distorted and suppressed through the imposition of a corporate bloc, as we have seen.[63] What emerges from the experience of local movements are the broad outlines of a radical democracy that rests upon a deeper conception of political involvement. First, democratic engagement must apply to every sphere of life—the workplace, neighborhood, educational institutions, even the family—as well as to the political system itself.[64] Second, the principal basis of legitimation is through grassroots forms of participation. Third, this type of democratic politics is integral to the general process of social transformation—that is, it incorporates both a substantive and a formal rationality. Fourth, this process indicates a decisive change of collective consciousness that would bring all persons into the structures of decision making. Finally, radical democracy is incompatible with strict hierarchies of truth and meaning in the sense that a truly open public sphere must tolerate ideological ambiguity.[65]

Democratization from below further suggests a generalized revolt against domination, which, as Bookchin argues, contains the most radical of all implications.[66] Social movements do not only or even primarily confront the reality of economic exploitation. To be sure, class relations are integral to the total structure of domination, but they do not exhaust the immense range of peoples' experiences and struggles in advanced capitalism. Domination in this sense refers to all forms of social hierarchy—not only class but also the bureaucratic, patriarchal, and racial forms—that must be confronted within the process of social transformation.[67] Each form of domination has its own history, patterns of development, and ideological expressions, yet each intersects with the others as part of a complex network of structural arrangements that is unique to each setting.[68] Thus, feminist and minority-based movements (ideally) encounter not only patriarchy and racism but the entire corporate and state spheres through which these ideologies are reproduced and enforced. They also stand opposed to a technocratic infrastructure which, through its command of specialized knowledge and expertise, rationalizes and legitimates the various types of domination. A break with this logic of domination is therefore far more complicated, and potentially more subversive, than the overthrow of capitalist forces of production as such; the assault on the larger ensemble of power relations involves diverse paths, diverse constituencies, and diverse ideologies.

If the proliferation of social movements indicates that class relations alone do not shape popular struggles, it simultaneously reveals a basic questioning of the material growth premises of the system. The challenge to productivism indicates a long-delayed recognition of the negative effects of a developmental model propelled by the relentless drive toward accumulation. The qualitative themes addressed by the new movements—egalitarian social and sexual relations, expanded public consumption, the attack on militarism, social conversion, decentralization of power, equilibrium between society and nature—can be understood as simply the first expressions of a deep crisis in the rationalizing mechanisms of the system. The growth-driven economy generates dysfunctions at every level: unemployment and decline of social services in the economy, devastation of the environment, an unprecedented concentration of political power, the prospects of nuclear catastrophe, and erosion of the quality of life for all but a privileged minority. More than that, industrialism destroys its own underpinnings as it devours the resources and ecological base it needs for further modernization. Thus, the clash between capitalist rationalization and the social demands of new movements lies at the heart of a whole new pattern of unfolding contradictions, cleavages, and conflicts.[69] What emerges is a far-reaching challenge to industrial culture, urbanization, and the fetishism of technological rationality—that is, to a permanent war economy that has exhausted its sense of invulnerability. The shift from a growth-oriented economy to a more rational, ecologically sound model compatible with modernity has immense implications for how people begin to define consumption and well-being.[70]

Vital to such a transition is the kind of "collective consumption" ethic that Castells found in his investigation of the Madrid citizens' movements and other urban struggles.[71] In Madrid what seemed to galvanize all neighborhoods and constituencies, despite their many differences, was the demand for a range of public services and programs that the state could not provide. The demand for socialized goods—education, urban transportation, health care, affordable housing, toxic-waste cleanup—was clearly outside the orbit of a growth-obsessed capitalism that produces goods more for private consumption (individual appliances, entertainment) and export than for public consumption. In this context the new movements assert social-use value over exchange value, human needs over commodities, even where such transformative language is rarely employed.

To varying degrees and in varying ways the new movements also seek to connect the personal (or cultural) and political realms, or at least they raise psychological issues that were often submerged or ignored by the traditional left. This is the cornerstone of radical and socialist feminism, but it also runs through movements concerning local autonomy, the environment, and antimilitarism. The crucial unifying thematic is alienation—that is, the pervasive sense of estrangement and powerlessness that popular struggles must confront if they are to advance their causes.[72] The familiar notion of empowerment refers to the recovery of social individuality that is simultaneously part of the de-

mand for community and democratization. From this viewpoint, alienation goes beyond the sphere of production and the workplace; it grows
out of the general relations of domination—in the case of feminism, for
example, out of the struggles of women around the issues of rape, abortion, health care, and the hegemony of male "experts" over virtually
every area of life.[73] De-alienation occurs through rebellion against ex-
ternally imposed social forms (class, patriarchal, bureaucratic, racist),
against the Hobbesian character of everyday life where violence, aggression, and egotism triumph over the communitarian virtues of reciprocity,
trust, and warmth. As part of an insurgent collective identity, therefore,
efforts to overturn alienation in its broadest manifestations necessarily
mean an enlargement of psychological options and human possibilities.[74]

Yet these new possibilities cannot unfold as a matter of individual
autonomy or personal self-expression, strictly speaking; they can take
form only in the context of larger social forces. For modern popular
movements, new sensibilities emerge as part of a sustained cultural
radicalism—an ensemble of relations that gives support to alternative
art forms (music, film, theater), popular media (radio, newspapers,
journals), and lifestyles (social and sexual relations). Cultural transformation according to this expanded definition corresponds to the
Gramscian theory of counterhegemonic struggles, which implies a renewal of the public sphere and a democratization of political discourse.

This process of cultural transformation is already visible in some
countries. For the United States, Yankelovich has marshaled an immense amount of survey data to show that momentous attitudinal
changes—the unfolding of a set of "new rules"—have occurred since
the 1960s. These attitudes concern issues of authority and participation,
the family, sexuality, relations between men and women, work and
leisure, and religion. Yankelovich shows that Americans have been
more ready to question familiar truths and to experiment with new
ideas and social arrangements. Among young people in particular there
has been a shift, though of course uneven, from one basic orientation
to another: from instrumental to expressive social relations, from self-
denial to self-affirmation, from a religious to secular worldview, from
work-centered to consumption-centered lifestyles, from traditionalism
to universalism.[75] If these changes are limited and partial, along the
sweeping contours of American history they do provide a glimpse of
dramatic changes in part born out of the new movements. As Altman
and Castells demonstrate in separate studies, gay communities became

preoccupied with lifestyles during the late 1970s—a trend that reinforced gay political solidarity and effectiveness.[76] This type of linkage is
equally visible in the peace movement. Two participants in Greenham
Common observe that "To oppose nuclear weapons requires a fundamental change in our attitude to life. Clarity of purpose and utter opposition is the only chance to reverse the threat that hangs over all our
lives. What we want to change is immense. It's not just getting rid of
nuclear weapons, it's getting rid of the whole structure that created the
possibility of nuclear weapons in the first place."[77]

Yet another theme running through the new movements, most explicitly in the peace organizations, is a principled commitment to nonviolent forms of struggle that can be traced back to the philosophy of
Thoreau, Gandhi, and Martin Luther King, Jr.,—to a tradition of civil
disobedience that embellishes direct-action politics. The assumption is
that the power structure rests upon a cycle of violence and destruction,
and that efforts to create a rational alternative must therefore break
with that logic. At this juncture the new movements pose two questions:
what should the methods of radical change be in a world shaped by the
threat of nuclear catastrophe, and what ideal of human behavior is
most compatible with a new (presumably nonviolent) social order?

The concept of nonviolent social transformation is a clear departure
from the Marxist dictum that overthrow of the old class system requires
a popular insurrection that, to a greater or lesser extent, will be violent
insofar as the traditional forces will defend their privilege with every
means of coercion at their disposal. The new context suggests that
insurrectionary politics can be avoided insofar as political institutions
are vulnerable to the incursions of an epochal cultural revolution. Nonviolence, moreover, points toward a critique and transcendence of the
"culture of militarism" that E. P. Thompson argues has pervaded the
deepest recesses of civil society in the West.[78] From this viewpoint, an
ethic of pacifism is counterposed to an ethic of militarism; the peace
movement is precisely what its name connotes—a pacific form of mobilization that would lose credibility if its adherents should resort to
violence. In turn, nonviolence introduces new ways of thinking about
politics as well as an entirely new approach to issues of national security
and military defense.[79] (On this question, of course, there is still much
debate even within the peace movement.) Finally, there is a linkage
between nonviolent methods and the struggle against multiple structures of domination. Both the peace and feminist movements, for ex-

ample, have emphasized the connection between the realm of *haute politique* and everyday concerns, thus allowing for a merging of feminist, antimilitarist, and pacifist sensibilities within a single framework of ideology and action.[80] This too suggests a complete redefinition of politics for, as the experience of the Greenham Common women shows, "we cannot achieve peace through violence. It is a fundamental contradiction in terms. Means and ends merge into one another and cannot be separated, so that anything won by violence has the seeds of that violence contained within it."[81]

A significant ideological component of the new movements is their affirmation of universal goals over particular interests. Unlike pluralist corporatism, which favors either bureaucratic influence or interest representation within the political system, the concern is for normative objectives that can have a societal (or global) impact: peace, collective consumption, environmental and consumer protection, new social forms and cultural expressions, democratic participation. The basic premises of interest-group politics are antagonistic to those of comprehensive social transformation since the demands of any single group cannot be identified with the (radical) priorities and needs of society as a whole.[82] To the degree that the new movements have no singular catalyst or focus and are rooted in no all-defining social contradiction, they are governed more by elements of normative choice than by material necessity.

There is, finally, a distinctly prefigurative dimension to modern social movements that flows from the overall thematic outlined in this section. Ultimate goals (e.g., peace, democracy, egalitarian social relations, ecological restructuring) are not separated from either the form or content of immediate political activity. Given a certain anticipation of the future in the present, new movements may embrace a unity of structures, processes, and objectives psychologically solidified by a sense of urgency and exuberant optimism. Effective social change occurs through a fusion of means and ends, methods and ideals, instrumentalities and visions in which there is a constant dialectic between actuality and possibility. As Rowbotham argues, this approach (for feminism) introduces an entirely new model of political action with its uniquely participatory language and style, its merger of organization building with everyday life.[83] Prefiguration thus has no real historical antecedents, despite some affinities with earlier forms of anarchism and council communism. In their radical emphasis on the unity of the personal, cultural, and political spheres, the new movements are clearly *sui generis*.[84]

On the basis of this interpretation, a number of misconceptions and myths about new social movements can be readily dispelled. For example, there is little evidence to suggest a romantic, antimodernist attachment to preindustrial society, much less a glorification of irrational and spontaneous impulses that receive such wide coverage in the media. An exception would be some of the fringe anarchist elements in the ecology and peace movements. Otherwise, the overall ideological thrust of the new movements is easily compatible with a mature (but restructured) industrial order. And surely the "narcissistic" components stressed by Lasch and others do not predominate in such a way as to distort the collective meaning of popular struggles. Nor can it be argued that movement activity is confined to the periphery of bourgeois society or that participation comes mainly from alienated youth or "Lumpen" elements. As we have seen, the movements have built popular strength within an immense variety of constituencies. Moreover, they have probably generated more support within the new middle strata than among the poor, unemployed, or otherwise marginalized. Finally, there is absolutely no basis for concluding that new movements have declined or become historical relics of the 1960s, even if certain forms of early new-left mobilization have largely disappeared. On the contrary, as I have argued, a good many of these movements have expanded in both size and impact during the 1970s and 1980s, and major themes originally associated with the new left seem as compelling as ever.

It might be argued that the very divisions within each type of movement undercut some of the ideological generalizations made in this section, and that there is the danger of idealizing the movements. This may very well be true up to a point, especially to the degree I have stressed the radical implications of popular struggles and have devoted little attention to competing tendencies. There is no denying that within the peace and ecology movements, for example, broad liberal reform currents prevail over leftist ones; much the same could be said about the women's movement. Since real divisions and debates do exist, it is impossible to project any uniform pattern onto the future, radical, liberal, or otherwise. There is no way of knowing how popular movements will develop separately or in tandem, or how they will be translated into political formations with a coherent ideology, organization, and strategy—or indeed if that is even possible over the long term. The very openness and indeterminancy of the movements rules out such a prediction. Still, it is useful to conceptualize broad historical tendencies and, where possible, to suggest a logic of social transformation that could render what is presently a dispersed reality more theoretically intelligible.

Here it might be appropriate to introduce Lucien Goldmann's notion of "potential consciousness." Writing in the tradition of Georg Lukacs, Goldmann poses a fundamental question for insurgent social forces and movements: what is the historically possible consciousness of a specific group or statum? This question implies that we must go beyond the empirical indicators of what people think at a given moment and inquire how they might think and act over time, that is, to project what changes are likely to occur within the realm of popular consciousness under certain historical circumstances. Of course, Lukacs, following Marx, insisted that the antagonistic location of the proletariat vis-à-vis capital would ultimately drive workers toward revolutionary consciousness, however limited their own understanding of this process might be at any given time. Goldmann observes that in the rapidly changing milieu of advanced capitalism the boundaries of popular awareness are being constantly expanded for a variety of social groups; the conditions of mass politicization seem irreversible.[85] Applied to the trajectory of new social movements, this observation might support prospects for their ultimate radicalization as they respond to the realities of economic decline, the authoritarian state, militarism and nuclear buildup, ecological devastation, and the disintegration of urban social life.

At the same time, the transformative potential of such movements depends upon at least three critical factors. First, there is the need for an ideological and organizational convergence of disparate and sometimes competing movements, a possibility that is often affirmed in theory but that remains practically remote.[86] It is surely the case, for instance, that the arms race and nuclear politics touch upon virtually the entire range of issues: economic crisis, political centralization, the environment, feminism, and of course human survival itself. Yet large sectors of the peace movement, committed to the nuclear freeze or other immediate tactical concerns, often hold tight to a single-issue focus that stays free of the murky concerns of ideology and politics. Important steps toward a linkage of movements have been taken in West Germany and England, but the process is not very far advanced. Second, there is the familiar and difficult problem of the state, a problem that I explore more fully at the end of this chapter. If social movements carry forward a revolt of civil society against the state—and thus remain largely outside the bourgeois public sphere—they typically have failed to engage the state system as a part of a larger democratizing project. In the absence of a coherent approach to the state, political strategy is rendered abstract and impotent. Third is the vexing question of how social movements can intersect with working-class struggles in the broadest sense, a question that must be posed on three levels: relations with traditional labor movements at the point of production, convergence with elements of the new middle strata (some of which already enter into the new movements), and a basic redefinition of working-class politics in terms of goals and organizational style, as filtered through new historical conditions. Strangely enough, practice seems to have run far ahead of theory in this area. Witness, for example, the spread of occupational safety and health groups, mobilization in response to the "feminization of poverty," and some ambitious projects in the area of economic conversion (linking the issues of jobs and military spending). As I argue in the concluding chapter, the theme of conversion (defined in broad transformative terms) may well hold the key to a unification of oppositional movements in the advanced capitalist societies.

MARXISM AND NEW SOCIAL MOVEMENTS

If the reality of popular movements in the West calls for fresh analysis and renewed vision, it simultaneously reflects a breakdown of the Marxist theoretical matrix. As we have seen, Marxist categories of thought and action have been challenged by a variety of tendencies since the 1960s; the search for a contemporary radical synthesis grounded in a new critical language is well under way. The question that presents itself, then, is this: in what sense, and to what degree, is the hegemonic theoretical status of Marxism on the left a phenomenon of the past? The study of modern social movements offers perhaps the most fruitful vantage point for exploring this problem.

Marxism presents the image of a bipolar world characterized by epochal struggle between two competing world-historical forces—wage labor and capital, proletariat and bourgeoisie, socialism and capitalism. Economic crisis leading to revolutionary transformation is the projected outcome of this dialectical confrontation. Such a polarized conflict (even when mediated by historical factors) was expected to produce a relatively homogeneous working-class community permeated with an anti-capitalist consciousness. However appropriate this scenario might have looked in earlier phases of competitive capitalism, when urban prole-tarian struggles did in fact commonly lead to civil insurgency, it now seems quite outdated in the more complex and fragmented world in-habited by the new movements. Advanced capitalism is increasingly shaped by multipolar relations, in which the traditional anchor points (production system, state, class, family, community) are extremely fluid and rapidly shifting. To retain a conventional Marxian framework—that is, one grounded solely in class analysis and class struggle—in the face of this fundamentally new historical reality is to reduce theory to a dogmatic, reified enterprise no longer capable of grasping social change. Of course Marxism has contributed immensely to our store of knowledge and analysis, but its utility as a comprehensive framework for understanding the nature of social conflict and political opposition in the new global situation has been exhausted. At the end of his long book on grassroots struggles in several cities, Castells concludes, "Our intellectual matrix, the Marxist tradition, was of little help from the moment we entered the uncertain ground of urban social movements."[87] This is so, at least in part, because "by definition the concept of social movement as an agent of social transformation is strictly unthinkable in the Marxist theory."[88]

This predicament is therefore hardly a temporary one waiting to be resolved by some new discovery or innovation; it goes to the very core of the Marxist theoretical structure. From this viewpoint the crisis of Marxism has three dimensions, each of which is highlighted by the durable impact of popular movements. First, there is within Marxism the philosophical commitment to a rather strict form of scientific ma-terialism, despite moments of ambivalence. The search for global laws of social development and universal principles of class struggle—the legacy of Enlightenment belief in a predetermined historical logic—has the effect of diminishing the space for human action and political initia-tive. (This tendency is especially visible within academic Marxism, given its positivist attraction to quantification and the processing of manageable data.) Second, Marxism is a productivist theory because its categories revolve around the mode of production, the dynamics of accumulation, industrial growth, and, of course, the familiar "labor metaphysic." This has one of two possible methodological implications: either material forces (political economy) occupy sole attention, or other spheres of social existence (authority relations, culture, the family) are reduced to the overarching rhythm of capital. Finally, Marxism has largely failed to confront the problem of domination in its multiple forms, at least in a way that points toward an overcoming of the social division of labor. Given a dialectic tied exclusively to production and class relations, the theory falls short when it comes to establishing a framework for analyzing the new movements and generating a viable political strategy in the West.

In contrast to the laws of regularity stressed by positivist methodology, social movements develop according to a rhythm of insurgency and disruption that defies rigorous quantitative analysis or scientific prediction. As I have argued, theirs is a turbulent world in which the established authority structures and social relations—indeed, the entire mode of communication itself—are subjected to perpetual challenge. In this context patterns of human activity are never really stable or routinized enough to permit elaborate statistical analysis. Popular struggles are scarcely reducible to discrete institutional forms and practices, though naturally there is always some overlap. It follows that the sphere of movements is in many ways outside of and antagonistic to hypothesized laws of historical motion. The very ideological substance of popular movements spills beyond the boundaries of scientific methodology, and thus beyond the parameters of Marxism itself. For example, there is the feminist demand for egalitarian social and sexual relations; the ecological commitment to a quantitatively new mode of economic development; the new populist concern for revitalized community life; and the generalized struggle for democratic self-management. None of these visions has been theoretically integrated into the Marxist tradition, at least in a way that points to a new synthesis, despite some efforts (mostly by feminists) to merge the concerns of Marxism and popular movements.[89]

The Marxist inclination to impose a single paradigm upon the fluid and sometimes chaotic social reality of local movements not only obscures the historical meaning of such movements but encourages a form of intellectual Jacobinism. Its elitist provincialism reflects the social division of labor within bourgeois society as a whole.[90] "Revolutionary" intellectuals, whether based in the party or the university, are considered to possess a store of scientific knowledge that permits them to grasp the "laws" of historical development more clearly than the "masses" who, however rebellious, generally remain confined to their social immediacy.

The autonomy of popular struggles, and with it their democratic thrust, is neatly dissolved within the universal laws of capital accumulation. This is yet another expression of the detached nature of university-based Marxism in most of the advanced countries, or, more specifically, the product of scholastic efforts to build formal theories that can resist the distorting effects of mundane historical conditions. But, as Karl Korsch observed in the early 1920s, the very attempt to construct a "purely theoretical critique" outside the flow of history sooner or later destroys the organic connection between theory and the world of political action. For an ostensibly praxis-oriented tradition like Marxism, such disconnection is ultimately fatal. Antihistoricism of this type can produce little more than "fixed metaphysical categories," which are inert from the viewpoint of social transformation.[91]

The relationship between scientific claims, a tendency toward social manipulation, and the denial of concrete experience becomes a rather transparent aspect of Marxism. Pretensions toward an absolute knowledge of social totality, accompanied by little ambiguity or skepticism, moves theory from the level of critique and analysis to that of an arrogant dogma parading as scientific truth. Often forgotten is the fact that categories of thought—including those emanating from the Marxist tradition—are themselves products of history; they are linked to a particular time and place. In this sense, the very ideological character (and limitations) of Marxism *tout court* have become increasingly visible with the passing of time. The result is a theory that in practice "can lead to anything and justify *everything*."[92]

The second theoretical point of conflict between Marxism and new social movements revolves around the familiar theme of productivism. Baudrillard's reference here seems appropriate: in many ways Marx's work was a "mirror" reflection of capitalist production,[93] since it was shaped by economic categories in a way that made sense within the context of an emergent industrial civilization, the material basis of which liberalism had obscured. The mode of production, value, labor, and of course the role of class were all guiding concepts for historical materialism. Marxism thus emerged as a theory *of* capitalism and as such its premises were confined to the contours and dynamics of that political economy.

In the twentieth century, however, the character of industrial capitalism has drastically changed: the very shape of the economy, labor, and class itself has been completely transformed. The growth of state capitalism, accompanied by the technological revolution, has altered the relationship between politics and economics, reduced the scope of the factory and the manufacturing system, diversified the class structure, generated new strata of technical, professional, and service workers, and marginalized larger and larger sectors of the population as a result of "structural unemployment." As we have seen, it is precisely these emergent social forces—the new middle strata and the marginalized— that furnish the main constituencies of new popular movements in North America and Western Europe. The traditional working class, many sectors of which are tied closely to corporatist interest-group politics, has scarcely contributed to such movements and in many cases (i.e., the women's, ecology, and peace movements) has consciously opposed their goals. When viewed historically, therefore, the notion of universal progress tied to the specific economic interests of the proletariat must be treated with skepticism. As Gorz puts it: "Capitalism has called into being a working class (or, more loosely, a mass of wage earners) whose interests, capacities, and skills are functional to the existing productive forces, which themselves are functional solely to the rationality of capital." [94]

If scientific Marxism expresses a theoretical mirror image of capitalist production, it simultaneously carries forward certain defining characteristics of the bourgeois order: fetishism of economic growth; technological rationality and the incessant drive to dominate nature; the efficiency of centralized economic planning; cultural traditionalism; and so forth. Marxism would inherit while also in some ways extending (and humanizing) the great achievements of capitalist development. One is therefore hardly surprised to find that throughout the twentieth century, as Wallerstein observes, socialism in its various expressions has become an integral part of world capitalism, even if still remaining mostly on the periphery.[95] Modern social movements, on the other hand, represent an historical break, however uneven and fragmentary, with this bourgeois model. Whether or not these movements represent a cohesive social bloc, their unifying thematic lies in a subversive ideological power directed against the capitalist project of economic rationalization and political integration. Despite a number of ambitious efforts toward theoretical reconstitution, contemporary Marxism still lacks an ecological, feminist, and democratic (not to mention cultural) critique of statist growth-oriented industrialism. The result is that popular movements that articulate such critiques inevitably clash with the narrowing confines of Marxist productivism.

Social movements can no longer be understood as secondary to class struggle or as tangential expressions of an assumed "primary contradiction"; they have a logic and momentum of their own that needs to be spelled out theoretically. There can be no denying that popular struggles grow out of real human needs, real historical processes, real social contradictions. Even though they interact with and are shaped by material factors, the economy as such has no automatic theoretical supremacy, no independent laws of development. In the final analysis, the new movements reflect a loosening of the (imputed) direct link between material necessity and political action, industrial expansion and human progress, the interests of the working class and the general struggle for social transformation. One can only conclude that Marxism narrows rather than widens the field of vision.[96] In its class reductionism it blocks efforts to comprehend the intricate relationship between the political, economic, and cultural spheres. Further, it obscures understanding of ideology and popular consciousness as anything other than the direct expression of class formations.[97] Productivist logic thus inhibits systematic analysis of nonclass processes and conflicts in the advanced capitalist setting.

This leads to the third area of tension between Marxism and the new movements: the thematic of domination and the related issue of democracy. The historic goal of democratization, taken up earlier by the anarchist, council communist, and new-left traditions, has been largely repressed within Marxism insofar as democracy was typically regarded as a bourgeois concern or was (in the Leninist case) simply equated with the dictatorship of the proletariat—that is, was viewed as the necessary outcome of class struggle to be resolved in favor of the proletariat. Although Marx himself wrote vaguely of proletarian self-emancipation and class self-activity, the institutional forms and practices expected to shape political power in the transition to socialism were in fact never seriously addressed. The assumption seemed to be that, once the mode of production was collectively appropriated and socialized, the issue of democracy would be naturally resolved. But the long history of both Leninist and Social Democratic parties and regimes conclusively refutes this assumption, for their legacies (either bureaucratic centralism or Keynesian welfare-state capitalism) are unquestionably statist, whatever their accomplishments in the realm of industrialization or social reforms.

Nor can this development any longer be understood as a transitory phenomenon ("the objective conditions simply weren't ripe") or misguided leadership. It has origins in the very theoretical basis of Marxism, which reproduces the logic of domination for reasons already mentioned. Marx's own writing embodied a recurrent tension between rationalization and democratization, but in subsequent Marxist theorizing (especially on the terrain of organized parties) the former always triumphed over the latter. This "subversion of the dialectic," to use Bookchin's phrase, ended up elevating the social reality of domination to the status of a natural (and irreversible) fact. Within such a paradigm the hierarchies of state, bureaucracy, party, and patriarchy would be left untouched. As Bookchin observes, scientism is at the root of the problem: "To structure a revolutionary project [Marxism] around social law that lacks ethical content, order that lacks meaning, a harsh opposition between man and nature, compulsion rather than consciousness —all of these, taken together with domination as a precondition for freedom, debase the concept of freedom and assimilate it to its opposite, coercion. Consciousness becomes the recognition of its lack of autonomy just as freedom becomes the recognition of necessity."[98]

Essentially non-Marxist in its inspiration, popular insurgency in the West has begun to challenge the legitimacy of authoritarian state institutions and, at least conceptually, has questioned the very efficacy of statist programs (nationalization, centralized planning, the command economy). New social movements embody a critique of bureaucracy and champion popular democracy by invoking a range of populist themes: neighborhood councils, workers' control, citizen enpowerment, economic democracy, personal politics, generalized self-management. Their stance toward the bourgeois public sphere contrasts with the institutional politics of Marxist movements and parties. At the same time, the orbit of state activity emerges as a focal point or at least one of the major areas of movement activity. This is so because protest movements are often spawned by those dysfunctions of expanded state activity—bureaucratization, the fiscal crisis, the crisis of legitimation— that seem endemic to advanced capitalism. The proliferation of movements reveals the simultaneous extension of the authoritarian state and its decomposition.

New social movements thus can be located at the intersection of state and civil society rather than in the factory or the traditional system of production alone, which Marxism has identified as the main arena of conflict. In this context, the movements defend social autonomy in the face of an encroaching bureaucratic state and corporate power with its enormous capacity to penetrate all areas of human existence. Here a familiar theme reenters the picture—the conflict between capitalist rationalization and democratization—which once again illuminates the gulf separating Marxist and popular-movement visions of change. Whereas Marxist strategy typically seeks to conquer state power (by means of either civil insurrection or electoral politics) with the aim of redirecting social priorities from above, the new movements often sidestep the bourgeois state apparatus in favor of local democratic structures. Because the entire system of domination in advanced capitalism is so complex, the scheme of revolutionary change laid down by Marx requires extensive reformulation.

Marxism puts forward a reductionist analysis not only of the state and bureaucracy but of other forms of domination. It offers a theory of these forms but loses sight of their historical specificity, as well as their explosive political impact, by forcing them into a productivist mold. Even neo-Marxism, with its greater attention to ideological and cultural factors, fails to generate an adequate theory of bureaucracy, technology, and sex roles.[99] In this vein, the celebrated unity or synthesis of Marxism and feminism has mostly turned out to be the absorption of the latter into the former. The Marxist tradition never really understood women's struggles as anything more than largely class or workplace-centered struggles, and its search for a materialist grounding of feminism has led to a variety of extreme formulations, including efforts to present women in the household as producing surplus value or to conceptualize the family as a capitalist institution. The result is that historical materialism in its varied expressions furnishes few dynamic insights into the distinctive character of gender and sexual oppression: rape and violence against women, prostitution, sexual objectification, abortion, and the like. It offers little understanding of the way in which women's everyday lives are shaped by patriarchal social relations as well as by capitalism. As a corollary, it contains practically no vision of alternative social and sexual forms. Contributions of this sort have come almost entirely from outside Marxism, through the development of contemporary radical and socialist feminism. It is hard to resist the harsh conclusion that Marxist categories possess a built-in sexist (or gender-blind) character that cannot be fully transcended within the present theoretical paradigm.[100]

So the historic gulf between Marxism and social movements appears to have narrowed very little. It is true that a good number of Marxists have in recent years become interested in new-movement themes and have begun to appropriate elements of the new discourse. But these overtures (whether opportunist or not) have made no real dent in the theoretical armor of Marxism, which borrows freely from competing intellectual traditions but fiercely resists any challenge to its basic scientistic and productivist assumptions. This theoretical rigidity alone indicates a loss of critical spirit; there is a fear of breaking with conventional epistemologies and political visions even as the framework loses explanatory power in a world radically changed since the time of Marx and Engels. Oddly enough, what originated as a revolutionary theory now encourages a shrinking of intellectual boundaries, a political and cultural conservatism, and the divorce of thought from the world of concrete social struggles.

On the whole, organized Marxist parties and governments have probably done more to block than to stimulate the growth of social movements. Within the classical (pre–World War I) pattern both social democracy and Leninism—whatever their strategic and organizational differences—conformed to the same elitist, bureaucratic premises: an intellectual-activist stratum, incorporated into a party vanguard, would bring advanced socialist consciousness to the masses in the form of "scientific" discourse. Both were, moreover, equally productivist in assigning supreme historical status to the industrial proletariat and in stressing the imperatives of economic and technological modernization. Consequently, both were suspicious of "spontaneous" popular struggles that the party could not manipulate for its power objectives, and of social and cultural priorities that might conflict with their productivist bias. With the Bolshevik conquest of power and the subsequent collapse of social democracy, Leninism soon became the hegemonic and seemingly most viable force on the European left. Within a decade after 1917 it had evolved into a bureaucratic centralism that in fact repressed social movements both within the Soviet Union and outside of it (e.g., Spain during the Civil War), either by transforming them into "transmission belts" or by destroying them altogether. Later, as Leninism lost its applicability to the postwar setting of advanced capitalism, the Communist parties that grew into mass-based organizations adopted a strategy of structural reformism (the "parliamentary road to socialism") that by the mid-1970s had become known as "Eurocommunism." These parties were clearly less hostile to the popular movements than were their Leninist predecessors, but they too had difficulty establishing a genuine presence in the movements or building a dynamic strategy around them. The Eurocommunists responded in one of three ways, each characterized by ambivalence if not outright hostility toward local struggles: sabotage (France), symbolic appropriation (Spain), instrumental cooptation (Italy). Whatever the pattern of Communist response, the new movements confronted party leaders with intricate dilemmas that they were unable to resolve.

The obsolescence of Leninist strategy in the West has been dealt with extensively elsewhere and need not detain us here.[101] It is enough to reaffirm that both the theory and history of Leninism have given rise to an authoritarian-statist legacy that, in its drive toward cohesion and unity from above, restricts the growth of popular democratic movements from below. Indeed, any sustained coexistence of vanguard party (or party-state) with autonomous local struggles is virtually ruled out by definition, all the more so once the state apparatus consolidates power around its project of "socialist construction." The historical reality of bureaucratic centralism in the Soviet Union and other Soviet-type societies bears this out: in every case the party's organizational imperatives have prevailed over the goals of radical insurgency. The most important exception—the brief success of Polish Solidarity—occurred in a society where party control had been extremely fragile.

Whatever its revolutionary claims, Leninism in fact reproduces within itself elements of the bourgeois division labor; it fetishizes the hegemonic role of intellectuals, leaders, and professional cadres. For this reason it cannot give credence to movements that demand egalitarian and democratized social relations, for to do so would contradict its very raison d'être. Whether in power or out, the preoccupation of Leninist elites with "correct" theory, organizational discipline, and seizure of state power necessarily cuts them off from the rhythm and flow of social struggles, especially those that advance essentially new themes. This separation of the political from the social spheres coincides with an instrumentalism that, in effect, serves to obliterate or at least devalue the personal realm. Thus an irreconcilable antagonism between Leninism and feminism, in both form and content, is largely unavoidable.[102] The fatal contradiction of Leninism is that a single party cannot ideally represent the interests or goals of diverse social constituencies and movements in advanced capitalism; a "master discourse" that seeks global unification of oppositional struggles is neither desirable nor possible.[103] Where the vanguardist mode succeeds—most often in preindustrial countries—the prospects for genuine democratic representation are typically held in check. Regardless (or perhaps because) of their modernizing accomplishments, Leninist regimes normally serve to extend the network of domination while negating the articulation of popular movements within civil society.

Since the late 1940s Leninism has developed into an increasingly marginal political force in Western Europe and North America. Prospects for repeating a Bolshevik-style revolution in the postwar West, where most countries have combined a long phase of economic growth with relatively stable liberal democratic institutions, seem virtually nil. The historic choice presented to the Marxist left has been: either jettison the Leninist model with its authoritarian illusions or risk degeneration into tiny, isolated political sects. The latter path was in fact the destiny of Marxist-Leninist (or Maoist) groups in every capitalist society where they have had any significant presence.

But leaders of mass-based Communist parties (notably in Italy, France, and Finland, and later in Spain and Greece) abandoned any pretenses of vanguardism and insurrectionary politics in practice if not in theory. In political reality, Palmiro Togliatti's vision of a "third road" beyond social democracy and Leninism—of a transition to socialism within a reconstituted, expanded liberal state and grounded in a broad alliance strategy—held sway even where various residues of Leninism persisted. This phase of "duplicity," as Italians called it, lasted until the early 1970s when, through the initiative of PCI leader Enrico Berlinguer and PCE leader Santiago Carrillo, the last vestiges of Comintern politics were officially discarded. Now largely independent of Soviet foreign-policy dictates and preoccupied with electoral politics, Eurocommunist parties grew more sensitive to domestic pressures and, ultimately, embellished a moderate reformism. The very notion of "smashing" the bourgeois state was no longer taken seriously, and opposition to NATO, the Common Market, and even multinational corporations was dropped in favor of "critical support." Before long, the parties evolved into a form of institutionalized opposition, with the "Communist" label offering fewer and fewer clues to actual political behavior.[104] But if the general strategic contours of Eurocommunist parties are similar, their developmental patterns, political situation, and relationship to the new social movements can be shown to contrast greatly.

In the case, first, of the French Communists, events have revealed how the theory of structural reformism was only partially and ambivalently internalized by the PCF leadership: its Eurocommunism was rather incomplete. In 1977 the PCF decided to drop Leninism as its official ideology, a delayed reaction to electoral pressures within France and to deradicalizing tendencies long at work in other Western European parties (notably the Italian). But the PCF was still wedded to traditional forms of organization and strongly resisted any real internal democratization. Though critical of the Soviet model, it continued to identify with the general aims of Soviet foreign policy (endorsing, for example, the military intervention in Afghanistan). More significantly, it held to an old-fashioned *ouvrierisme* that severely inhibited its capacity to build new bases of electoral strength within the emergent middle strata. At a time when the manufacturing sectors were beginning to decline, with a simultaneous expansion of new constituencies, the PCF clung to a heroic vision of the proletariat standing face-to-face with capital that was more appropriate to an earlier capitalist period. Immersed in working-class culture, the party championed traditional virtues linked to religion, family, hard work, and clean living, a posture that could only alienate it from the majority of youth, students, intellectuals, and other elements of the new middle strata. This social location in French politics explains why the PCF could so energetically support traditional growth-oriented programs (including use of nuclear power) while self-consciously distancing itself from new-movement themes.[105]

At the same time, the PCF was more committed than ever to electoral politics and to pluralist democracy as a matter of principle. The party was stranded somewhere between a deep social-democratic instinct and a Leninist vanguard image it hoped to preserve under changing conditions, much like the Italian party of the 1950s and 1960s. For this uneasy dualism and wavering the French Communists were to pay a heavy electoral price.

In the 1981 election, won by the revived Socialists in a smashing victory, the PCF vote dropped to 15 percent (from a consistent postwar level of more than 20 percent) and to forty-eight seats in the National Assembly, by far its worst showing since 1936. This decline continued through the 1983 municipal elections, with the Communists barely able to hold their strength at 10 percent, precipitating a new crisis of morale among party members. The postwar alignment that transformed the PCF into the largest, best organized, and most influential force on the French left was shattered. In part this can be seen as the delayed consequences of the May 1968 events, when the party hierarchy fiercely opposed the mass mobilization of popular groups, insisting that the moment for social upheaval was not "objectively" ripe and that direct action would lead only to misguided adventurism and, ultimately, to the growth of reaction. Given this outlook, the leadership tried to sabotage the May insurgency, toward which end it worked (successfully) with the Gaullist regime to transfer the center of political activity from the streets and barricades into parliament. Whatever the immediate wisdom of that policy, the long-term result would be a chasm between the PCF and new social forces that persisted into the 1980s. The explosive new-left themes given impetus by the May Events—the efficacy of direct action, *autogestion* (self-management), feminism, ecologism, cultural radicalism—were forced outside of and against the party organization. This was politically crippling, since even if the new social movements were not able to sustain a concrete presence in French society after the late 1960s, the themes they embodied were pervasive throughout the middle strata. Hence, while the PCF was striving to discredit the Socialists as just another bourgeois party, it was they rather than the Communists who emerged as the beneficiary of middle strata support in the early 1980s.[106]

Ironically, the PCF's resolute defense of bourgeois institutions against the spontaneous incursions of the new left served to weaken its stature in the eyes of the French electorate; it was a victim of its own ideological inertia and organizational rigidity. By the mid-1980s French Communism stood essentially as a political relic, a conservative bureaucratic machine cut off from the social forces around it, its base reduced mainly to the "Red Belt" industrial areas around Paris and in the North. Unless it alters course drastically, it can look forward to long years of isolation, futile opposition, and a dwindling mass base. The new social forces have passed it by.

In contrast to the PCF, the Spanish Communists—less numerous and more confined to the political periphery than their French counterparts—looked expansively in the direction of the new movements from the outset, hoping to appropriate their energy as a means of building a mass party.[107] During the 1970s a broad range of popular forces emerged from long repression under Franco's dictatorship: the workers' commissions, local neighborhood organizations, feminist groups, the student left, and movements for regional autonomy (e.g., in the Basque country). The PCE leadership saw in these forces powerful movements that would reshape prospects for democratization—and ultimately pave the way toward resurgence of the Spanish left. In the first elections after Franco's death, in 1977, the Center-Right was swept into power, leaving the PCE on the margins of political life (with only 9 percent of the vote and twenty parliamentary deputies). However, no single party was able to capture the support of the new constituencies. From the standpoint of the general electorate, the PCE, whatever its new-found strategic flexibility, was still too associated with its Stalinist past and its ambiguous Civil War legacy.

By the late 1970s, nonetheless, the PCE was moving steadily in a Eurocommunist direction under the stewardship of Santiago Carrillo. It jettisoned Leninism, harshly criticized Soviet domestic and international policies, and set out to implement a PCI-style alliance politics with hopes of building a progressive social bloc. In this fashion the PCE sought a framework for simultaneously breaking with Francoism and initiating the transition to socialism. It had become perhaps the most adaptive and "liberal" of all nonruling Communist parties, despite the vocal resistance of a sizable old guard. The party's Ninth Congress in 1978 was open and participatory to an extent unprecedented for Communist parties. Spain thus appeared as a major testing ground for Eurocommunist strategy, which sought to integrate the best of the Marxist tradition, liberalism, and the social movements. Yet, within a few short years, this hope collapsed amidst a stunning Socialist electoral triumph in 1982 that gave the PSOE not only a clear majority but uncontested hegemony on the Spanish left. The PCE came out of the debacle with only 3.6 percent of the vote and thirteen deputies in the Cortes—an outcome that effectively reduced it to a minor force within the political system. It now faced a predicament from which it was unlikely to recover.

Carrillo, who was removed from the party leadership in the aftermath of the defeat, blamed the outcome on "external" factors such as the attempted military coup preceding the elections. But the PCE's problems went much deeper. The party leadership, aging and cut off from the most dynamic social forces in Spanish society, was still tied to the past in ideological if not organizational terms: its conservative style alienated many voters, especially young people who were put off by the party's cultural traditionalism and patronizing attitude. In this context a far more youthful and culturally adaptive PSOE leadership could step into the void—made even larger by the collapse of the right—and appeal to the new constituencies without having to explain away historical anachronisms. The PSOE skillfully played on the themes of local self-government, antimilitarism, feminism, and cultural renewal. The PCE, for its part, tried valiantly to appropriate these themes but in the end did so in a much less enthusiastic and convincing manner. This limited and largely symbolic attachment to the new movements was surely dictated by a profound ambivalence within the party shaped by residues of Leninism and workerism.[108]

The Italian version of Eurocommunism (the *via Italiana*) departed rather significantly from the French and Spanish patterns. If the PCF's relationship to the new movements was largely one of avoidance and conflict, the PCI, after an initial phase of hostility, looked upon them as a source of political momentum. Whereas the PCE sought to build roots in the popular forces but failed, the PCI accomplished its project —at least to the extent that it could make electoral advances in the 1970s that brought it to the doorstep of national power. Of all Eurocommunist parties, the PCI alone rode the crest of the social movements. Yet the outcome for the movements themselves was ambiguous, since the PCI's strategem was essentially cooptative and instrumental within a narrowly defined electoral framework. Thus, the large and militant Italian new left, which began as an "extraparliamentary opposition" in the 1960s and then evolved into more stable "emergent" movements during the 1970s, was simultaneously enfranchised and domesticated.

The PCI was transformed from a small underground organization into a mass party with over two million members during the Resistance struggle against fascism at the end of World War II. From this position it gradually extended its presence into broad sectors of Italian society during the 1950s and 1960s, including trade unions, peasant associations, cooperatives, and local governments. It broadened its base among the middle strata (as Togliatti had enjoined), thereby increasing its electoral support from 20 percent in the late 1940s to nearly 35 percent in 1976. Togliatti's structural reformism paid electoral dividends as the PCI finally achieved near parity with the long-dominant Christian Democrats while solidifying its position as the world's largest nonruling

Communist party. Although the Communists did not enter national government, they did become (in alliance with the Socialists) a ruling force in many provinces, cities, and towns. The result was that, in contrast to the PCF and PCE, the Italian party enjoyed an overwhelming hegemony on the left throughout the postwar years. (Although the Socialists were part of governing coalitions since the early 1960s, their share of the vote rarely exceeded 10 percent.) Moreover, after years of difficult struggle to create an image of respectability, the PCI did appear to offer a viable and realistic alternative to an entrenched power structure. By the 1980s it had developed into a party with an established (nonrevolutionary) identity, despite internal conflicts over how far to move along the Eurocommunist path.

From this position of institutional and ideological strength—and with deep roots already in the middle strata—the PCI leadership could make genuine overtures to the social movements. It did so, however, with the aim of integrating them into a parliamentary-centered politics that restricted popular initiatives from below and narrowed the movements' objectives.[109] The PCI actively proselytized white-collar workers, professionals, intellectuals, students, women, and local activists—all the more so once (after 1973) it became preoccupied with entering national government, first through the *compromesso storico* tactics (a governing alliance with the DC) and then through the vision of a "left majority." By incorporating both the movements' themes and constituencies, the Italian Communists could stem insurgency from their left and weaken the challenge of new parties (Radicals, Proletarian Democracy) while also revitalizing their own membership and base.

But this scheme presented its own dilemmas, since the PCI leadership was willing to bend only so far to integrate the real interests and priorities of new movements. Such interests and priorities would be taken seriously only to the point where they would not alienate more supporters (e.g., Catholics, blue-collar workers, old-line militants) than they might attract. In this vein the PCI championed peace and opposed deployment of Pershing II missiles in Sicily, but remained lukewarm toward the peace movement itself and was very careful not to extend its criticism of this American policy to the whole of NATO or the Common Market. And though it ultimately took up the "woman question" directly in the mid-1970s and fought for progressive divorce and abortion legislation (though not without much prodding from below), it strongly resisted taking up the broader range of feminist concerns, which it argued would be divisive for party members and supporters. Of course the PCI could always offer the promise of concrete economic and social reforms along with expanded female participation; but feminist issues like child care, birth control, more liberal abortion laws, consumer and health-care services, and the quality of neighborhood life were either dropped or pushed back into an acceptable cultural matrix.[110] Finally, the PCI proclaimed its commitment to local democratic forms (e.g., neighborhood councils, committees of the base) that had emerged out of the radical left, but the party simply absorbed them into its hierarchial structure and subverted most of their popular content. For the PCI, as for other Eurocommunist parties, "democracy" had little meaning beyond *pluralist* democracy. Indeed, it never really formulated a theory of democratic socialism that transcended the old political boundaries. This was predictable enough, given the degree to which the party had become institutionalized.[111]

The PCI was compelled to instrumentalize social movements because its statism and productivism (however modified) could not possibly accommodate the radical side of these movements. Having long ago abandoned Leninism and the Soviet model, Italian Communism evolved in the direction of northern European social democracy. Once in power, the PCI would most likely set out to rationalize the political system and economy within a state-capitalist framework, hoping to overturn traditional barriers to growth that have chronically plagued Mediterranean countries.[112] On the other hand, as a mature electoral machine the PCI could hardly afford to ignore or reject the new movements, especially since it could provide a pole of attraction to social forces that, out of a sense of frustration and impotence, might turn to the Communist party as the best hope for winning *some* political gains. The fact, too, that the new left in Italy differed from similar radical currents elsewhere in its continued adherence to Leninist and workerist ideology no doubt facilitated this uneasy marriage of convenience.[113]

The experience of all three of these parties reflects the incapacity of Eurocommunism to establish a presence compatible with the main thrust of the new movements. The reality is that Eurocommunism constitutes not so much a fundamentally new strategy as a transitional phase in the European left, between an outmoded Leninism and the emergence of new oppositional forms. Structural reformism embodies the tense merger of two contradictory elements: a Marxist (or even Leninist) theory and an eminently social-democratic practice. Efforts

to resist the logic of social democratization in favor of the old commitments, as in the case of the PCF, can lead only to further isolation and
powerlessness. Both the PCE and PCI seemed ready to adapt to this
logic—and to accept its ideological consequences—but only the PCI
was strong enough (and tactically wise enough?) to effectively pursue it
and thereby allow for a partial opening to the social movements. In
none of these experiences, however, is it possible to speak of a new
oppositional model that departs significantly from the past. The theory
of structural reformism, despite its pretenses of a "third road," actually
ends up recycling the Bernstein–Kautsky synthesis that governed the
Second International.[114] Today, at a time of intensifying global economic crisis, this model can be seen in a more critical light—as an
elaborate strategem for overcoming the crisis in particular capitalist
societies through a project of rationalization.[115]

Where nominally Marxist parties like the PCI have managed to exert
a powerful leverage within the state system, their institutionalization
over time obstructs initiatives toward mass mobilization and popular
democracy. This strategic impasse is far too historically embedded to
be reversed by an immediate shift in leadership or policies. In the final
analysis, institutionalization simply broadens the division between state
and civil society and, correspondingly, between parties and the more
radical expressions of popular movements. From this viewpoint, the
very notion of a viable *Communist* party in the historical definition of
that term is meaningless. The vanguardist, productivist, and workerist
ideologies that reflected the Bolshevik and early capitalist experiences
simply lack resonance in the West.

FROM SOCIAL MOVEMENT TO POLITICAL STRATEGY

The emergence of diverse social movements on a large scale is a dramatic new phenomenon in the history of advanced capitalism and,
potentially, in the evolution of a new radicalism. In their challenge to
vanguardism and statism, productivism and workerism—in their demand for a reconceptualization of politics—the new movements reflect
the limits of traditional modes of opposition that revolved around the
poles of social democracy and Leninism. As a critical and ecumenical
source of fresh theoretical insights, popular struggles call into question
the classical scenario of an economic crisis leading to explosive ruptures

within capitalism that will sooner or later produce a revolutionary outcome: the new crises, and the strategies employed to confront them,
will necessarily be political and cultural as well as economic. Modern
social movements have already begun to demystify not only the premises
of bourgeois domination but those of the Marxist left as well, insofar as
both embrace, in rather different guises, an Enlightenment schema of
capitalist rationalization. And it is a pattern of economic development
that, as Wallerstein observes, is becoming manifestly irrational on a
world scale.[116]

Yet this is only a small part of the story. Although Piven and Cloward
are correct to observe that popular struggles as disruptive, anti-institutional forces can have a greater impact on social change than formal
mass organizations, the fact remains that the historical experience of
new social movements as such has typically been one of frustration and
impotence. There have been few concrete political victories. Movements
come and go, often leaving behind quite ambiguous legacies. Consider
the fortunes of the French May, the Italian revolutionary left, the West
German SDS, and the American new left. Although it remains true, as
I have argued, that many durable organizations (urban, feminist, environmental, antimilitarist) have superseded these earlier failures, the
immediate political results have not been any the less disappointing.
The reality is that, whatever their transformative potential, new social
movements have shown a marked incapacity for confronting the imperatives of political power.[117]

A great difficulty is that most of the movements, often according
to their own self-definition, choose to operate at a distance from the
political system itself.[118] Under these circumstances the winning of concrete objectives is always extremely problematic, with the result that
movement activists and supporters can easily become disillusioned.
Where this occurs organizations can easily be overwhelmed by a collective mood of despair, which can take any number of forms: privatized
retreat, escapism or spiritualism, cultural inversion centered on community building, even terrorism. Another possibility, described by Castells,
is the steady encapsulation of a social movement (e.g., the gays in San
Francisco) into a more or less self-contained subculture.[119] Finally there
are the prospects of simple absorption into the political system, with a
single-issue organization evolving into a legislative and/or bureaucratic
interest group. In this latter example, of course, the activity is no longer
that of a movement.

Even though mass defiance can surely win intermediate reforms, in the end it will deliver nothing more than limited and sporadic expressions of revolt—with the reforms themselves often nullified at a later stage. Refusal—the withdrawal of legitimacy, the questioning of authority, the assault on traditional values—cannot itself generate real change, let alone structural transformation. In other words, the new movements alone cannot be agents of historical change, for it is the *political context* that gives popular struggles meaning and vitality, direction and potential, and, perhaps most important, the capacity to contend for power. It follows that the predicament of local movements is tied to the problem of strategic translation, to the struggle for a durable ideological and organizational expression. Without some kind of organic linkage between vision and methods, between theory and politics, the most radical and energetic commitments will only yield to a paralyzing futility rooted in the disintegrative tendencies already mentioned.

For this reason it is necessary to place in sharp relief the dynamic element of politics—the role of state power, legislatures, party systems, interest representation—that the new movements (and their theorists) so regularly and self-consciously avoid. Of course the sphere of movements is eminently that of the "social," the extra-institutional, of civil society in the broadest sense; their dialectic has been antibureaucratic and antistatist, part of historic attempts to carve out realms of autonomy shielded from authoritarian incursions of the bourgeois state. But this fetishism of civil society leaves unresolved the question of how radical goals can be achieved without completely restructuring the state system itself. A purely negative, reactive stance is not adequate to this task. Thus the lack of a distinctly political (and therefore strategic) outlook can be expected to produce one of two outcomes: either the well-known lapse into spontaneist and localist impotence, or retreat to more manageable liberal reform efforts where minor victories are possible. Here a critical rediscovery of politics suggests a dialectical and transformative thrust that integrates the dual imperatives of popular initiative *and* state reconstruction. Such a framework appears to fit the realities of advanced capitalism, where the political arena constitutes the focal point of social conflict and interest representation. Indeed, it is hard to conceive of significant radical-democratic struggles ever bypassing this terrain. Democratization involves first and foremost the growth of social movements, but it also requires new institutional forms and practices—emergent processes linked to the decomposition of the old state apparatus—and this cannot be achieved by popular struggles confined to civil society. The problem, however, is not only to unite politics and social movements but to redefine this relationship in such a way that any return to vanguardism and statism is precluded.

What new-movement experiences bring to this project is a reconceptualization of the familiar concerns of state, power, and democracy, including a broadened understanding of the ways in which the forms of domination permeate every sphere of social life. The boundaries of power and authority cannot be viewed as solely within the confines of discrete institutions and formal processes, since the ensemble of relations intersects civil society and the political system. As Nancy Hartsock argues, an analysis of domination-based gender as well as class relations demands a more comprehensive theorization of power than can be found in either liberalism or Marxism.[120] Insofar as social and personal dynamics are embedded in patterns of domination, the themes of sexuality, of male and female identity, of women's "material life activity" must enter into the struggle to reconstruct and democratize political institutions.[121] Thus, feminist sensibilities begin to redefine the very character of power. Kathy Ferguson suggests, further, that feminism embodies a powerful, if still incipient, transcendence of the stale, cold, instrumentalized discourse that shapes the existing (bureaucratic and patriarchal) public sphere. As such, it renders problematic the "mass-based permanent organizational" model typical of Leninist, social-democratic, and most liberal reform efforts. Feminism represents a "submerged discourse" that stands outside the male-dominated framework of public debate and action.[122] In Ferguson's words: "To be firmly located in the public realm today is, for the most part, to be embedded within bureaucratic discourse; to be firmly grounded in the non-bureaucratic is to be removed from the arenas of available public speech."[123] Democratization, therefore, involves considerably more than a challenge to authoritarian state power; it necessarily extends to those institutions, processes, and ideologies tied to the multiple forms of domination.

In looking at the political context of the new movements, the most vital (and perhaps most difficult) challenge is to reconstruct power in such a way that the polar extremes of statist "conquest" and romantic detachment are broken. Rather than a posing of civil society against the state, there must be a dialectical tension, or reciprocity, between the two involving a merger of the social and political realms. This entails far more than normative prescription, for it recognizes that in advanced capitalism the separation between state and civil society, state and economy, has narrowed or become blurred to the point where the boundaries are no longer clearly distinguishable. Each sphere is part of an overlapping and interlocking network of institutions and processes. If the state exists as neither prime mover vis-à-vis other social forces nor strict instrument of class domination—that is, if civil society has no real independence from the state—it follows that any transformative strategy will have to move on two levels. Poulantzas' conception of the state as a shifting ensemble of forces rather than as a discrete formal entity standing above civil society, is a suggestive point of departure.[124] Employing this logic, popular struggles would not seek to control or attack the state apparatus so much as to work through it with the aim of reconstituting the entire political system on egalitarian and democratic foundations.

Still, there is an unavoidable tension between the prefigurative style of social movements and the necessarily instrumental concerns of winning, securing, and administering political power. Strategic translations of popular struggles are bound to involve conflict between the social and the political, local and national, movement and party.[125] On one side there is the sphere of mass disruption, democratic claims, and perhaps a certain romantic attachment to community; on the other there is the realm of bargaining and compromise, organizational routine, and commitment to modernity. Of course there are no easy strategic formulas for resolving the conflicting pressures that accompany any dynamic process of social transformation. The Marxist left has typically asserted the political over the social, instrumental over the prefigurative, and modernizing over the democratic or communitarian realms. What the thematic of new movements introduces, as we have seen, is precisely the reverse side of this dualism. A truly radical strategy, however, would arrive at a synthesis of the two, creating a political framework in which vital linkages—between divergent types and levels of movements, for example—could occur in a more or less organic, non-Jacobin fashion. Such a strategy is unthinkable in the absence of a convergence between party and movements, institutions and community, parliament and local councils, electoral and direct-action politics. Thus the future vision must be nothing short of an entirely new system of authority, a new kind of state.

All of this revives a theme stressed at the outset, the struggle for a post-Marxist theory and politics. Of course the constituent elements of a new synthesis cannot be anticipated in detail, if only because the character of social movements it must comprehend is emergent and still tenuously defined. At a minimum, however, it will have to rely upon a critical, nonobjectivist epistemology, a nonproductivist social theory that takes into account the diverse forms of domination, and a democratic political theory compatible with the ideal of a nonbureaucratic, self-managed society. But it cannot dismiss the Marxist preoccupation with material and class forces because it would then no longer be possible to make sense of either national or global development. The political formations (e.g., parties) likely to give expression to post-Marxist currents will be socially and ideologically heterogeneous, probably quite fragile, and vulnerable to assorted internal contradictions. I have incorporated such already-existing formations under three broad categories: Eurosocialism (Mediterranean Europe), new populism (United States), and the Green tendency (northern Europe). Since the late 1970s there has been a vigorous political opening—as well as new theoretical directions—that makes it possible to analyze these initiatives. The remaining chapters of this book will explore each strategic model with the purpose of arriving at generalizations concerning their long-term transformative potential.

3
EUROSOCIALISM
AND THE SEARCH
FOR A THIRD
ROAD

Of the three identifiable post-Marx-
ist alternatives, the Eurosocialist phenomenon in the Mediterranean
has been the most politically far-reaching. In 1981–82 alone Socialist
parties won unprecedented electoral victories in France, Greece, and
Spain; by 1984 not only these countries, but Italy and Portugal as well,
were governed by Socialists either alone or in coalition. The Socialist
tradition, historically associated with northern and central European
countries and viewed by many as simply the progressive side of capitalist modernization, had apparently received an infusion of new life.
Eurosocialism had become a critical pole of attraction for the nonsectarian left.

The Mediterranean Socialists gathered strength at a unique point in
postwar European history. A convergence of economic, political, and
ideological forces seemed peculiarly advantageous to new radical initiatives. Advanced capitalist societies were approaching an end to economic growth in a context of energy crisis, spiraling military costs,
and fierce struggle for competitive advantage in the world market. The
consequences—massive unemployment, balance-of-payments deficits,
fiscal crisis, decline of social services—were exacerbated by the failure
of statist Keynesian techniques to reverse the downward spiral. In
southern Europe, this predicament was further sharpened by a chronic
technological dependency upon the developed countries (the United
States, Japan, England, West Germany). There was also a gradual (but

marked) transformation of the class and social structure resulting from the erosion of old manufacturing sectors and the expansion of new sectors tied to the public and service domains, technology and communications, culture and the "knowledge industry." It occurred, moreover, at a time of mounting popular disenchantment with bureaucratic structures that, in countries like Spain, Portugal, and Greece, produced an intensive assault on an authoritarian state connected for years to fascist or right-wing military rule.

From the standpoint of leftist strategy, the Eurosocialists found themselves in a position to step into a huge ideological vacuum created by the eclipse of Marxist (and Leninist) models on the one hand and the corporatism of organized labor on the other. Earlier fascination with Soviet, Chinese, and other Third World models had been exhausted, and Eurocommunism—after its brief moment in the mid-1970s—was unable to fulfill its promise. In this fluid situation the search for alternative vehicles of change, for new strategies of social transformation, was both possible and necessary. It was the Socialists, unencumbered by outmoded ideological and organizational formulas, who now began to occupy this terrain. The Eurosocialists, by all appearances, had become bona fide heirs to the European radical tradition or, put another way, the locus of a refurbished post-Marxist dialectic.

An important source of Socialist revitalization was the explosion of new social movements in the preceding two decades. To be sure, electoral successes as such cannot be mechanically explained by the presence of new movements, especially when the actual weakness of such movements in some countries is taken into account. Yet it is my contention that outside the historical reality of the new movements—that is, outside the universal themes, visions, and constituencies which they encompass—the Eurosocialist project is unintelligible. The movements of feminists, ecologists, peace activists, youth, and urban groups, whatever their specific ebbs and flows, did establish a political momentum in the 1970s that helped to rekindle a democratic political culture that could be recuperated by the non-Communist left. Eurosocialism held out hope for a new kind of radicalism, or democratic socialism, attuned to broad social and participatory concerns of the new movements, rooted in diverse constituencies, and intent upon exercising governmental power in a new way. This would be no mere recycling of welfare-state politics but would constitute an ambitious departure along the elusive "third road" beyond both social democracy and Leninism.

THE SOCIAL-DEMOCRATIC IMPASSE

Eurosocialist leaders, from François Mitterrand in France to Felipe Gonzales in Spain to Andreas Papandreou in Greece, have sought to distance their parties from the legacy of European social democracy, which in their view had become fully absorbed into the logic of capital. What was the character of this historical impasse? How did the Euro-socialist alternative define its strategic course vis-à-vis its ideological precursor? And most significantly: to what extent have the new departures been successful?

At its inception, beginning in the 1890s, social-democratic theory—filtered mainly through the German party (SPD) and the influence of Karl Kautsky—clearly defined its mission as one of socialist transformation. It was Marxist and resolutely anticapitalist, even if the methods it chose would generate certain insurmountable dilemmas. In the thinking of both Kautsky and Eduard Bernstein, which centered on parliamentarism despite their different theoretical premises, the overriding goal was to merge socialism and democracy. Later, even as virtually every Social Democratic party in Europe became institutionalized within the bourgeois state system, thereby giving expression to interest-group politics, national chauvinism, and ideological moderation, the ultimate (Marxian) objective of socialist revolution was still loudly proclaimed. After the Bolshevik Revolution, most Social Democratic parties, by now debilitated as a result of their overt class collaborationism during the war and their failure to intervene effectively during the post-war crisis, converged upon a militant anti-Communism that would forever stamp their development. Beginning in the 1920s, the Socialist (Second International) and Communist (Third International) parties would compete for working-class support and would also, on occasion, join together in short-lived Popular Front governments (France, Spain, Italy). At one time or another, mass-based Socialist parties took root in at least a dozen European countries and, except for Italy where the Communists remained strong, exercised varying degrees of hegemony within the left. With the notable exception of Spain, their commitment to electoralism and gradualism seemed to fit the mood of popular constituencies in the period after 1923; civil insurrection was no longer a real possibility. Simultaneously antifascist and anti-Stalinist, the social-democratic tradition was the main bearer of a secular liberalism between the wars, upholding the ideal of a socialist order still more or less inspired by Marxism.

By the early 1950s the newly created Socialist International (SI) was composed of thirty-nine member parties, the majority of them in Western Europe. This number grew to fifty-four parties with 15 million members in 1970. Increasingly removed from the Communist orbit, the postwar Socialist tradition evolved into a moderate, even centrist, force during the 1950s and 1960s, a trend that was reinforced when several parties (in France, Sweden, Austria, and Norway) were voted into power. These parties presided over a continuous expansion of the welfare state, but they generally did not propose (much less implement) any broad anticapitalist reforms. The gulf between Marxist theory and liberal practice became much too visible to ignore, with the result that the former was explicitly and officially abandoned by one party after another, starting with the SPD's Bad Godesberg declaration in 1959. The very idea of a proletarian revolution, or indeed any kind of socialist revolution, in the conditions of advanced capitalism was dismissed as utopian.

Yet the long-term transformation of social democracy was infinitely more complex. The problem was that a strategy of incrementalism and parliamentarism adopted by party leaders was incompatible with any systematic attack on the centers of bourgeois economic and political power. Absorption was inevitable, given the logic of winning and maintaining power within the framework of pluralist democracy: preoccupation with immediate results, vague appeals and programs, the balancing of diverse interests, institutional stability, and catering to large capital as a source of new investment. Such pressures typically conflicted with the imperatives of popular mobilization.[1] In the end electoral politics created a distance between the party apparatus and the mass constituencies, which could only reproduce class fragmentation rather than class unity and solidarity.

The political consequences were predictable enough: postwar social-democratic governance in several European countries in effect allowed for the expansion of domestic capital, the multinationals, and an EEC based in the monopolies—not to mention a strengthening of the NATO alliance. Of course the welfare structure did improve the quality of life for a large percentage of poor people and workers, and Keynesian mechanisms did soften the worst features of the capitalist cycle. But these economies were still controlled by private capital, income distribution was scarcely altered,[2] and the bureaucratic side of the state grew. The historical role of social democracy was to manage the crisis tendencies of capitalism, administer the economic and political system more efficiently, and rationalize the process of accumulation by means of state planning, fiscal controls, and technological innovations. In this way the Social Democratic parties became instruments of bureaucratic order, technological rationality, and the mixed economy, an outcome far removed from what even Bernstein and Kautsky envisioned at the turn of the century. Their ideologies were closer to the reality of liberal pluralism than to the ideal of socialist egalitarianism. Their fear of losing electoral support was matched only by a fear of civil crisis that might force them to break with the logic of capital in order to preserve their "socialist" image and working-class support.

The prototype of social-democratic integration was the West German party, which governed through a Socialist-Liberal coalition (with the Free Democrats) from 1969 to 1982. In the period when the SPD was carrying out extensive social reforms, it further solidified its position as a statist, modernizing, cold-war party committed to preserving established class and power relations. Even before its stunning defeat in the March 1983 elections, the SPD was an exhausted and depleted party incapable of presenting a real alternative to the Christian Democrats, a predicament that went much deeper than Helmut Schmidt's particular brand of cautious, managerial leadership.

In the political sphere the SPD presided over an authoritarian "security state" that, among other things, enacted measures barring leftists from public employment (*Berufsverbot*). The West German state apparatus, always a powerful ally of capital, was bolstered by a renewed social contract involving government, big business, and unions designed to guarantee growth-oriented production on a foundation of regulated class conflict.[3] The security state functioned to mediate group interests while setting clear limits to popular participation. Economically, the SPD-engineered Modell Deutschland followed three lines of development: encouragement of a free market with the export sector playing a decisive role, technological restructuring of industry, and expansion of trade with Soviet-bloc countries. Only the broad range of social reforms, implemented during the early 1970s, distinguished this accumulation model from more strictly capitalist models introduced elsewhere —but even so, the main beneficiary of these reforms was the middle class.[4] All of this was designed to bolster the already privileged position of West Germany in a period of sharpening international economic competition. In foreign policy the SPD energetically followed the U.S. lead and endorsed the guiding cold-war assumptions and policies: a stronger NATO, U.S. nuclear supremacy over the Soviets, deployment of the Euromissiles, and so on.[5] Even Willy Brandt's earlier *Ostpolitik*, or "opening to the East," was intended to fit the American preoccupation with detente at that time. SPD criticisms of U.S. intervention in the Third World, moreover, were generally timid and lacking in conviction.

By the late 1970s the SPD encountered its own celebrated crisis of political identity, which was less a crisis than the actual loss of identity as an oppositional force in German society.[6] Now a catch-all electoral party with a remote relationship to its popular base, it drifted away from even that minimally cohesive leftist culture which sustained it throughout the 1950s and 1960s. Tied to an old-style bureaucratic politics rooted in technocratic pragmatism, it could never make contact with the new social forces sweeping Germany during this period.[7] As SPD programs and policies became less distinguishable from those of the Christian Democrats, the likelihood that it could offer solutions to the mounting economic crisis had become distant. Neither the party leadership nor the labor movement seemed capable of, or interested in, overcoming a long-ingrained corporatism.

In this context the SPD, lacking any transformative ideology or commitments, could only fall back upon platitudinous slogans and a manipulative realpolitik. As Oskar Negt writes, "categories such as class struggle, exploitation, and classless society are gone for good, and are openly replaced by the postulates of Christianity and morality." Beneath this the SPD, "when considered as an electoral party, in terms of party structure, in terms of the social composition of its leading bodies and congresses, is a party of clerks and public servants."[8] It would appear that Michels' famous concept of "embourgeoisement," applied originally to the SPD just after the turn of the century, had lost none of its validity for the German setting.

A second variant of the social-democratic model is found in the Italian Socialists (PSI), who have been junior partners in a national governing coalition for most of the past two decades. If the SPD is understood as the classical mass-based integrative party with decisive influence on societal development, the PSI can be seen as a meditating power broker within the Byzantine maze of Italian political groupings. A party much smaller than the SPD—with a peak of 11.4 percent of the vote in 1983—the PSI has typically sought a moderate "balance" between right and left, between the Christian Democrats and the Communists. To this end, particularly under the modernizing leadership of Bettino Craxi, it has stressed the need for large-scale "grand reforms" that would give the Socialists identity and leverage vis-à-vis the Christian Democrats while simultaneously neutralizing the Communists or at least undercutting their claim to a role in government.[9] For Craxi, the ideal is a "complex equilibrium" of political forces within which the PSI could play a leading, or at least influential role.[10] In reality, however, the PSI has been more or less absorbed within the ruling coalition dominated by the DC. Thus, its effectiveness in pressing for real social reforms, beginning with the *apertura alla sinistra*, or "opening to the left," in the 1960s, has been extremely limited.

The problem with the PSI, aside from its relatively small electoral base, is lack of clear political identity and ideological direction. In this respect the Italian Socialists are devoid of even the rationalizing coherence typical of the German and Swedish parties. Since he was named party secretary-general in 1976, Craxi has frequently pointed to the SPD as a model for the Italian party. (Of course the SPD has had, until the rise of the Greens, no competition on the left, whereas the PSI has been completely in the shadow of the Communists.) Like the SPD, the PSI long ago abandoned Marxism, but in contrast to the northern European parties it never fully embraced the shift toward capitalist modernization—although since Craxi became prime minister in 1983 there have been gestures in that direction.[11] The reality is that the PSI remains a diffuse, patronage-based party organization without a serious long-range strategy or vision; its evolution is confined largely within the orbit of the DC. It offers no program critical of monopoly capital or the multinationals; its concept of democracy and decentralization lacks specificity; and it favors an austerity policy for labor, having in 1984 weakened the mechanism of wage-indexation (the *scala mobile*) that stood as a symbol of trade-union gains in the 1970s. Moreover, it adheres to an uncompromisingly pro-American and pro-NATO foreign policy that included a strong endorsement of Euromissile deployment. A party of civil servants, teachers, and cultural workers, with little presence in the labor movement, the PSI has been as distanced from the new movements as has the more labor-centered SPD. This paradox is explained by the party's brokerage role and its *clientelismo*, both of which favor an extreme instrumentalism quite at odds with the thrust of popular struggles.[12]

Since 1945 the progressive role of Social Democratic parties in many Western European countries has been associated with a phase of capitalist prosperity, increased state planning, and expanded social services. It has been a period, too, of strengthened working-class economic and political power.[13] By the late 1970s, however, this model seemed to have reached its historical limits, not merely as a source of oppositional politics but as a form of governance within capitalist society. The Keynesian welfare state, anchored to a corporatist social contract designed to reconcile class interests, began to unravel in the midst of global crisis and repoliticization of social forces outside the state system, which could no longer maintain its productivist legitimation supports. One response to the decline of social democratic integration was return to an anti-Keynesian conservatism (monetarism, supply-side economics, reprivatization), which helps to explain the success of politicians like Reagan, Thatcher, and Kohl.

Beneath this historic shift lies a pattern of development that is both continuous and predictable. The social-democratic version of structural reforms, at least in its postwar incarnation, was never meant to challenge or overturn the capitalist mode of production—or the bourgeois state; it was conceived from the outset as a means of streamlining the system in order to alleviate its crisis tendencies, introduce new social priorities, and improve the living standards of the general population. As we have seen, this project centered on several dynamic elements: a rejuvenated welfare system, social planning, technological modernization, fiscal and monetary controls—all meant to eliminate obstacles to smooth accumulation and growth within a mixed economy. At the same time this model depended upon investment of the bulk of political resources in the bourgeois public sphere (notably, in electoral, parliamentary, and interest-group activity). The outcome in most cases was a party of corporatist assimilation, cut off from the process of mass mobilization when out of power and a responsible partner in crisis management when in power. (The Social Democrats were better prepared than conservative parties to satisfy those imperatives, given their base of support in the labor movement and their enlightened rationalizing ideology, which set them apart from both the narrowly capitalist and preindustrial groupings.) This phenomenon is hardly new or unexpected; it was built into the Bernsteinian strategy of "evolutionary socialism" at the turn of the century, and the full unfolding of embour-geoisement was simply a matter of time.

The social-democratic predicament stems in great measure from col-lapse of the Keynesian synthesis—from the crisis of a state-managed network of production, social control, and class reconciliation. Histori-cally, several factors have contributed to this turn of events. First, be-cause of the dramatic slowdown of economic growth in the advanced countries, overall demand for public services could no longer be met at the old levels, thereby undermining one of the key programmatic rationales of social democracy. As Keynesianism confronted the fiscal crisis of the state, it was impossible to sustain both social programs and the existing tax structure, full employment and balanced budgets, wage increases and dynamic investment policies. Second, environmen-tal pressures made capital accumulation (Keynesian or otherwise) more difficult. The dysfunctions of poorly planned industrialism and urbani-zation—blighted cities, depleted land and water, polluted air, toxic wastes—imposed new material and ideological obstacles to further economic expansion. Moreover, the diminished supply of natural re-sources (or at least the added expense of obtaining them) meant that development was more problematic than in the preceding era of "eco-nomic miracles." Third, Keynesian solutions naturally brought new levels of state intervention and, with it, the bureaucratization of social life that eventually gave rise to popular resistance in the form of grass-roots movements. With the state apparatus supplanting or complement-ing the market as a regulatory framework and thus having to resolve a wider range of problems, it began to absorb systemic contradictions to the extent that the very fragility of state power became more visible.[14] Fourth, growing numbers of workers refused to accept labor discipline and austerity policies imposed by governing Social Democratic parties in their efforts to counter economic stagnation. The social contract made less and less sense, especially once it became clear that restructuring programs were throwing large numbers of workers out of jobs. Finally, this predicament was aggravated at a time of structural fragmentation of the global economy. In the absence of a rational system of coordi-nation beyond the nation-state (or small regional groupings of states like the EEC), the cyclical and anarchic tendencies of international capital inherent in a competitive market were likely to get out of con-trol.[15] The absence of any "Keynesian" mechanism on a world scale meant, for example, that multinational corporations could pursue their interests largely outside the fiscal and monetary regulations established by particular governments. It also meant there could be no viable collective planning instrument for shaping investment policies or counteracting the dysfunctions of uneven development.

For these reasons, the social-democratic model that seemed to operate so smoothly through the postwar growth period was destined to fall under the weight of its own contradictions. Responding to intensifying pressures of the global crisis, it had no alternative but to adapt to the priorities of capitalist accumulation: profits, productivity, balance of economic interests, austerity, export-driven growth. In such circumstances Keynesianism could not possibly move beyond the parameters of market competition, whatever social goals it might project and whatever ideological attachment to welfare-state democracy it might have.[16] From this viewpoint it would have been difficult to imagine, within the European social-democratic experience, a real shift toward socialized forms of investment, popular control of the state and economy, and egalitarian class and social relations. The illusion that mass-based Social Democratic parties with a claim to governmental power could set in motion a transition to democratic socialism, whatever their own limits and contradictions, was now finally dispelled.

THE EUROSOCIALIST ALTERNATIVE

The revitalized Socialist parties in the Mediterranean can be understood in terms of both continuity and rupture with the familiar social-democratic pattern: continuity in that they originated and developed as parties of the Socialist International, rupture to the extent that they offer an image of ideological rebirth and dynamism in contrast to a stale welfare-state politics. The Eurosocialist upsurge of the early 1980s had its origins in the 1960s, in the new-left upheavals typified by May 1968 and the later proliferation of social movements. It signaled a fresh start toward deep structural transformation that had historically eluded the Social Democrats and Communists—and which seemed beyond the capacity of the new left. It held out an eclectic and imaginative ideology, an open and nonbureaucratic style of leadership and organization, a populist form of mobilization, and a youthful membership in touch with new constituencies, new ideas, new possibilities. Eurosocialism was post-Marxist insofar as it rejected the singular dialectic of class struggle, viewed history as an open field of forces, questioned the primacy of material conditions, and dismissed prospects of an economic crisis leading to cataclysmic revolution. At the same time, it retained a conventional social-democratic faith in electoral politics—now more broadly defined—and in the familiar parliamentary road to socialism. In a few short years the Eurosocialists did in fact expand the sphere of political struggle, as well as the very conception of socialism. At issue was whether they could preserve and concretize their commitments while laying the basis of a promised "third road" strategy for the future.

Among southern European Socialist parties, the French were clearly in the vanguard of this tendency. With the old SFIO weakened and in disarray, and Gaullism still more or less hegemonic, the May Events jolted the established political alignments. Beneath the post-1968 institutional recuperation of the Fifth Republic came a marked political fluidity, a leftward shift of popular consciousness. One outgrowth of this unsettling process was a reborn French Socialism that, in the period 1969–71, experienced a profound radicalization from bottom to top. A massive influx of youth, women, ecologists, young workers, and Christian militants (most of whom identified with Michel Rocard's PSU, or Unified Socialist party) transformed the party from a stagnant bureaucratic institution into a dynamic activist organization more in touch with the social and cultural changes sweeping France.[17] In the wake of an ideological renewal stimulated by the involvement of *gauchistes* active in the May Events, the PSU turned its back not only on its own social-democratic legacy but even more emphatically on the Communists, who were seen as hopelessly attached to an outmoded Stalinist apparatus and steeped in cultural conservatism. Galvanized by a new stratum of leftist intellectuals, who thought in terms of a "break with capitalism," the Socialists pressed for novel approaches and fresh solutions grounded in a radical critique of bourgeois society.

Integral to Socialist growth and renewal in the 1970s was a creative and nonsectarian leadership drawn largely from the ranks of progressive sectors of the new middle strata (teachers, professionals, cultural workers, and some civil servants). Though moderate by party standards, François Mitterrand epitomized these leadership qualities; his organizational rebuilding campaign was simultaneously visionary and pragmatic, freed from past ideological formulas and clichés. Indeed, there seemed to be ample room within the party for a coexistence of both old and new left, Marxists and non-Marxists, workers and middle strata.[18] Party membership grew from a low of 10,000 in 1969 to 40,000 in 1973, then skyrocketed to 165,000 in 1977 and nearly 200,000 in 1981. The PSF-affiliated trade-union confederation, the CFDT, reached a level of 1 million members by 1980.[19] Moreover, at a time when the PCF was losing support despite its Eurocommunist turn, the Socialists were able to run up almost equally remarkable electoral gains, outpolling the PCF in 1978 by 22.6 percent to 20.6 percent only a decade after the SFIO had been left for dead. With the PCF still immersed in a workerist politics, the Socialists were shrewdly constructing their own version of alliance strategy or *fronte de classe* designed to build a left majority that could win governmental power (ideally, without the PCF).[20]

The surprising 1982 electoral victory of the PSOE symbolized revitalization of the Iberian left after several decades of fascist rule. Even before Franco's death in 1977 the beginnings of democratization were well under way, in part the result of popular reaction against an authoritarian model of industrial development (and political control) that had kept Spain on the margins of Western Europe. Already by the late 1960s, an expanded public sphere outside the dictatorial state made possible the rise of grassroots movements—workers' commissions, neighborhood struggles, and a variety of new-left, youth, and women's organizations. As in the French case, such popular mobilizations served to rejuvenate the long-dormant Socialists (and to a lesser extent the Communists) during the mid and late-1970s. The PSOE emerged from the Franco period organizationally weak and ideologically compromised, its image one of order and traditionalism.[21] Its main political objective was the liberalization of Spanish society—a gradual and peaceful transition from fascism to bourgeois democracy within the confines of the monarchy. Beyond that it had no clear identity or mission.

After 1977, however, the PSOE experienced an uneven but steady process of radicalization. Transformed in great measure by the popular movements, which were fueled in turn by widespread anti-Franco sentiment and economic crisis (with 15 percent unemployed), the Socialists were able to build a new leadership around the influx of thousands of young militants, a good number of whom had participated in assorted new-left, anarchist, and Trotskyist groups. Their concerns went far beyond restoration of liberal democracy or Spanish entry into the European community, encompassing a creative blend of economic, political, and social demands that challenged the centers of privileged interests. More populist than workerist, the PSOE appealed to diverse social groups but had no real presence in the trade-union movement, a deficiency it tried to correct in 1977 by setting up its own labor confederation (the UGT). In 1979 the party leadership, following the pattern of the French Socialists, turned to the dynamic Felipe Gonzales for new guidance and a fresh beginning. Gonzales, whose charismatic appeal did much to ensure the party's rapid growth, envisioned a distinctly progressive but non-Marxist course with the aim of putting the PSOE at the head of a majority social bloc. As the membership consensus at the 28th Congress reaffirmed, such a departure would allow for the development of innovative programs, enabling the Socialists to occupy a terrain distinct from both centrist social democracy and the PCE.[22] What the PSOE did share with these tendencies, of course, was an abiding commitment to electoral politics.

This Socialist strategy produced results that surprised even the party's most dedicated supporters. From a tiny sect in the early 1970s it rapidly grew into a mass party ready to contend with the "centre" and right for governmental power. The rise of the PSOE was hastened by several conditions: widespread anti-Francoism, the economic crisis, fragmentation of the center-right (UDC), and the remarkable impasse of the PCE. In the 1977 national election the Socialists won 29 percent of the vote (compared with 9 percent for the PCE), setting the stage for their astonishing performance in 1982. Membership increased from less than 4,000 in 1975 to 200,000 in 1979, and then built steadily over the next few years.[23] Vigorous grassroots organizing activity was carried out in all parts of the country, with the result that by 1982 the Socialists were easily the largest and most dynamic political force in Spain—an impressive achievement in the span of barely a decade.

Like their French and Spanish counterparts, the Greek Socialists experienced rapid organizational growth and ideological renewal during the 1970s just as the old political alignments were being upset by emergent popular movements. And like the Spanish party, the Greek PASOK was an expression of strong democratizing tendencies impatient with years of right-wing authoritarian rule. But in contrast to the French and Spanish Socialists, the Greek party originated more or less de novo; its roots in the traditional left were tenuous at best.

Founded in 1974, PASOK created a grassroots presence through sustained populist activism, building its membership to 150,000 by

1977 and its electoral support to 22 percent of the vote and ninety-three parliamentary seats in the same year.[24] It fed on popular hostility to the traditional power structure—to social forces that had kept Greece on the European periphery for so long: the military, the church, multinationals, the EEC, and of course a corrupt and repressive Greek state. Much of this hostility was channeled into local (urban and rural) citizens' movements and a variety of new-left groups that eventually formed the backbone of PASOK. Party strength was quickly consolidated through the development of more than 1,500 branch and local committees in towns and villages throughout the country. Much like the French and Spanish parties, PASOK set out to construct a broad multiclass alliance with hopes of mobilizing an electoral majority. It emerged as a party not only of the middle strata (which were smaller numerically than elsewhere in Europe) but of the disenfranchised—urban workers, peasants, petty bourgeoisie, the poor. The result of these efforts was a stunning Socialist triumph over Karamanlis' fading New Democracy forces in 1981.

The PASOK leader, Andreas Papandreou, epitomized the new type of Socialist leader represented by Mitterrand and Gonzales. As an intellectual from an academic background, he saw in PASOK a vital source of new ideas for Greek development—a party freed from conventional social-democratic attachment to Keynesian reformism, bureaucratic solutions, American hegemony, and cold-war ideology. One key to Papandreou's success was his ability to synthesize the concerns of democratic socialism and Greek nationalism. (Because of a closer identification with Third World struggles, owing in part to the peripheral location of Greece itself, PASOK was less anxious than either the French or Spanish parties to jettison Marxism entirely.) Thus Greece would have to break decisively with its dependent past and follow its own "third road" outside the dictates of the Socialist International, which PASOK saw as a tool of American and Western European monopoly interests.[25] The absence of a strong social-democratic tradition in Greece, along with the division of the Communist left into two small competing parties, would presumably make this task easier.

After barely a decade of political revitalization, therefore, the Eurosocialist moment arrived in the early 1980s, securing a Mediterranean outpost of resistance to the rising tide of conservatism in the West. First, in May 1981 the French Socialists won a lopsided victory over a demoralized and divided Gaullist Right; the PSF's 38 percent of the vote and 283 seats in the National Assembly ensured it an absolute working majority for five years, making France the first advanced capitalist country to elect an explicitly leftist government to national power. Mitterrand became the new president with a promise to radically alter the political landscape of the country and, with it, to perhaps inspire changes elsewhere in Western Europe. As new social constellations came to the fore, the terrain of discourse and struggle—the sense of what was historically possible—seemed to expand almost overnight. The PSF breakthrough instilled a mood of optimism and exhilaration—and even more astonishingly, a spirit of unity on the left—that had been absent from France through most of the postwar years. Thus, while the Communists dropped from 20.9 to 15.4 percent of the vote and from eighty-six to four seats in the legislature, they entered the Mitterrand government and accepted four cabinet portfolios, though not without some ambivalence. Overall, the obstacles to far-reaching structural change seemed very manageable.

Both the Greek and Spanish parties duplicated these results within the next eighteen months. In October 1981 PASOK won a governing majority in parliament (172 out of 300 seats) and the presidency with 48 percent of the vote. The conservative New Democracy returned only 115 deputies while the two Communist parties were able to elect only 15. Papandreou characterized this turn of events, which ended a half-century of right-wing rule, as a critical historical shift that would permanently alter the face of Greek politics. PASOK followed its national success a year later with a string of local electoral victories that included 175 mayorships out of the 276 contested.

The PSOE followed suit in October 1982, winning 48 percent of the vote (nearly double its showing of 1977), giving it 202 of 350 seats in the Cortes, control of the presidency, and complete supremacy over the debilitated UDC (now reduced to 22 percent of the vote and 65 deputies). The Socialist victory further ensured the downward slide of the Communists, who dropped to 3.8 percent of the vote and from twenty-three to five seats in the legislature. Gonzales' appearance in Madrid on election night was celebrated by a large tumultuous crowd that appeared to sense the historical meaning of the Socialist landslide: it was a moment that symbolized the final, dramatic break with Francoism and the legitimation of liberal democratic institutions. Indeed, Socialist popularity no doubt grew in the wake of a failed military coup the preceding year and subsequent rumors of new attempts. The PSOE further solidified its national gains with new successes in the May 1983 municipal elections, where it won an absolute majority on sixty-five city councils representing urban areas of more than 100,000 population. As in France and Greece, the Socialist ascent to power in Spain created large new areas of political space within which popular struggles could be articulated and advanced.

Before we look at the actual record of the Eurosocialist parties in power—and the strategic dilemmas they have encountered—it may be useful to explore more fully the political outlook they share. Of course there are a number of historical and theoretical differences among the French, Spanish, and Greek Socialists. Still, in programmatic terms it is possible to identify four broad commonalities: democratization, non-Keynesian economic restructuring, cultural renewal, an independent foreign policy. On the strategic level, each party is committed to a "third road" version of parliamentary socialism that requires a multi-class social bloc of forces, ideological-cultural transformation, and the gradual rebuilding of economy and state quite distinct from the old crisis-polarization-upheaval scenario. Eurosocialism represents a blend of novelty and tradition, new approaches and old commitments, radicalism and moderation, which, as I shall argue, is a source of both strength and weakness as reflected in the reappearance of some familiar predicaments.

The Mediterranean Socialist project suggests first and foremost a new phase in the long struggle for democratization; its slogan could well be "democracy first, then socialism." This theme can be understood as an expression of three complex and interwoven dimensions: the historical context in which the parties came to power, their style of political mobilization, their long-range ideological objectives. Thus, for the Spanish and Greek Socialists electoral victory signaled the rupture with a long period of fascist governance during which the left was suppressed and marginalized, whereas for the French it meant a return to left hegemony following more than two decades of Gaullist authoritarianism. The context was one of a rather sharp (and perhaps durable) realignment of political groupings built upon a popular wave of anti-authoritarianism. This shift in itself constituted an important step toward democratization. For each party, moreover, success depended upon a lengthy prior stage of grassroots organizing and popular initiatives by diverse social movements. The electoral breakthrough was essentially the culmination of democratizing changes within the political culture, as I have argued. Finally, in opposition to both Leninism and classical social democracy, Eurosocialist parties were firmly committed to the goal of democratic socialism—to the concept of self-management, workers' control, and local autonomy—in contrast to the bureaucratic model, which views the state (or party-state) as the decisive agency of change.

In the case of French Socialism, democratization meant overturning the entire legacy of statism, or *dirigisme*, that goes back to Napoleonic centralism in the period of the French Revolution. The PSF matured in the 1970s as a party of *autogestion*—as an expression of the new-left participatory spirit that it incorporated from the May Events and carried forward into the 1980s. Its goal was to broaden the decision-making base of all French institutions: the welfare apparatus, large-scale industries, trade unions, the educational system, and of course the state itself. To this end the CFDT called for a new type of unionism centered on "control" issues as well as broad social demands, although this emphasis declined after 1981. Decentralization of managerial functions would take the form of democratic planning, which would give regional and local bodies greater decision-making power vis-à-vis the elite corporate and technocratic stratum. The PSF would be the vehicle of a "capillary democracy" that filters up organically from below, ultimately transforming the state in the process.

For the Spanish party, on the other hand, the critical task was to curb the immense power of the military, which had been a dominant force in the country since 1868 and which remained a bastion of extreme reaction even after Franco's death. The PSOE promised to expand civilian control over the military, reduce its size and budget, and professionalize all of the branches (thereby, presumably, undercutting the fascistic bent of the officer corps). The PSOE also campaigned on a platform of attacking state bureaucracy, decentralizing the political system, and overhauling the Francoist legal code and court system. The Greek Socialists emphasized more or less the same priorities. They declared their intention to reduce the power of the church, the military, and multinational corporations—although their first priority was the public sector, which they set out to "modernize" by eliminating the long-ubiquitous practice of *rousteti*, or "corruption." PASOK additionally focused its attention on the proliferation and strengthening of local committees and producers' cooperatives in both the rural and urban regions of Greece, and on the regeneration of grassroots branch activity within the party itself.

The second Eurosocialist goal—basic restructuring of the domestic economy—was both as vague and as ambitious as the concept indicates. At the most general level, of course, each party proclaimed its long-term commitment to a socialized economy in which resources would be collectively owned and equally shared, class divisions would be abolished, and foreign dependencies would be severed. More immediately, Socialist programs stressed the theme of economic modernization that (particularly for Spain and Greece) would enable the Mediterranean countries to overcome their poorly competitive and semicolonial position within the international market. Allowing for differences of emphasis and context, the programs identified three vital tasks: public supports for technological development, democratic planning for social and economic reforms, the gradual breaking down of exploitative monopoly interests. Assuming significant momentum in this direction, the intermediate result would be a post-Keynesian mixed economy in which a nonstatist public sector and market forces would combine in a dynamic, growth-oriented, democratized system. The process of restructuring was expected to be relatively nonantagonistic. Riding the crest of huge popular mandates, the Socialists envisaged rather sweeping changes; yet the anticapitalist substance of these changes, not to mention the political means for achieving them, remained fuzzy.

The French Socialists came to power with a promise to restore industrial growth, combat unemployment, and initiate the transition to a more egalitarian economy. Their first priority was massive new infusion of public funds into the high-technology sector (e.g., electronics and computers) with the goal of boosting its profitability and competitive position in the global market. If this scheme was successful, the high-technology sector could become the accelerator for French economic expansion in the 1980s and 1990s. The PSF was also prepared to carry out a new series of nationalizations in the leading industrial banking, and commercial sectors, but within a more democratic framework (based upon the spirit of *autogestion*) than was previously the case. Technology-inspired growth, along with significant increases in public investment and control, was expected to generate new jobs, raise workers' standard of living, lessen demands on the welfare system, and of course reverse the always-precarious balance-of-payments deficit. Ironically, these expectations actually depended upon a modified Keynesianism that shared a number of traditional social-democratic premises.

As for the Spanish and Greek parties, they too had become preoccupied with growth and modernization. The PSOE counted on intensive technological progress to set in motion a rationalization of the country's archaic industrial sectors, which would finally permit integration of Spain into the European community from which it could derive all the benefits of modernity. This was less a matter of creating super-competitive technology sectors as such than of applying technology to enhance productivity in all areas of the economy. In contrast to the PSF, the Spanish Socialists were reluctant to embark upon any significant nationalization projects or otherwise expand state power. Modernization itself, with heavy emphasis on the market, was expected to produce a dynamic sequence of changes that, at the very least, would significantly reduce unemployment (which reached 16 percent in 1982). Once the economy was thus reinvigorated, the Gonzales government would presumably be in a position to initiate more sweeping social reforms.

PASOK's efforts to transform the Greek economy were likewise tied to technological rationalization, but with perhaps a greater sense of urgency, given the country's more peripheral status. A project of state-directed technological research and development was designed to improve overall productivity, stimulate growth, and cut the balance-of-payments deficit, with the hope that this would ease the worst manifestations of the crisis. At the same time, PASOK took a more radical (and nationalist) position toward the role of internationally based monopolies than either the French or Spanish parties. Although Greece had joined EEC in 1979, when the Karamanlis regime was in power, PASOK promised to reassess a relationship that, it argued, simply perpetuated Greek colonial status and economic backwardness relative to Western Europe and the United States. Aside from strong encouragement for small businesses and producers' cooperatives, however, the actual means by which monopoly power would be effectively broken (or even curtailed) were never clearly defined. Surely PASOK had no ambitious plans for further nationalizations (60 percent of the economy was already state controlled), or for regulating the huge export-trade sector exemplified by Greek shipping. Socialist leaders anticipated that such challenges—and probable confrontations—could be deferred.

In its concern with pursuing a "third road," Eurosocialism energetically took up themes—feminism, the environment, culture—to a far greater extent and in a different way than had social democracy (and of course Leninism). The impact of new social movements was very much in evidence. Still, the parties' programmatic content was rather tentative and vague—in part because this was novel terrain, in part because the global crisis forced the leadership to give first priority to economic issues. Further, insofar as the Socialists championed an ideology of secular modernity, there was a general belief that economic progress itself would trigger large-scale social and cultural changes that in turn would undermine traditional values. It was thought that efforts to impose such changes through state policy might end up being counterproductive.

In each country the most urgent area of social concern appeared to be women's issues, which entailed three levels of change: a call for reforms that had been central to the feminist movement (liberalization of abortion and divorce laws), broader female participation in Socialist parties and governments, and the abolition of sexist practices in society. Environmental problems were less directly attacked, although the parties did outline general plans for developing solar power, fighting air and water pollution, and reversing urban blight. Because France is more highly industrialized than Spain or Greece, and possibly owing to the earlier inroads made by the ecologists, the PS seemed more prepared than either the PSOE or PASOK to carry out immediate environmental reforms. The very appealing but poorly defined vision of "cultural renewal" was likewise taken up by each of the parties. Tied to a certain rekindling of economic and political nationalism, the struggle for cultural revitalization meant above all expanded public subsidies of creative work in film, art, music, and literature which, it was thought, would strengthen those progressive indigenous traditions already predominant in Mediterranean culture. Finally, the Eurosocialists pushed for broad secularizing changes in the educational system (less church intervention) and the legal code (more liberal censorship laws, and the like), especially in Spain and Greece, where traditionalism persisted and even bourgeois democratic freedoms had long been denied.

Yet it is in the sphere of international politics that the Eurosocialists seem to have departed most emphatically from the traditional social-democratic pattern. The major Social Democratic parties were without exception pro-NATO and anti-Soviet. They viewed the U.S.-designed Atlantic Alliance as the fulcrum of political and military strategy, which of course in the postwar years was directed against the Soviet bloc. The new Socialist foreign-policy orientation taking shape in the Mediterranean, however, began to resist the hegemony (or aspired hegemony) of both superpowers and challenged the very legitimacy of the bloc system, which it saw as dangerously destabilizing—the source of an arms race that could precipitate nuclear war at any time. Thus the French, Spanish, and Greek parties all expressed ambivalence (and even hostility) toward the NATO alliance to one degree or another. For this reason they hoped to frame an independent foreign policy that could provide new political leverage for Western Europe (and perhaps for the continent as a whole) in a realigned global structure. For the Third World, this meant creating an alternative to both U.S. imperial control and the Soviet developmental model—a "democratic socialism" that would, given a progressive balance of forces, receive support from the advanced countries. The strategic means for implementing such a novel foreign policy, however, varied greatly from party to party.

For the French Socialists an independent role in world politics served to justify further extension of the nuclear *force de frappe* that was inherited from de Gaulle. For Mitterrand, the concept of balance between the two blocs suggested not so much reduction of military forces or disarmament as a project of nuclear modernization that could give credibility to a deterrent force separate from that of NATO, the United States, or England. Though this stance obviously distanced the French from NATO, it did not lead to a policy of outright rejection; the goal was instead one of mutual coexistence within a shared anti-Soviet framework. The PS was perfectly willing to live with a strengthened NATO, including deployment of the Euromissiles, so long as this did not encroach upon French prerogatives. The Socialists came to power with the aim of increasing military spending and bolstering the French position in Europe, based upon the merger of a left political vision and a nationalist realpolitik.[26] Neither Spain nor Greece possessed such a nuclear potential, however, so that the Socialist fear of bloc politics gave rise to a more rejectionist attitude toward NATO and the continued U.S. military presence in southern Europe. Both the Gonzales and Papandreou governments spoke of terminating relations with NATO (the PSOE promising a national referendum on the issue) and closing down American bases in their countries, although this would necessarily be a very gradual process. Each party was supportive of grassroots peace initiatives—in contrast to the self-conscious indifference of the PS—and each opposed the U.S. decision to station the Euromissiles, even though neither Spain nor Greece was chosen as a nuclear site. Their foreign policy was motivated by the historic struggle against subordination to the industrialized powers, which infused it with a "Third

World" dialectic of the periphery challenging the core while also emu-
lating it in certain ways. For both parties there was also an obsession
with curtailing the power of a military apparatus in which reactionary
ambitions were still very much alive. Whatever the points of convergence within Eurosocialist foreign policy, therefore, the tensions produced by these critical differences were bound to surface as each Socialist government began to stake out its strategic perspective.

From the outset Eurosocialism, insofar as it could be seen as a unified
tendency, represented a novel departure made possible by the bankruptcy of social-democratic and Leninist strategies in the European
setting. It promised a new phase of radical politics in the Mediterranean
and perhaps elsewhere. Moreover, it appeared at a time when Marxist
theory (at least its politicized expressions) seemed to have exhausted its
potential, when Soviet global prestige was at a low ebb, and when
hopes for a Eurocommunist breakthrough (notably in Italy) failed to
materialize. In many respects the strategy of these Socialist parties was
reminiscent of post–World War I Austro-Marxism, which entertained
the idea of a "third road" between Bernsteinian social democracy and
Bolshevism grounded in a new theoretical synthesis that was never fully
worked out and that, in any case, produced little in the way of practical
results.[27]

Whatever the nature of the Eurosocialist "synthesis," it clearly has
much in common with classical social democracy while also departing
from it in significant ways. It shares with its predecessor a firm commitment to parliamentarism, winning incremental reforms within the
political system, and building multiclass alliances. It foresees no total
break with the bourgeois power structure—that is, no civil insurrection
leading to a new type of state. To the degree that it anticipates no
epochal crisis or collapse of capitalism, it projects an evolutionary and
relatively peaceful model of change not too far removed from the theory
of Bernstein. But Eurosocialism differs from social democracy not
simply because of its ideological eclecticism and social diversity but
because of its more expanded political vision, resulting in great measure from the impact of the new popular movements. Whereas social-
democratic parties were typically comfortable in their historical role as
rationalizing agents of capitalism, the revitalized Eurosocialists present
an image of democratic socialism that embellishes a fundamentally new
kind of society. The vision is one of a fully democratized and culturally
rejuvenated order that could never be achieved through simple utili-

zation of the bourgeois state apparatus for socialist ends. On the contrary, it suggests the reconquest and ultimate reconstitution of state institutions by means of a lengthy series of democratizing structural reforms. The path to socialism would therefore be neither a direct overthrow of the power structure nor a smooth evolutionary process in which the old forms gradually yield to the new. The long-term outcome, presumably, would involve a complete overturning of the complex system of domination rather than yet another recycling of efforts to administer that system more humanely and efficiently.

At the same time, Eurosocialist parties have appeared as little more than faint echoes of their distant Marxist origins; their hallmark has been a willingness to rethink old ideas, programs, strategies, and methods. They assign no privileged status to the industrial working class or labor movements; they anticipate no explosive crisis of capitalism; they are suspicious of old-fashioned productivist solutions (whether Marxist or Keynesian or conservative) that rely upon the benefits of growth; and they view the sphere of ideology and politics—not the economy—as the key arena of social transformation.

Yet in their efforts to construct a popular electoral base the Socialists have upheld an image of moderation, caution, and conciliation—to the extent that their programs are infused with a vague and minimalist language. Quite clearly their leaderships are wary of being perceived as too radical by the majority of voters, most of whom are not yet prepared to accept fundamental changes in the economy or political system. Thus, during electoral campaigns the parties have typically emphasized safe issues (peace) or vague promises (economic stability and more jobs) under the rubric of broad slogans—*por el cambio*, "for a change" in the case of the PSOE, *Megali Allaghi*, "Great Change" in the case of PASOK. They have tried to project a sense of optimism and progress tied to modernizing advances that, though understandable from the standpoint of Mediterranean countries looking to break the cycle of dependency and marginality, was bound to conflict with the themes and priorities of the social movements. Moreover, aside from occasional references to socialism as an ultimate goal, party statements have never adequately specified the methods required to carry out even intermediate objectives. Even prior to the Eurosocialist ascent to power, therefore, the ideological limits of this peculiar brand of structural reformism seemed evident, whatever the grandiose claims of exuberant supporters. But such ambiguities could not nullify an overriding historical fact:

within a relatively brief time span the Mediterranean Socialist parties had become large and successful post-Marxist formations with at least some linkage to the new movements.

Eurosocialist victories brought not only a mood of euphoria to southern Europe but an expanded left-wing institutional and legislative presence enabling the parties to implement long-delayed economic and social reforms. And in each country the Socialists did introduce measures for progressive change within the structural-reformist framework. Within a year of their electoral successes the parties swept away all outward appearances of conservative hegemony while carrying out a flurry of reforms in virtually every area—the economy, the state, culture, family life, religion, the military. Only in the realm of foreign policy did they refrain from undertaking any significant new departures.

On the reform front the French Socialists were clearly the most ambitious and, in the period from May 1981 to late 1982, they announced one series of far-reaching political measures after another. Nationalizations—previously a focal point of tensions between the PS and the Communists—were extended to about 90 percent of banking and credit enterprises and to several key industrial sectors: electronics, computers, steel, glass, armaments, and aluminum. With public control of investment funds greatly expanded (to roughly 35 percent of the total), the state could stimulate and protect favored areas of growth (such as electronics and computers) so as to bolster the French economy in the world market. Welfare and social security benefits were extended, the minimum wage was increased by 10 percent, and unemployment was countered through higher levels of public spending (including a large boost in the military budget). The Mitterrand government also moved to decentralize the structure of power—that is, to reverse the seemingly inexorable tendency in France toward technocratic statism. In March 1982 the PS announced a law "on the rights and liberties of communes, departments and regions" that gave new authority to local and regional bodies while curtailing the legendary authoritarian domain of the prefects. At about the same time the Auroux Laws were enacted to reinforce the bargaining rights of trade unions. In other areas the government established a ministry of women's affairs, embarked upon two large solar projects, doubled the funding for French arts and culture, abolished the death penalty, and broadened occupational safety and health regulations. From all indications the Socialists were able to push through these and other changes with only minimal resistance from the right opposition and from conservative managerial elites.[28]

If the Spanish and Greek Socialists achieved less during their first year or so in power, they nonetheless managed to generate the same atmosphere of change and dynamism; they projected an innovative leadership more open and ready to challenge established patterns. In February 1983 (just five months after taking office) the Gonzales government decided to nationalize the Rumasa conglomerate, Spain's largest business empire with a work force numbering 300,000, and close down eighteen banks. Although the PSOE conceded that this had more to do with restructuring inefficient or failing enterprises than with any move toward socialism, it did provide the government with new leverage over investment. Meanwhile, the Socialists introduced measures that would reduce the political role of the Catholic Church and professionalize the military, although the expected purge of conservative senior officers was proceeding quite slowly. On social matters the government sanctioned divorce, legalized marijuana, and made serious (but still limited) efforts to bring more women into political life. Perhaps most important, the PSOE brought an energetic and youthful leadership to a Spanish society that had been dominated since the late 1930s by a very closed fascist (or semifascist) hierarchy.

Roughly the same pattern unfolded in Greece. Once in power, the Papandreou government embarked upon new projects with a fervor and optimism unprecedented in modern Greek political history. In 1981 the country was swept by a populist spirit. PASOK did not immediately nationalize any large-scale industrial or financial enterprises, but it did act to overturn the rigid monetarist policies that the Karamanlis regime introduced in 1979. At the same time, it also enacted a more progressive taxation scheme, expanded some welfare benefits, and permitted small businesses to obtain loans under more favorable conditions. During their first year in power the Socialists granted wage increases keyed to the level of inflation, froze consumer prices, and broadened social security benefits. In the political sphere they pushed for a liberalization of trade-union and labor laws, greater separation of church and state, and professionalization of the civil service — reforms that would clearly take many years to carry out fully. In February 1983 the Greek parliament approved sweeping changes in family laws which, among other things, would make divorce easier and give women legal equality. In early 1984 women were guaranteed equal pay for equal work. As in France, the

Socialist government more than doubled the budgetary support for indigenous cultural and artistic programs.

Contrary to what many observers had anticipated, the Eurosocialists
refrained from initiating any profound shifts in foreign policy, a consequence in part of their greater preoccupation at the outset with domestic
issues. The PS, as we have seen, felt compelled to follow the dictates of
Gaullist nationalism; their only deviation was a modicum of support
for some Third World anti-imperialist movements (for example, in
Central America). The early foreign policy record of both the PSOE
and PASOK might be summed up as one of loud words (directed against
NATO, the EEC, and U.S. hegemony) but relatively little action. Unlike the PS, however, the Spanish and Greek parties did oppose the
Euromissile plan, even if Gonzales seemed to waver from time to time.
But the PSOE delayed a promised referendum on Spanish participation in NATO, and PASOK stepped back from its earlier commitment
to have U.S. military bases removed from the country and to reassess
its EEC membership. By 1984 both the Gonzales and Papandreou governments seemed ready to coexist, however uneasily, with the hegemonic reality of NATO and the EEC, raising the question of whether
Eurosocialism did in fact represent a final break with traditional social
democracy on international issues.

But this question could not be restricted to the realm of foreign
policy, since within only three years of the historic Eurosocialist breakthrough even the most far-reaching domestic initiatives were engulfed
in a wave of conservatism and retreat that sapped the momentum and,
ultimately, the popularity of the parties. This development, moreover,
must be understood as more than a temporary setback or tactical maneuver, for it can be traced to a particular set of ideological, strategic,
and historical factors that in the end were destined to block Eurosocialist progress in the direction of a "third road." These factors had
begun to impose a series of dilemmas similar to those previously confronted by social democracy.

THE DILEMMAS OF STRUCTURAL REFORMISM

An emphatic turn toward political moderation and ideological retreat
within Eurosocialism, which by 1984 would dash the radical expecta-
tions of even the most optimistic partisans, could be observed in three

broad areas—the economy, structure of state power, and foreign policy. In some cases (for example, the international policies of the French Socialists) this conservatism reflected not so much a shift or "retreat" as it did a single continuity from previous goals and priorities. For the most part, however, this process did involve a significant (if not altogether surprising) retrenchment in terms of earlier party commitments, and indeed even of reforms implemented during the triumphal first months of governance. The overall Eurosocialist reality very quickly turned into a rather dramatic turning away from promises the parties made in the midst of postelectoral euphoria. Such a reversal can be understood above all as a response to external conditions or pressures emanating from the global economic situation. At the same time, the shift was internal to the extent that the parties themselves failed to articulate or press for a comprehensive radical, anticapitalist solution to the crisis.

Once in power, the Mediterranean Socialists understandably enough became preoccupied with economic matters and therefore chose to defer their qualitative social and political goals. The historical context dictated an approach calling for "development first, then socialism," as the Spaniards put it. The consensus among party leaders was that in the absence of dynamic economic development, qualitative demands would ultimately be blocked or distorted. The fact is that a good deal of initial reformist activity, despite some very real changes, was largely expressive or symbolic. Broad programmatic options were narrowed in order to combat various manifestations of the crisis—a narrowing spiral that sooner or later would converge with the logic of capitalist accumulation.

While the Eurosocialists were driven to stabilize their respective national economies within the international capitalist division of labor —a task viewed as the first step toward socialist transformation—their efforts bore few immediate results. Of course, their reform initiatives did allow the state broadened discretion for making investment decisions, but only to a limited extent. And party leaders were convinced that workers and the poor should no longer be forced to shoulder a preponderant burden of the crisis. Nonetheless, by the end of 1984 France, Spain, and Greece were beset with the same continuing problems: sluggish growth, high levels of unemployment (8.2, 19.5, and 10 percent, respectively), shrinking investment capital, growing budgetary deficits, unstable currencies. Only the decay of urban social services was slightly reversed. The fact is that these countries were essentially trapped within their peripheral relationship to the international market economy; they seemed unable to break the vicious cycle of dependency and stagnation.[29] The prospects for genuine progressive reforms, whatever the theoretical inclinations or political intentions of Eurosocialist leaders, were by 1985 probably as remote as ever.

The economic dimension of this Eurosocialist reversal was rooted in three interrelated elements: technological restructuring, austerity, and movement toward a neo-Keynesian market economy. From the viewpoint of party leaders, as we have seen, survival in an increasingly competitive world capitalist system called for a shift in the direction of high-technology production, to be subsidized and protected by the state. The manufacturing sector would have to be modernized if these countries hoped to compete effectively within the international market. To this end the Mitterrand government heavily invested public funds in research and development for the strategically vital, but still limited, electronics and computer industries. In order to stimulate productivity throughout the economy it began an energetic rationalizing project that, in 1983–84, resulted in massive worker layoffs in the auto, steel, and shipyard sectors. Restructuring along these lines eliminated roughly 30,000 jobs in the steel industry alone.[30] In several cases plants that had been unprofitable were simply shut down by the government. Those most harshly affected were poorly skilled, low-paid African workers who had recently entered French basic industries in large numbers. In May 1983 a drastic anti-inflation program was carried out, including tax increases, wage limits, utility rate hikes, severe restrictions on the number of francs that could be spent abroad, and cutbacks in spending for some social services. This coincided with a modest Keynesian initiative—deficit spending accompanied by increased transfer payments—to help counter the worst effects of restructuring.[31] At the same time, in order to stimulate new investment the PS looked more and more to the private sector, or at least to a tight partnership of government and business; fearing capital flight, it courted the involvement of multinationals. By 1984 the kind of entrepreneurial mood that had been prevalent in Gaullist France seemed to have returned with a vengeance.

Yet such efforts to insulate the French economy from the harmful vicissitudes of global crisis—always problematic from the standpoint of socialist objectives—eventually cut deeply into the leftist government's base of support. Restructuring and austerity policies were met with militant resistance both from within the labor movement and the African community, where the jobless rate had climbed to 40 percent. Protests by hundreds of workers at the Talbot auto plant in 1983 led to a series of confrontations with riot police.[32] Later in the same year a wave of protests, strikes, and even plant occupations swept Peugeot, which, with government approval, had laid off some 2,000 workers (mostly Moroccan immigrants). In early 1984 more than 30,000 steelworkers marched through the streets of Paris to protest plant closings and layoffs. At the same time millions of government workers staged a one-day protest strike in opposition to austerity and repressive wage policies. The PS minister of industry, J. P. Chevenement, resigned his post out of exasperation with Mitterrand's economic programs. More significantly, the Communists, no longer interested in supporting these policies or enduring the consequences, exited from the governing coalition in June 1984—a split that would not seriously erode government stability (the PCF held only four cabinet posts) but would further undermine Socialist credibility in the labor movement.[33] By late 1984 Mitterrand's popular support dropped to a favorable rating of 33 percent in public opinion polls.[34] Perhaps even more revealing was the party's terrible showing in the spring 1984 European parliamentary elections, where it received only 21 percent of the vote compared with 37.5 percent in the 1981 general election. Several months after this debacle, the Socialists, now on the defensive, finally abandoned their last piece of overtly progressive legislation—the educational reform bill —following a wave of massive right-wing demonstrations. A measure of further decline was the poor outcome of the March 1986 parliamentary elections, where the PS dropped to 33.1 percent of the vote (with 212 seats), thereby losing its legislative majority along with the premiership to the Conservative coalition. Despite this defeat, however, the Socialists remained the largest single party in France, with a level of support that actually exceeded the predictions of many observers.

The PS government's embrace of austerity policies, or *plan de rigeur*, signaled the abandonment of the idea of rupture with the capitalist system; the guidepost now was the neoliberal ethos of a mixed economy.[35] Socialist goals were inevitably devalued—and not merely deferred into the distant future—by most currents in the leadership. Familiar capitalist methods of governance exacerbated many of the familiar economic problems, resulting in: increased unemployment, reduced purchasing power for workers and the poor, continued social inequality.

PS leader Lionel Jospin spoke of the need to respect the "laws of capitalist economics" in order to arrive at realistic solutions, and Michel Rocard called for a reduction in state power so that free enterprise would have more space to flourish. These sentiments were validated with the party's shift to the right at the Toulouse Congress in October 1985. With the emergence of Laurent Fabius, a smooth, pragmatic technocrat, the model increasingly upheld by the PS was that of the SPD, British Labour, and Swedish Social Democracy.[36]

Like the PS, the Spanish and Greek Socialists sought to avoid any head-on confrontation with the centers of domestic and international capital. They, too, relied heavily on new infusions of private investment to reverse the downward spiral. For the PSOE, the private sector (with state involvement, to be sure) was the lynchpin of technological rationalization and, by extension, of the breaking down of barriers to full participation within the EEC. The Gonzales government moved to close down unproductive enterprises and banks, establish wage limits, and pursue foreign capital. The idea was to create a high-technology infrastructure enabling Spain to capture an expanded share of the global "postindustrial" market. In contrast to the French approach, however, this strategem did not depend upon large-scale nationalizations. Even in the case of the Rumasa takeover by the state, within a year the PSOE decided to return the bulk of its assets to private groups and foreign investors. But in general the Spanish case fit the overall Eurosocialist pattern: a program of technological restructuring, austerity, and neo-Keynesianism paved the way for a new technocratic structure that in effect marginalized the left and the trade unions while solving few economic problems. By 1985 the Socialists had still not been able to revitalize the productive system, even within the parameters of capitalism, so that unemployment hovered near 17 percent, social services lagged, and budget deficits continued to grow. The result was that Gonzales, too, suffered a drop in popularity. Austerity policies and layoffs were protested by tens of thousands of workers, who staged brief general strikes in the northwest and the Basque country. More than 20,000 shipbuilding workers were laid off in 1983, while the state-owned Altos Hornos del Mediterráneo steel plant was being phased out with a loss of 8,000 jobs.[37]

The fact is that restructuring made a shambles of Socialist promises to cut unemployment by nearly a million; between 1982 and 1985, on the contrary, about 700,000 jobs were lost in all, with youth joblessness rising to nearly 50 percent.[38] PSOE economic policies came to differ little from those of Thatcher and Reagan.

The Greek situation followed more or less the same dialectic. As in Spain, the PASOK-engineered marriage between the state and big business was arranged without even the pretense of a structural-reformist attack on the monopolies and multinationals, except that in Greece far greater attention was devoted to the rejuvenation of small-scale enterprises and farms. Less than a year after the election that brought the Socialists to power, hostile references to the EEC, the multinationals, and even U.S. hegemony were markedly toned down. Such a confrontational posture, after all, was bound to disrupt even a modest start toward technological restructuring. In fact, the Greek project was far more limited than either the French or the Spanish for at least four reasons: a more narrow resource base, a draining military budget that accounted for 7 percent of GNP, a less-developed industrial base, and a feeble state apparatus that itself was badly in need of modernization. Thus, efforts to redirect investment—for example, toward research and development, social services, subsidies to small businesses—did not go very far even where they were successful. As Papandreou's initially harsh attitude toward EEC abated and PASOK stepped up its appeals to private capital, the market became a legitimate vehicle for development in Socialist thinking.

In order to extricate itself from a position of semiperipheral dependency, Greece under PASOK rule sought to stimulate incentives for new public and private investment that, ironically, included strong appeals to outside capital (both Western and Soviet). Within the public sector PASOK was preoccupied with improving efficiency, professionalizing the civil service, and cutting labor costs. There was simultaneously a turn toward monetarism, labor discipline, and wage controls. Although some labor benefits were increased, on the whole workers were asked to tighten their belts for the sake of the badly needed modernizing changes.[39]

Unfortunately, this path turned out to be no more fruitful for Greece than for France or Spain. After three years of "Great Change" politics the country's economic burdens persisted, with levels of unemployment, inflation, and fiscal deficit remaining about the same. Still, Papandreou lost little of the popularity he enjoyed in 1981, despite these economic problems and a series of labor demonstrations against austerity, which began in January 1983.[40] He enjoyed continued support because, in the context of recent Greek history, PASOK remains a dynamic symbol of democratization and national unity, whatever the limits of its domestic policies. Its continued strength was reflected in the June 1985 parliamentary elections: the Socialists won 46 percent of the vote (with 161 seats), compared with 41 percent for New Democracy and 10 percent for the KKE. The election showed that most Greeks were still committed to basic change, despite the difficulties encountered by PASOK, and seemed willing to be patient with Papandreou's leadership.[41]

Eurosocialist restructuring of the Mediterranean economies would, if successful on its own terms, integrate them more fully into the regional EEC system and the international division of labor. Insofar as structural-reformist programs adapt to the workings of the global and domestic market, they become increasingly detached from modes of action consistent with the requirements of socialist transformation. To some extent this logic is rooted in deep-level historical tendencies that operate independently of leadership motivations or stated objectives. Because the crisis of modern capitalism further sharpens economic and technological competition, giving rise to a situation in which only a few countries can be "winners" and most are "losers," radical alternatives easily give way to ideological moderation and fear of mass disruption. Socialist theorists argue that, in the present historical juncture, the only realistic choice is detente with private capital, both global and national. Should left-wing governments deviate from this logic, they risk losing sources of investment, which in turn means destabilization of the whole economy (thus nullifying any restructuring plans) regardless of other reform initiatives. There can be no immediate break with the world system, no avoiding the imperatives of accumulation within existing structural arrangements. In accepting this logic the Eurosocialists opted for a broadening of market forces alongside statist forms of social investment and planning—without which economic modernization would be inconceivable. This amounts to a kind of "local Keynesianism" designed to manage the crisis of regional capital.[42] As such, it signals a basic retreat from the unique version of structural reformism originated by the French, Spanish, and Greek parties.

Under these circumstances "socialist" goals become increasingly remote within the ideological framework of Eurosocialism. Organizational activity coheres around a "pragmatic" center dominated by skillful and adaptive functionaries for whom "modernization" becomes the ideological guidepost.[43] As the presumed first stage of progressive social change, modernizing concerns take on the character of an instrumentalized final goal, with all future stages essentially reduced to an abstract utopia. As one close observer of the PSF concluded, "Socialism, in its original inspirational meaning, as a working-class movement to change society, is quite simply being liquidated in France."[44]

The central political issue, therefore, revolves not so much around Eurosocialist adaptation to global market pressures—this is inevitable to some degree—but rather the extent to which there has been a full-scale, self-conscious retreat from the commitment to set in motion a transition to socialism. From this standpoint it is possible to speak of both *external* (global economic) and *internal* (strategic) factors in accounting for Socialist retrenchment. Accordingly, if we reflect upon the dilemmas at work within the party organizations, a different side of the problem becomes visible: party leaders never really formulated an alternative economic model consonant with their (socialist) ideological aims. Once in power, they seemed to lose the capacity for political imagination that had won them so much electoral support prior to 1982.[45] They presented no comprehensive framework within which specific policies or reforms might be justified or make sense to their broad base of members and supporters, despite initial efforts to move beyond familiar liberal or social-democratic prescriptions. Perhaps the very ideological vitality they derived from the constituencies (new middle strata) and themes (qualitative demands) associated with the new social movements was simultaneously a source of weakness in the sphere of economics. Or perhaps their orientation toward the new middle strata—and the corresponding narrowness of their labor support— pushed them into the arms of private capital as they struggled to consolidate their governance.[46] Whatever the case, quite clearly the Eurosocialists did pull back from their assault on the EEC, the multinationals, and the market system.

In France, this retrenchment was painfully recognized within what remained of leftist currents in the PS, especially those grouped around CERES, which attacked the leadership for its failure to develop a radical economic strategy that could at least confront the crisis directly. Without a coherent anticapitalist program or vision, they found themselves backpedaling toward a (more rationalized) mixed economy that implicitly follows the Japanese model, with its emphasis on free-enterprise restructuring combined with technocratic integration, near full employment, an extensive welfare system, and strong labor discipline. For the Eurosocialists this shift amounted to a form of neoliberalism with a thin leftist veneer.[47]

In political terms, therefore, restructuring suggests a new phase of corporatism based upon a partnership between state and capital, but with trade unions relegated to a lesser role than under traditional or postwar social democracy. Given the extent of state domination over civil society required by this form of economic modernization, the long-term impact of Eurosocialist hegemony can favor only mass demobilization rather than active politicization, and this indeed has been the trend: the brief postelection period of triumphal popular enthusiasm was followed by a profound passivity and cynicism. As the politics of modernization, institutional stability, and class collaboration begins to prevail, party leaders have little choice but to discourage active struggles or grassroots mobilization.[48] The decline of social movements in France, Spain, and Greece probably has as much to do with this dynamic—that is, with the capacity of left governments to absorb and domesticate oppositional energy—as with any internal collapse of the movements themselves.

This pattern of economic retreat cannot be separated from the sphere of politics because changes in the state and party system are profoundly influenced by restructuring processes. As we have seen, the Latin parties all share a firm commitment to democratization—or, in their more visionary moments—to democratic socialism. And they have concretized this goal in practice as they move to consolidate liberal democratic structures and values against the recent legacy of authoritarian regimes (Gaullism, Francoism, the Greek colonels). In this respect Socialist rule has been constructed upon decidedly popular foundations.[49] But the process of democratization has run up against severe limits, theoretically and practically, largely because the mode of capitalist rationalization being carried out by the parties demands broadened statist intervention. Centralized state power works to streamline the accumulation process, in the form of planning, subsidies, taxation and fiscal policies, regulation, research and development, labor discipline. Further, the state helps to legitimate restructuring by framing and justifying both immediate and long-range goals. The pull of technological efficiency and administrative stability comes to outweigh that of popular participation, decentralization, *autogestion.* Indeed, the emancipatory elements of democratic politics so vital for party programs were largely

dropped without much debate. The twin emphases on growth and politics as usual began to submerge the democratizing themes that grew
out of the social movements.

In France, for example, the initial burst of decentralizing activity
was quickly negated by a return of traditional *dirigisme*, centered in a
large and well-entrenched elite technocratic stratum that the Socialists
cultivated for their restructuring purposes. Lacking roots in any genuine process of mass mobilization, the Mitterrand government initiated
its reform project largely from above; political boundaries were established and protected by the state. The PS set out to bring the state and
productive apparatus together into a unified structure that went beyond
the realities even of Gaullist technocracy, for the state was now able to
direct an enlarged scope of economic activity and also constitute itself
as the most important forum of interest-group mediation. The Socialists in effect were looking toward a type of capitalist socialization that,
if successful, would lay the groundwork for a more institutionalized
system of industrial relations. In this vein Kesselman comments that "a
review of socialist reforms suggests that the government is serving as a
midwife to ease the transition to a mode of pluralist and corporatist
regulation long prevalent elsewhere."[50] With the passing of time, the
PS leadership demonstrated less and less interest in aligning with social
struggles from below, and indeed wound up *opposing* many of their
goals. The ideal of *autogestion* was largely discarded; decentralizing
reforms took on an increasingly formal-administrative or even cosmetic
character; and routinized organizational politics began to typify Socialist
governance.[51] The distinctively electoral nature of Mitterrand's victory,
and with it the displacement of popular activity, was more apparent
with each passing year.

This shift away from democratization more or less fits the Spanish
situation as well. In Spain, too, statism is a long and deeply ingrained
tradition, though without the parliamentary trappings. The restructuring policies of the PSOE, though less ambitious than those of the PSF,
carried forward and refined many of the centralizing features associated
with Francoism—state planning, regulation, labor controls, and the
like. At the same time, the parliamentary system itself—or, more accurately, the transition from authoritarianism to liberal democracy—is
still rather fragile in Spain. For some observers the issue of bourgeois
democracy (and basic civil liberties) versus Francoism or military rule
is still unresolved.[52] On the one hand, the Socialists helped to consoli-

date the young parliamentary system with its fragile but nonetheless important protection of general political freedoms. They have also initiated judicial reforms and, more significantly, have undertaken an ambitious program of reorganizing the armed forces with the purpose of undermining their potential for political intervention. On the other hand, the Gonzales government has on occasion resorted to repressive police methods in handling mass protests and demonstrations, including those conducted by the left. In 1983, after continuous prodding from the right, the Socialists enacted stringent antiterrorist laws that could be applied to virtually any type of oppositional activity. Moreover, there is the strong personal role of Gonzales, who has been able to set the agenda for discussion and action both within the party and government. An effective power-oriented politician, Gonzales established himself as an unchallengeable leader who could shape policy, disarm opposition, and in general act as a counterweight to democratizing reforms, which in any case have been mostly superficial. The PSOE has molded a governing apparatus according to the norms of stability and moderation, necessary not only to its modernizing commitments but also a function of its consuming fear of political disruption and class polarization (which in turn stems from justifiable anxieties concerning the return of fascism).

In Greece, however, the process of democratic transformation appears to be firmer and deeper. Not only does the PASOK government enjoy a broader base of support than does the French or Spanish, but reversion to right-wing dictatorship seems quite unlikely in the present circumstances. More significant, the Socialists have managed to introduce the spirit, and to some extent the form, of popular involvement that goes well beyond parliamentarism, as part of their effort to decentralize the state. PASOK itself was built on a foundation of hundreds of local branches, many of which are sustained by lively mass participation. Grassroots mobilization in Greece has become a reality in small towns and rural communities, where cooperative and local assemblies began to flourish on a new scale and with a new sense of purpose. Still, there are the familiar problems and dilemmas that have beset Eurosocialism in general. Despite its anti-EEC and pro-small business stance, PASOK remains closely tied to large corporate and financial interests, while its modernizing project depends upon a state infrastructure that has always been integral to Greek capitalist development.[53] Restructuring tends to reproduce this type of statism and its natural outgrowth, a weak civil society. Moreover, the cult of a strong leader exerts an overwhelming influence in Greek politics. Papandreou has been able to control the party and government to an even greater extent than do Mitterrand or Gonzales, owing in part to his charismatic style.

In its rather ambitious efforts to streamline the state bureaucracy, PASOK in effect has generated a new system of highly concentrated power. The struggle to replace archaic clientele networks had given rise not only to a more professionalized civil service but to a new stratum of Socialist bureaucrats, which has sought to establish firm control over both labor and the popular movements. "Participation" is increasingly managed from above. The initial attempts to organize formal self-management councils were largely abandoned as the local forms gave way to government-controlled "advisory councils."[54] As the party merges with the governmental structure, the divorce between PASOK's democratic ideology and its quasi-authoritarian practice becomes more visible and a greater source of alarm for many militants.

On the terrain of democratization, then, Eurosocialism represents a clear advance toward liberal forms of governance—no minor achievement—but its vision of democratic socialism has been obscured to the point of being almost completely forgotten. The renovated party systems made possible by emergent popular forces now seem to require for their functioning a political culture shaped less by activism and engagement than by passivity and detachment—except, ironically, for those labor protests directed against the Socialist governments. This peculiar relationship between economics and politics has two distinct but interwoven consequences: just as "socialism" comes to signify a regrouping of old centers of power around new rationalizing ideologies, popular movements themselves wind up absorbed by the hegemonic state or otherwise lose their momentum.[55]

In international politics, it is far more difficult to generalize for all Eurosocialist theory and practice. Indeed, one can detect unique patterns for each of the parties: a strongly Atlanticist, anti-Soviet orientation (France), a resolutely anti-American, anti-NATO ideology (Greece), and a position best described as ambivalent but leaning toward the West (Spain). However, though the official political lines may vary greatly, the actual conduct of Socialist foreign policies reflects the same loyalties and commitments owing to the compelling pressures brought to bear by U.S.-dominated regional and global structures.

Eurosocialist dilemmas parallel in many ways those of classical social democracy, which in the postwar years endorsed the ideal of balance between the superpowers but which in practice never strayed from the NATO orbit. It seems clear, too, that Socialist retreat on the domestic front is bound to have far-reaching implications for the parties' international behavior.

The founding convention of the French Socialists at Epinay in 1971 actually departed little from conventional social-democratic premises: the PS consensus was that the European left should locate itself between the major blocs, while at the same time, the PS insisted that progressive social change would have to be pursued within the existing Western European alignment of forces since immediate overthrow of bourgeois institutions was out of the question. Thus, the PS initially rejected any dramatic break with the United States or NATO, whatever its (largely nationalist) differences with American foreign policy.[56] In a formal sense the Socialists faithfully adhered to the principle of balance, a perspective reinforced by the Gaullist vision of an independent nuclear deterrence that would presumably give France, under any government, a more powerful role in European affairs. In reality, however, PS loyalty to the United States and NATO was never in question, if for no other reason than its own intractable legacy of anti-Sovietism (stemming in part from its domestic competition with the Communists). It might even be argued that, since 1981, the Socialists have been more pro-Western than their conservative predecessors.[57]

Since their ascent to power, the French Socialists have moved closer to the West Germans and the United States even as they adhere to the irrepressible *force de frappe*. Their hostility to the Soviet bloc, along with an ardent nationalism, has given expression to a cold-war ideology that was downplayed long ago within the political discourse of other Western European countries. The centerpiece of Mitterrand's foreign policy has been to enlarge and modernize the French military, above all its nuclear arsenal. Despite austerity programs, military spending has increased yearly by an average of 8 percent, the largest growth rate for any advanced capitalist society. One component of restructuring has therefore been an ambitious campaign to produce and deploy more sophisticated atomic weapons, including the neutron bomb. For French political life this means acceptance and even glorification of the country's military role and perhaps of militarism. The logical corollary of PS policy is a tendency to view with cynicism all arms-control schemes (which would make secondary powers like France even less consequential) and the European peace movement, which the Socialists like to vilify as a misguided assemblage of romantic pacifists. On the first point the Mitterrand government has been counted upon as perhaps the strongest defender of NATO's Euromissile deployment; as for the second, the PS has frequently sabotaged efforts to broaden peace mobilizations in France.[58] An example of this latter tendency was visible at the Mannheim Conference held in May and June 1984, which brought together French and German Socialists with representatives of European peace organizations to outline a common agenda. The PS blocked agreement on virtually every issue with its uncompromising anti-Sovietism and its insistence upon the viability of nuclear deterrence.

As a long-time *Atlantiste*, Mitterrand has steered French foreign policy in the direction of Reagan's global priorities. As Diana Johnstone writes, the PS "has served to forge a consensus and a new version of Gaullism subservient to American 'global security' concepts."[59] In this sense a distinctly French deterrence force, however loudly championed, has little practical significance for world politics insofar as there is no way it can ever be effective. For the French Socialists, however, nuclear nationalism furnishes the illusion of military strength and international credibility, which explains their understanding of the peace movement and "pacifism" as a tool of Moscow. The July 1985 bombing of the Greenpeace vessel *Rainbow Warrior* in New Zealand by French agents intent upon sabotaging protests against French nuclear testing in the South Pacific revealed this nearly hysterical obsession with the nuclear *force de frappe*.

The ambivalence of Spanish foreign policy under the PSOE grows out of two conflicting pressures: a longstanding skeptical attitude toward Atlanticism reinforced by the memory of U.S. support for Franco and continued fear of American hegemony, and the previously mentioned desire for entry into the Western European economic community. With the Socialists' lack of progress toward a post-Franco foreign policy, they have fallen back into the pro-NATO camp more or less by default. During the 1982 electoral campaign, for example, Gonzales promised a national referendum on Spain's involvement in NATO. After two years of delay, the government decided to go ahead with the referendum, but with the proviso that the PSOE leadership was now in favor of continued NATO membership since Spain must honor its obligations toward the "collective defense of the West."[60] The overriding fear was that, in the event the country should withdraw from the alliance, its prospective EEC membership would be in question. Under these circumstances the Spaniards predictably enough yielded to pressures from the United States, West Germany, and other Western European governments to remain within the Western military bloc. In March 1986 Spaniards voted overwhelmingly (by 8.8 to 6.7 million) to remain within NATO. The outcome was clearly a personal victory for Gonzales, who campaigned vigorously and was credited with almost single-handedly turning around the strong anti-NATO (and anti-American) sentiment in the country. Indeed, the month preceding the referendum witnessed a series of large anti-NATO demonstrations in several Spanish cities, including one of 750,000 in Madrid, sponsored by more than 150 peace, ecology, and leftist organizations united within the Pro-Peace Committee. A poll in October 1985 showed that only 19 percent of the populace was ready to endorse Spain's participation in NATO.

The notion that Spain could somehow be detached from East-West politics was, given the magnitude of its economic crisis and its desire to modernize, nothing but self-deception. Thus PSOE ideology, too, evolved in the direction of a cold-war anti-Sovietism; most of its justification of the Euromissiles, acceptance of U.S. military bases, and dismissal of the peace movement was premised on the need to combat "Soviet expansionism." By 1985 its foreign policy differed from that of the French Socialists only in being less stridently nationalistic. And, despite uncertainties about the referendum, Spanish participation in NATO had solidified since the Socialist rise to power: Spain is represented on virtually every alliance body, including the vital Defense Planning Committee.[61] With full integration into NATO and the EEC (admission was granted in June 1985), Spain thus appeared to be on the road to its long-cherished "Europeanization." In this context, continued Socialist references to peace and disarmament—and to a reduction of the U.S. military presence in the country—seemed rather empty.

In contrast to the French and Spanish parties, the Greek Socialists have held to an (attenuated) anti-NATO and anti-imperialist position since their founding in 1974. From the outset PASOK called for Greece to disengage from any international organization or alliance that compromises the country's independence, that reinforces its postwar status as an American colony. It opposed the idea of military blocs and called for a "federated Europe." From this viewpoint both the EEC and NATO were regarded as simple tools of U.S. hegemony, which PASOK argued would be incompatible with Greek socialist development or even modernization. In May 1984 Papandreou delivered a scathing attack on U.S. foreign policy, characterizing its designs as those of "expansionism and domination." Meanwhile, PASOK's relations with the Soviet bloc grew warmer, to the point where Papandreou could praise the Jaruzelski military regime in Poland (thus becoming the only Western European Socialist leader to effectively oppose Solidarity). Before the 1981 election PASOK threatened to close down the several U.S. military installations on Greek territory, and although the issue was temporarily settled in 1984 (in favor of keeping the bases), public opinion remains opposed to the American military presence. In spring 1984 the government refused to prevent striking workers from blockading entrances to several U.S. bases. Earlier, Papandreou voiced strong opposition to the Euromissiles but was willing to compromise on a sixteen-month postponement in hope that the Geneva arms control talks would reconvene and arrive at a solution. Beginning in 1981 PASOK pushed for a nuclear-free zone in the Balkans, making it one of the few parties in the Socialist International to endorse such a scheme.

What factors make the Greek Socialist approach to international politics unique? One decisive element would seem to be PASOK's deep roots in the peace movement, which in Greece was composed of three relatively large and active organizations. In the early 1980s Athens was a center of perpetual rounds of demonstrations, meetings, and conferences in connection with the arms race, militarism, and Third World issues.[62] This ideological milieu is reinforced by the small size of the country and its peripheral location in Europe, which helps to explain its identification with anticolonial movements and regimes. Equally important has been NATO's special postwar relationship with Turkey— Greece's historical competitor in the Aegean—and its assistance to the Greek military dictatorships. Whatever the underlying factors, this radical consensus concerning foreign policy goals has been a significant unifying force binding together PASOK's leading cadres, especially since it is clear that nationalist mobilization helps to legitimate party rule.[63]

Yet the Papandreou government has taken no dramatic steps toward a break with the West. Party ideology and rhetoric have not worked to produce concrete shifts in policy. One observer suggests that Socialist foreign relations have been governed by little more than a series of "symbolic empty gestures."[64] Thus, after four years of PASOK governance, Greece remained solidly within the EEC and NATO, although the Socialists did insist upon the right of "selective participation" in NATO field maneuvers. In 1984 Greece negotiated a five-year extension on the four U.S. military bases (and about twenty minor installations) with the proviso that the arrangement can be terminated in 1988. Apparently, PASOK leaders felt that any real departure from the Western alliance would only benefit Turkey (militarily) and harm Greece (economically) by discouraging foreign investment. They insisted that the appropriate tactics were to "struggle from within" regional European structures. This logic was bound to give rise to a partial retreat on the terrain of foreign policy, but within an ideological framework of anti-Atlanticism that rejects conventional cold-war politics.

The general problem for Eurosocialism is that it did not really formulate an alternative socialist conception of international relations or collective national security. Only the Greek Socialists made even tenuous initiatives in this direction. Lacking such an alternative, the parties sooner or later tend to revert to the old ties. Moreover, the costs and sacrifices likely to accompany full disengagement from the EEC and NATO for any Mediterranean country are likely to be formidable. The enormous economic, political, and military pressures brought to bear by the United States through its powerful role in the world capitalist system can be overwhelming, especially in southern Europe where crisis and dependency are especially acute. For this reason Eurosocialist moderation in foreign policy is probably less a matter of support for U.S. militarism or strong anti-Soviet feelings than of simply adapting to the requirements of economic and political modernization. This dynamic separates Eurosocialism from postwar social democracy, which thoroughly and enthusiastically identified with U.S. interests in Western Europe.[65]

Yet the Greek Socialists' rather firm challenge to the cold-war framework suggests that the rudiments of an alternative foreign policy can be established without the need for complete disengagement from the world market (virtually an impossibility in any case). Again, the critical factor would seem to be the degree to which these parties can retain close ties with popular movements that have created space for the development of a post-Marxist radicalism. PASOK's novel departure would be unthinkable in the absence of a large and militant peace movement that, in the end, will surely be one of the driving forces behind progressive social change in Europe.

THE CONSOLIDATION OF BOURGEOIS HEGEMONY

The rise to power of rejuvenated Mediterranean Socialist parties in the early 1980s occurred in something of an ideological vacuum: not only liberalism but Keynesian social democracy seemed to have exhausted its potential, Leninism and the Soviet model were more discredited than ever, and the promise of Eurocommunism as a left alternative simply never materialized. In this context Eurosocialism appeared as the best hope, finally, for realization of the elusive "third road" to socialism—meaning that France, Spain, and Greece would form the terrain of a newly unfolding dialectic. Not only did the Socialists assimilate the energy of the new popular movements, they also enjoyed the legacy of a renewed structural reformism with its immense optimism regarding electoral politics and the prospects of a broad-based social bloc that espouses transformative goals. As we have seen, in its initial phase the Socialist triumph was accompanied by widespread political activism that helped to revitalize the public sphere. The space for progressive advances was dramatically enlarged. But the subsequent retreat demonstrates that the Eurosocialists were ultimately unprepared to occupy this vacuum and pursue the opportunities it furnished. Although 1981–86 is a relatively brief period by any historical measure, it is nonetheless adequate for identifying fundamental patterns or directions of economic and political development.[66] It is difficult to resist the judgment that, whatever its claims or pretensions to the contrary, the Eurosocialist phenomenon represents not so much the subversion as the *consolidation* of bourgeois hegemony in those countries where it has governed and established its programs.

Of course this is a familiar criticism of European social democracy, except that in the postwar years those parties never pretended to challenge the power structure, never claimed to represent democratic socialism or a "third road" strategy. The governing legacy of social democracy has been unambiguous: capitalist rationalization in the economic sphere, welfare-state reformism in the area of social programs, statism alongside a broadening of pluralist democracy in the political system, and defense of U.S. and NATO strategic interests in foreign policy. In the end social democracy served to reproduce and legitimate while also humanizing the structures of domination in bourgeois society. Put in the simplest terms, Eurosocialism seems to have become reabsorbed into this traditional framework. It offers a new image and speaks a new language, but the underlying premises and attachments are roughly the same even if many of the concrete policies differ.

In the evolution of the southern European parties, then, the dynamics of Socialist retrenchment can be located on two levels—productivism in the realm of the economy, statism and parliamentarism in the political arena. First, insofar as the industrial restructuring project is the cornerstone of Eurosocialist programs, there has been a definite shift away from ultimate goals and toward adaptation to immediate pressures. Those pressures, of course, are linked to the process of capital accumulation in the narrow sense rather than to any alternative path of development or to the transition to socialism. It is true that most governments, East and West, are forced to borrow money in order to finance their economic projects. During a period of international crisis and intensified national competition, as in the 1980s, there are added pressures to maximize exports, reduce imports, and cut public spending. Even governments on the left are compelled to take up the concerns of technological rationalization, industrial growth, profit maximization, and austerity—all consistent with capitalist priorities of securing a good climate for business investment. Since Eurosocialist parties want to attract rather than drive away capital, they have been generally solicitous of commercial banks, the multinationals, and various EEC institutions. Thus, given the importance they assigned to economic modernization at the outset, they were were obviously prepared to adapt to the logic of capital—or, more accurately, to the logic of technocratic state capitalism—with all of its political implications.[67] In fact, Socialist governance has resulted in an even greater concentration of capital in both public and private sectors than was the case under previous conservative regimes.[68]

Insofar as Eurosocialism has in reality jettisoned any political vision that goes beyond this convergence of state and market, it has likewise abandoned its interest in qualitative social change and grassroots mobilization. Both processes would obviously clash with the imperatives of accumulation dictated by a restructuring agenda. As in the case of classical social democracy, leftist governments have emerged once again as rationalizing vehicles of capitalist production and social organization.

Whether such a schema could ever be successful under present conditions, even within the parameters of capital, is highly problematic. Restructuring generates its own contradictions, and collaboration with the agencies of international capital brings new dysfunctions. Even the conventional social-democratic promise to expand social services and reduce unemployment—integral to Keynesianism—cannot be fulfilled today since rationalization shrinks the demand for labor, while the failure of Keynesian solutions at a time of declining economic growth means that the public sector no longer functions to ameliorate systemic conflicts and strains. Still, despite a wave of worker protests that have accompanied Eurosocialist initiatives, the reality is that this "left" productivism has done much to stabilize bourgeois institutions in the Mediterranean.

This stabilizing dimension of Eurosocialist rule is dialectically linked to the political contours of party strategy. It is clear that the Socialist victories, whatever they owed to popular movements and constituencies, took place almost exclusively on the terrain of electoral politics. Parliamentary majorities were built through the ballot box after lengthy periods of electioneering. The overriding goal in each case was to win institutional power at the national level. Although this reflected important advances for the left, the problem was that party structures were largely detached from any sustained process of local mobilization, cut off from the dynamism of grassroots struggles. As mass-based national organizations with societalwide priorities, they were consumed with one sphere of political activity: parliament, the party system, state bureaucracy. (Although Socialists do have a presence in local and municipal governments, this fact does not basically alter their strategic relationship to popular movements and constituencies nor the character of power that is wielded.) Under these circumstances the parties inevitably made their peace with the pluralist world of interest-group bargaining and bureaucratic control—that is, with the very neocorporatism that typified social democracy. From the standpoint of left strategy, parliamentarism and technocratic statism can thus be understood as twin expressions of the same historical process.

This predicament reveals the inherent flaws of structural reformism, which go back to the earlier theories of Kautsky and Austro-Marxism and to the later refinements of Togliatti, Carrillo, and other Eurocommunists. The main thematic continuity of structural reformism is a definition of the electoral-parliamentary arena as the primary locus of social transformation. Although lip service is paid to local movements and structures, there is no coherent theory or practice that unites the two dimensions of electoral politics and grassroots struggles. In this sense it is possible to identify a broad tradition from Kautsky through Eurocommunism and, finally, Eurosocialism.[69]

The structural reformist impasse is graphically illuminated by the experience of the southern European Socialists—all the more so, given their undeniably sincere efforts to chart a "third road." The evidence shows that parliamentary institutions tend to reproduce a division between elites and masses, party and movements, state and grassroots, insofar as participation is commonly limited to either voting or interest-group bargaining. Typically, the "electorate," whatever its ideological character, is anything but a dynamic social bloc capable of autonomous action. On the contrary, it is often composed of a fragmented, passive, and in some cases alienated network of disparate constituencies unable to exert political leverage outside the legitimate framework of power. The disruptive potential of mass struggles can be easily neutralized within the stabilizing pressures of party and interest-group politics.[70] In this respect parliamentarism, where it is a hegemonic force, tends to carry forward and even strengthen the political division of labor, thereby narrowing or depoliticizing the public sphere.[71]

A second problem is that even massive shifts in parliamentary alignments—as occurred in France, Spain, and Greece—do not normally constitute any real attack on the centers of power and privilege that lie outside parliament and the party system. This observation does not refer merely to the familiar argument that legislative bodies in the advanced societies have declined in power relative to the executive branch of government. It is more a question of the decisive influence of dispersed institutions of economic, political, and social power beyond the reach of parliaments: the multinationals, international banks, the military, churches, the bureaucratic state itself. To reconstitute parliament according to the vision of structural reformism—in other words, to create a shifting equilibrium of electoral forces favoring the left— does not in itself amount to a fundamental transformation of power and class relations. As the experience of many left governments during the past forty years has borne out, the once-celebrated "parliamentary road" cannot lead away from the dominant order; it leads mainly to further absorption of oppositional forces.[72]

Third, the very commitment to party politics within complex legislative and bureaucratic structures has a profoundly moderating and institutionalizing impact over time. The decision to participate fully and not just tactically encourages a logic of institutional adaptation and class collaboration endemic to pluralist catch-all parties, the modus operandi of which is shaped by interest-group conciliation, social conservatism, bureaucratic style, and fear of instability and disruption. To some extent this can be viewed as a return to the Michelsian dilemma —how to sustain large-scale, mass-based electoral forms without abandoning ideological dynamism—except that in modern pluralist systems this deradicalizing impulse may be even more compelling (if still not quite an "iron law") than Michels' critique of early German Social Democracy suggests. The corporatist relationship between parliament, the party system, and the national state apparatus today is such that integrative pressures are stronger than they were during earlier phases of capitalist development. In any event, there are no historical instances of mass-based Communist or Socialist parties that have pursued a structural-reformist strategy being able to resist this institutionalizing pull.[73]

The implications of such an emphasis on electoral politics for Eurosocialism, therefore, have been to further legitimate the structures and norms of pluralist democracy. Although the parliamentary arena has a popular dimension that can give expression to mass struggles, its stability ensures that radical incursions can go only so far—to the point where the integrity of the power structure is threatened. Thus, an electoralism that rules out extraparliamentary activity (the center of gravity for popular movements) necessarily enforces the code of bourgeois hegemony. Here, as elsewhere, the intimate linkage of economics and politics is abundantly evident. Structural reformism thereby reinforces a system-sustaining dynamic that narrows the range of debate, closes off policy alternatives, and forces social programs toward (at best) a moderate welfare statism. This is part of the reason why Eurosocialism had little choice but to opt for a modernizing economic project, an instrumental politics, and a foreign policy committed to NATO. Quite clearly, then, its ideological "retreat" occurred because of the conflicts involving global economic pressures and domestic strategy, and not because of leadership betrayal, historical accident, or bureaucratic laws.

Yet it cannot be denied that the parliamentary road allows for a conquest of governmental power, such as took place in France, Spain, and Greece. Despite the fact that such a conquest does permit leftist parties or coalitions to implement far-reaching reforms like nationalizations and progressive taxation schemes, leftist advances are essentially formal insofar as the bastions of power remain largely outside the political system as such and even beyond national boundaries, especially in the Mediterranean. This formal aspect of parliamentary democracy, however, does not basically alter the reality of statism. Socialist governments have introduced technocratic planning mechanisms, public ownership and control of industries and banks, and vital welfare measures in more than a dozen countries since the 1930s, but none of these governments has ever challenged the rules of capital accumulation or pluralist democracy.[74] So it has been a statism of a peculiar sort, one that coexists with all of the trappings of a representative system. The boundaries of structural reformism seem rigidly fixed. If mass constituencies are depoliticized and parliament wields relatively little power, then the most likely prospect—but hardly a radical one—is for a regrouping of privileged interests around the state and the corporations.

Still, it would be misleading to conclude that popular movements have been fully assimilated into a new corporatist bloc managed by the Eurosocialists. Mass politics continues on many levels—labor protests against austerity, peace mobilizations, urban movements, feminism, and so forth. Yet one immediate outcome of Eurosocialist retrenchment has surely been the demobilization of movements within the orbit of party activity; their demands and goals have either been instrumentalized by electoral politics or blocked altogether by the turn toward productivism and statism. Perhaps grassroots militancy, where it has been a major factor, was disarmed by the unprecedented visibility of a leftist government that symbolizes progressive change and promises extensive reforms. If so, such quiescence is not likely to endure for long in a context where ruling Socialist parties have lost their political vision and where neoliberal domestic and foreign policies are being offered as the only alternative. The point is that Eurosocialism, within a few short years, has in effect placed a range of obstacles in the way of democratization and qualitative social change. In many respects the "revitalized" Socialist parties now stand in opposition to those radical ideals that were the impetus for their original successes.

This deradicalizing outcome raises once again the question of whether a mythical "third road" is possible, given the unyielding pressures of global capitalism and the imposing power of pluralist-democratic institutions in the West. The obsolescence of Leninism and the Soviet model for the industrialized societies, the marginalization of council-communist, anarchist, and Trotskyist alternatives, and the impotence of structural reformism calls for a fundamental rethinking of past strategies. Lacking in all of these approaches, whatever their stated objectives or their accomplishments, is a dialectical conception integrating two distinct realms of political practice: national and local, party and movements, institutions and community, parliament and popular assemblies. Such a conception would presumably be more solidly grounded in the new social movements than were previous strategies, yet would require an organizational presence to coordinate these movements in a project of societywide change. Such a radical-democratic strategy would, at least in principle, be compatible with different forms of ongoing insurgency against the privileged centers of power.[75]

Two emergent strategic paradigms of this sort, both post-Marxist in their inspiration and outlook, will be explored in the following chapters. These are the new populism (centered mainly in the United States) and the Green tendency (situated primarily in West Germany). Both are identified with the struggle for new forms of democracy and innovative styles of radical politics; both stress qualitative social goals associated with feminism, ecology, and the peace movement; both seek to mobilize disparate constituencies largely outside of labor and the trade unions; both emphasize the "limits to economic growth"; and, above all, both are convinced that real progressive social transformation is possible despite the familiar array of obstacles and external pressures. For new populists, the key objective is to capture positions of local power through a combination of grassroots mobilization and electoral politics in order to set in motion a process of molecular change throughout the entire society. The Greens, too, are preoccupied with community-based movements and emphasize the struggle for local power, but they have devoted much of their energy and resources to establishing a national party (sometimes called an "anti-party party") in the West German parliament. It is to these newly evolving strategies that we shall now turn.

4

THE AMERICAN CONTEXT
FROM NEW LEFT
TO NEW POPULISM

The sharpening institutional, economic, and cultural crisis of American society has given rise, since the 1960s, to resurgent populist movements on both the right and left. These movements and the organizations they have spawned reflect an erosion of the Keynesian welfare-state consensus that has shaped two-party politics since the 1930s. Set in motion by the fiscal crisis and bureaucratization of the state, the two populist revolts share an anti-statist, decentralizing vision with deep roots in U.S. history. Both legitimate their goals through appeals to democracy, the community, self-help, and the everyday concerns of the common person, and both envision gradual but militant struggles to restore civic participation against the encroachment of powerful interests. Further, both offer solutions to the present crisis that contain a strong moral as well as economic and political thrust. The right-wing populists, who helped catapult Ronald Reagan into the presidency, urge a return to the mythic free-enterprise economy, with its glorification of unfettered individualism, self-regulating market forces, and private incentives, and to traditional values embodied in an old-fashioned work ethic, the neighborhood, religion, patriarchal sex roles, and patriotism. A weaker, more fragmented left looks toward the broad anticorporate politics of structural reforms grounded in "economic democracy," or what might be called a "new populist" strategy: the extension of new democratic forms into every sphere of life, the socialization of resources as a step toward a more egalitarian, ecologically balanced society.[1]

In terms of any real democratizing potential, it is difficult to take rightist populism very seriously. Beneath its antibureaucratic rhetoric lies an elitist and corporatist project designed to strengthen multinational corporations, the military, and the authoritarian state. Poorly camouflaged by symbols of traditional morality, self-reliance, and "supply-side" economics, the corporatist "solution" is little more than a cover for policies beneficial to the affluent and powerful and cynically brutal to workers, the poor, minorities, and the vast majority of women. It follows that Reaganism could not for long reconcile the rationalizing imperatives of capital accumulation with a populist legitimation urging a return to early capitalist principles, or laissez-faire myths, appropriate to the frontier. Something had to yield—in this case, the new-right ideology of a free-market economy already suffocated by the requirements of both monopoly and governmental expansion. Still, the ideological success of a right-wing populism that has strong appeal among blue-collar workers, urban ethnic groups, Christian fundamentalists, and small proprietors has been impressive.[2]

The broad diffusion of populist sentiment, even where its ideological content remains highly variable and unpredictable, signifies a fundamental shift of American social and political forces that was well under way before the 1980s. If the right wing (and the Republican party) appears to be the main beneficiary in the short run, the direction of change could be altered in the long run to the degree that space for leftist mobilization is extended. A dynamic left-wing populism has already appeared in many parts of the United States in response to a wide variety of concerns: housing, energy, antinuclear campaigns, abortion, plant closings, health care, and so forth. The rebirth of progressive politics at the grassroots above all constitutes a response to the shrinking of the public sphere in national politics of the sort discussed in Chapter 2. This shrinkage has been particularly visible in the American system, spanning from the inertia of welfare-state liberalism to the narrowness of the old social contract and the hegemony of cold-war anticommunism. The result is that in most areas of national competition the two-party system has suppressed or avoided real debate on important domestic and foreign-policy issues, leading to a pervasive sense of disenfranchisement. Even the powerful impact of Jesse Jackson's 1985 campaign for the Democratic presidential nomination was felt largely within specific local communities. The prospects of Jackson's making serious inroads into the larger party structure were minimal from the outset. Widespread powerlessness has the effect of alienating many local constituencies from the central political system, of detaching them from the ideological symbols that legitimate a politics of indiscriminate growth, waste, and destruction.[3]

New-populist struggles on the left thus indicate a revival of efforts to recover the public sphere obliterated by large-scale corporations, the military, and the authoritarian state. In some areas of the United States these movements have achieved durable forms of organized political expression and thereby a modicum of presence that was lacking in the 1960s and 1970s. However, in contrast to the Eurosocialist parties, which were in a position to conquer national power and which defined their strategies accordingly, new-populist organizations like the Campaign for Economic Democracy (CED) in California looked almost exclusively to the local sphere—to the neighborhoods and municipalities—with hopes of initiating a long process of molecular social transformation. While far more limited in scope and immediate political impact, the new populists grew in close proximity to the new social movements and were thus able to combine their electoralism more fully with popular themes and goals. During the early 1980s several new-populist organizations won significant electoral victories and in some cases were able to take control of municipal governments—for example, in Santa Monica, Santa Cruz, and Berkeley, California, and in Burlington, Vermont.

Viewed in historical terms, the new populism represents a species of structural reformism, with all of its characteristic dilemmas and limitations. At the same time, its leaders and theorists espouse a concept of progressive change broader in many ways than earlier populist, left-liberal, trade-unionist, or social-democratic approaches. The core element of this theory is "democratization"—a process of evolutionary change that, building upon the most progressive elements of liberal democracy, would ostensibly lead to expanded popular involvement in the political system, workplace, and community.[4] New-populist activists often identify with the insurgent legacy of the 1960s or, more precisely, with its most "mature" expression at a time of retrenchment in the 1970s. They seek an indigenous language presumably more relevant to 1980s-style politics than the stale discourse of both old and new left. The new populism therefore seems to offer an effective and vital sense of realism that appeals to many leftists confined so long to the margins of American political life. Its concrete gains, within a relatively brief time, have in fact been quite remarkable. But these successes, however dramatic in their local communities, could turn out to be illusory from the standpoint of more far-reaching social transformation. To confront this problem, it is necessary to examine new-populist assumptions about the nature of capitalism, power, the state, and democracy.

NEW POPULISM, MARXISM, AND THE LEFT

In its commitment to build upon the long tradition of American citizens' movements as an alternative to importing foreign models of social change, the new populism represents a conscious turning away from Marxism and (more ambiguously) from European social democracy. As Harry Boyte argues, the "abstract theoretical model" of Marxism is rooted in a narrow, class-based framework that has never really struck a clear resonance in the American experience. With its excessively optimistic view of proletarian revolutionary potential, Marxism tends to devalue the "raw materials of populist insurgency"—for example, those issues linked to neighborhood and community struggles as well as distinctive national or religious traditions that have inspired major twentieth-century popular movements.[5] According to Boyte, this explains why organizing efforts based upon conventional Marxist premises have achieved such limited results in the United States. Marxian socialism has marginalized itself, its isolation stemming as much from its own outmoded theory as from external forces such as political repression or cooptation.

Boyte's hostility to Marxism more or less typifies new-populist theory. Tom Hayden, for example, considers Marxism an old-fashioned theory "meaningful only for a certain historical stage—and not for the age we are gradually entering." The underlying problem is a pervasive "economism" that stresses productive relations over politics, material forces over culture and consciousness. Hayden argues that "the predictive or explanatory power of Marxist class analysis is hampered by its inherent tendency to dismiss *other* factors as merely part of the superstructure. Yet in the past generation, millions of Americans have been motivated by race, sex, age, by disability, by moral and religious desires, by consciousness. The superstructure itself, rather than the base, often seems to be a determining or at least operative factor in change. But because of a necessary adherence to materialist dialectics, left groups have been left out, tending to view such movements as merely 'progressive' but not 'fundamental' because they did not arise from class factors."[6] Hayden thus concludes that the central flaws of Marxist theory—the primacy of class over community, insensitivity to the problem of state bureaucracy, worship of industrial growth—are so deeply embedded in its very logic that Marxism loses all strategic relevance for the advanced countries.

The new populism shares with Eurosocialism a post-Marxist vision tied to "qualitative" themes but goes even further in distancing itself from the Marxist theoretical legacy *tout court*. To some extent this difference can be attributed to an American "exceptionalism"—that is, to the development of a more pervasive liberal hegemony and a more corporatist and conservative labor movement than exists in the relatively class-polarized Mediterranean societies. As Mark Kann observes, Lockean political culture has had an immense staying power in the United States; not only has liberal consensus set clear boundaries to class conflict and party politics, it has also allowed for the growth of a "radical liberalism" tied to progressive movements that are uniquely American in their ideological and organizational substance. In this context Marxism and socialism could only be viewed as imported doctrines completely devoid of political value. They only served to inhibit the left from coming to grips with the distinctive American reality, thereby blocking new opportunities and alternatives.[7]

The obvious fact is that neither the Communist nor the Socialist parties were able to establish a mass presence in American political life throughout the postwar years. Historically, the bulk of oppositional energy was channeled through the two-party system. By the 1960s these traditions came to be viewed as political fossils out of touch with the new social movements and the democratizing impulses they exemplified. Various Marxist organizations, whatever their official line, were bypassed by emergent social forces that the old theories could scarcely comprehend. In the turbulence of the 1960s and 1970s the old left appeared to embody the norms of political authority, social order, and cultural conformism: on the Communist side there was an authoritarian image of the Soviet model, on the Socialist side the vision of a recycled welfare state. With the eclipse of new-left radicalism in the early 1970s, the "rediscovery" of Marxism (or "Marxism-Leninism") led to a romantic fetishism of Third World struggles (e.g., Chinese, Cuban, Vietnamese). By the late 1970s none of these alternatives seemed very compelling as a source of leftist strategy in the United States—or, for that matter, in any industrialized country. And of course none was remotely successful. "Westernized" or neo-Marxist currents retained some appeal insofar as they questioned the conventional productivist, class-based paradigm, but they (like the variants of Trotskyism and anarchism) lived on essentially within tiny educational forums detached from mass politics. This state of affairs set itself in opposition to the tiresome elitist and workerist tendencies of the Marxist left.[8]

If Marxism as conceived by the new populists is hopelessly outdated, what then can be said of social democracy, which long ago abandoned any pretense toward Marxism or revolution? Consistent with the belief in an American exceptionalism, new-populist theorists have paid little attention to what they regard as foreign traditions (including social democracy and Eurocommunism). They distance themselves from such theories and strategies partly for class reasons (refusal to make labor the axis of struggle) and partly because the new-populist concern with democratic self-management, consumer interests, and cultural renewal clashes with previous "left Keynesian" efforts to rationalize capitalism. Preoccupied with state intervention for purposes of redistributing income and stabilizing the business cycle, postwar European social democratic parties have carried out programs that differ little from liberal welfare-state policies, except for a greater willingness to nationalize large (often failing) industries and introduce technocratic planning.[9] Since the mid-1970s both of these approaches have given rise to new obstacles and contradictions—stagflation, the fiscal crisis, bureaucratization. Moreover, even where social democracy succeeds on its own terms (as in Scandinavia), the results fall short of the types of reforms envisaged by the new populism.[10]

The rejection of social democracy as a model, however, has not ruled out the possibility of drawing upon certain of its positive achievements. Thus, Carnoy and Shearer take inspiration from Sweden, where they find impressive reforms in the area of workers' control and democratization of authority relations within Swedish enterprises, which in their view lays the foundations of a more progressive welfare state than exists elsewhere. Even though the Swedish economy is hardly socialist in even the broadest meaning of the term, since investment remains largely within private hands, Carnoy and Shearer argue that the Swedish government "has intervened massively in the economy and has done so on behalf of the organized labor movement it represents. It has entered directly into the bargaining process between capital and labor, tilting the process in favor of labor to a much greater extent than in other industrialized countries, on the one hand, and guaranteeing profits to capital, on the other." [11]

The new populism departs from social democracy not so much re-garding its acceptance of a "mixed economy" as in its more expan-sive vision of economic priorities and democratization. The language, themes, and appeals employed by the former are more congruent with the traditions of civic democracy and grassroots political pluralism than are previous welfare-state models. New-populist structural reformism offers a choice beyond either the free market or Keynesianism; it looks to collective, responsible, and socially useful forms of investment that would be cycled not only through government but through "alternative enterprises" run on the principle of workers' self-management. Accord-ing to Carnoy and Shearer, this is the essence not of state capitalism but of an entirely new kind of "democratic social contract whereby government, responsible entrepreneurs, labor, and consumers would share equally in decision-making." [12]

It promises more than a recycled welfare state insofar as it seeks a basic shift of power from corporate elites to "the people"—a gradual relocation of political and economic decision making. Although, as Boyte concedes, the populist notion of people or community might lack the analytic rigor of the Marxian theory of class, it nonetheless allows for an understanding of change rooted in a "majoritarian bloc of forces." This requires "free social spaces," the essence of a reconstructed public sphere, within the framework of representative democracy. [13] A critical task addressed by new populists is how to create such free spaces for citizens' initiatives without forcibly overthrowing the dominant institu-tions—or, viewed from another angle, without destroying the firma-ments of established culture and community. But this would seem to require, in turn, a significant transfer of resources from the private to the public sector. [14]

The anticipation of a powerful citizens' movement sweeping the United States derives from the assumption that broad social change occurs through mass opposition to elite domination rather than the struggle of labor against capital. The new populists see the spread of grassroots revolt in the 1970s as a validation of their strategy. The decade was, after all, a period of emergent community struggles over tenants' rights, the environment, feminist and gay issues, welfare cut-backs, occupational health and safety, and affirmative action. [15] These struggles, despite their unpredictable ebbs and flows from the 1960s to the 1980s, did bring a new dynamism to American politics. On one level they reshaped popular attitudes on a broad range of issues: race, sex, authority, culture, foreign policy.[16] On yet another level they altered the political system insofar as they exposed the state—particularly in the local arena—to new forms of democratic influence.[17] In other words, social movements expanded the terrain for challenging established institutional arrangements, social relations, and ideologies. The new populism set out to fill a void in American politics created by the erosion of corporate liberalism and the continued marginalization of the Marxist left.

Filling this void implies recognition of the state, rather than economic relations per se, as the primary sphere of conflict and change. The new populism operates on the premise that grassroots mobilization must take place largely within the political realm insofar as the state is the main locus of economic contradictions, popular movements, and efforts to achieve a viable radical strategy. Not only have social struggles created an opening or fissure in the system, but intensified conflict over fiscal policies and social programs has placed the public sector at the center of class antagonisms. The welfare state itself has given rise to new constituencies and interests that engage in battle almost exclusively on the political terrain.[18] For the new populists, this fact represents an historic opportunity to advance the prospects of democratization against the imperatives and priorities of capitalism.

With this outlook the new populism can adopt a more flexible strategy that distinguishes it from the conventional leftist modus operandi. Thus it adheres to no single agency of transformation; its leaders claim no "scientific" monopoly of knowledge; it encourages alliances with "bourgeois" organizations; it participates energetically in the existing political-institutional sphere (including the Democratic party); and it openly courts the support of party, trade union, and even governmental notables. All of this corresponds to an ideological pragmatism and openness that the populists celebrate as a "non-sectarian" or "winnable" approach to issues, goals, and campaigns. In practice this has meant avoidance of Marxist groups—though not of course popular movements that may have a linkage to such groups—as well as abandonment of any serious effort to build an independent anticorporate or labor party. The unique technical (and ideological) restraints of electoral competition in the United States, along with the historical attachment of the vast majority of people to the two-party system, are viewed as insurmountable obstacles to this type of venture.[19] As Hayden once stated, "It's not really possible to have a third party in this country. Any serious person would reconcile themselves to that immediately and choose between either a protest kind of movement or the Democratic Party as a forum or an arena."[20]

One of the striking features of this approach is the coexistence of an amorphous post-Marxist theory with a strategy and tactics that is anything but amorphous. In this respect, too, it is much like Eurosocialism. New populist practice is cohesive, disciplined, and planned, with a sense of direction typically found in established Marxist parties. Organizations like CED, for example, are methodically efficient in their pursuit of limited, tangible objectives. Political and financial resources are mobilized to support mainstream activities—election campaigns, lobbying, fundraising, legislative reforms, conferences—designed to build a power base in relatively small communities. In the case of CED, the capacity to establish a grassroots presence sufficient to control the Santa Monica city government (and emerge as a powerful force within the California Democratic party structure) derived largely from its catalyzing role in tenants' rights struggles.[21]

If Marxism was discarded without a trace of ambivalence, the influence of social democracy on the new populism is more pervasive than most leaders seem willing to admit. As Jeff Lustig points out, new-populist strategy recalls in many ways the tradition of Eduard Bernstein within the Second International, with its strict emphasis on political evolutionism, electoral participation, and internal restructuring of the bourgeois state.[22] Indeed, Bernstein can be seen as the main precursor to contemporary structural reformism in its various phases and definitions. It is inaccurate, however, to characterize new-populist movements and organizations as simply the most recent expression of social democracy. The differences are many and in some cases profound. Social democracy built its strength on labor constituencies, looked to a national conquest of power, and strived to implement a Keynesian rationalization of the accumulation process. The new populism, on the other hand, rejects a labor focus in favor of the emergent social movements, adheres to an essentially localist strategy, and views Keynesian policies as contributing to rather than solving the economic crisis. As a distinctly American phenomenon, moreover, the new populism is far more removed from the Marxism tradition than is social democracy, which has roots in the Second International and remains, for all of its limitations, an emphatically European tendency. This helps to explain why social democracy has been relatively statist whereas the new populism champions grassroots democratization within both its own organization and the institutions of state power. Much like Eurosocialism, new populism is composed of far more diverse social forces and eclectic ideological strains than was generally true of social democracy.

Of course, there is the influence of the original U.S. populist tradition, as reflected, for example, in the idea of mobilizing "the people" against the privileged elites, in the concern for popular democracy, and in the desire to build local bases of power around community issues. Like the pre–World War I populists, the new variant exemplifies a general (but often vague) hostility to the status quo shaped as much by cultural as by material inspirations. There is also a common distrust of establishment politicians and, to a lesser extent, of intellectuals, a theme further linked to a profound skepticism of progress through economic growth. What Lawrence Goodwyn writes about the earlier populists could be equally applied in the modern context: the meaning of their revolt grew out of its "cultural assertion as a people's movement of mass democratic aspiration," out of its "expansive, passionate, flawed, creative . . . assertion of human striving."[23] From this viewpoint both forms of populism represent generic types of protest, with no sharply defined class basis yet no longer understood merely as a transitional phase of political struggle.[24] The profound differences between agrarian and urban contexts does not obscure their common pursuit of local autonomy. At the same time, this commitment to autonomy, however militant and visionary, could easily be assimilated into a liberal framework.

Second, as we have seen, there is a political culture deeply rooted in American liberalism, characterized by a distinctly indigenous pluralism and civic forms of participation more than two centuries old. In contrast to the celebrated Marxist crisis theory, which foresees a dramatic rupture with the capitalist order, the new populists conceive of radical politics as an extension rather than an overturning of pluralist institutions and norms. A new democratic political culture requires constitutional and legal freedoms, civil rights, and tolerance of dissent and opposition. Social transformation occurs through a maturation of tendencies that (in the United States) are presumed to already exist, developing from the voluntarist premise of a freely given consent that could galvanize popular movements against the privileged centers of wealth and power.[25] Finally, there is a strong residue of the new left, with its ideal of revitalized community life, participatory democracy, broad social goals, and cultural transformation. The new populism has carried forward a 1960s-style attachment to alternative institutions that, where durable, can provide the firmament of "living social change": cooperative markets, media groups and publications, bookstores, rent-control boards, rape crisis centers, medical clinics, toxic-waste projects, research organizations, and so forth.[26] Around these institutions the themes of small-scale activity ("human-scale" development) and grass-roots self-management have been carried forward from the 1960s to the 1980s—except that the new populists reject the insular, back-to-the-country type communes of the counterculture in favor of a more urban-centered, institutional approach. Here, as in other areas, this model has emerged as a response to the limitations of the new left—its utopian romanticism, its spontaneism, its rejection of stable organization and leadership (at least within some of its most visible tendencies). As Andrew Feenberg observes, the capacity of the new left to generate "cultural action from below" was a major source of its uniqueness and appeal, but the very innovative character of the movement meant that it would have great difficulty containing its own energy. The result was a kind of spontaneism that embellished a "politics of self-definition."[27]

Given such ideological pluralism, the new populism can be understood as a new kind of political formation, more democratic and culturally expansive in its outlook than the old populism, while at the same time irreducible to any of its major sources. These sources are above all American, not only in their remoteness from Marxism but in their shared commitment to citizen participation—to the ideal of democracy linked to community and progressive change.[28] As will become evident later in this chapter, it is this uniquely American dimension that gives the new populism both its strengths and its weaknesses.

THE CONQUEST OF NEW POLITICAL TERRAIN

Much along the lines of Eurosocialism, new populists in the United States have been extremely impatient to translate theory into practice. Hoping to avoid the seemingly endemic political isolation of the American left, they have struggled to win new positions of institutional power, mainly but not exclusively in the realm of electoral activity. In the decade beginning with the mid-1970s, new populists took advantage of the immense opening created by the proliferation of community-based movements as an outgrowth of the earlier phase of radicalism. For this reason, and given the structure of the American electoral system, new populists geared their activities toward taking power at the local or municipal level.

New-populist formations achieved their success in part because of a unique capacity to reach people concerning neighborhood issues. This was less a matter of possessing correct theory than of simple grassroots organizing. They were able to combine the instrumental concerns of electoral and administrative work with the rhythm and flow of popular movements, so that the image conveyed was one of concretizing the radical and qualitative demands of the new left. Local mobilizations of the 1970s and 1980s differed considerably, however, from the Alinsky model of organizing that predominated after the 1930s. With the breakup of many urban communities and the emergence of the new left, the recent thrust of popular struggles was not only more diversified but, more significantly, infused with the energy of the new social movements. Thus the feminist, ecological, cultural—and of course democratic—components of revolt came to replace the more simple and direct efforts of the earlier period, which pitted cohesive groups of inner-city poor people against a rapacious outside enemy (city hall, developers, corporations). Whereas the traditional Alinsky-style efforts were essentially defensive in their orientation, the new populists have stressed a positive, forward-looking commitment to building alternative political, social, and economic forms.[29]

The contemporary vision is one of a transformative populism. But like the Alinsky-type groups that preceded them, many of the new organizations present a self-conception that goes "beyond" existing ideologies —whether conservative, liberal, Marxist, or anarchist—enabling them to touch broad constituencies where anxiety to recapture the integrity of family, neighborhood, and community is widespread. By 1985 literally thousands of such organizations had sprung up in virtually every part of the country. In turn, these groups contributed to the growth of political coalitions that, in their readiness to contest for power and influence, would begin to make their mark on American life. Notwithstanding a strong ambivalence toward the party system, new populists have become active in the left wing of the Democratic party and have established a presence in Congress, where in 1984 a Populist Caucus (with fifteen members) was formed in the House of Representatives.

The most well-known new-populist formations include ACORN (with a nationwide network of chapters), the aforementioned CED (based in California), Massachusetts Fair Share in Boston, the Ohio Public Interest Campaign, COPS (in San Antonio), Berkeley Citizens Action, and the now-defunct DARE.[30] Though ideologically similar, these groups vary considerably in their tactical approaches: some emphasize lobbying and legislative reforms, some are primarily educational, others embrace electoral politics and the struggle for governmental power. The extent of their willingness to initiate or support forms of direct-action politics varies greatly.

ACORN, founded in 1970 and sometimes referred to as a "union of the community," is the largest grassroots organization in the United States, with branches in more than twenty states and close ties with some labor unions (notably public employee organizations like AFSCME), local governments, community projects, and the women's and minority movements. Its aim has been to mobilize people, within and outside the electoral arena, on the terrain of taxation, consumer rights, and welfare services—and it has succeeded not only in building large constituencies (especially in the Midwest) but in winning some important battles.[31] Through all of its activities ACORN has campaigned for democratic accountability of public institutions and officials along with immediate reforms, as part of a commitment to citizen "empowerment"—but with only marginal success. A major factor in ACORN's dramatic growth, and perhaps one of its great liabilities, has been its straightforward "nonideological" approach to issues.

CED, on the other hand, was a product of Tom Hayden's strong but unsuccessful campaign for the U.S. Senate in 1976. Constructed initially around Hayden's political machine and personal stature, CED gradually expanded to fifteen active chapters throughout California, with linkages to environmental, tenants, women's, and peace groups. It created an efficient organizing apparatus that reached a large public, much of it university and college students, on a variety of issues: rent control, community services, toxic wastes, the feminization of poverty, crime, and even foreign policy concerns (for example, the arms race and U.S. intervention in Central America). CED's presence was critical to several new-populist electoral victories between 1978 and 1984 and was instrumental in securing strong rent-control ordinances in a number of cities. It was also indispensable to Hayden's election to the California Assembly in 1982 and 1984.

Successful election campaigns were particularly important for new populists insofar as the idea of "winning" governmental power had been central to their outlook from the beginning. In California alone, progressive majorities were established on city councils in Santa Monica (April 1981), Santa Cruz (October 1981), and Berkeley (November 1984). Electoral representation was achieved in Yolo, Humboldt, and Butte counties and in the cities of Bakersfield and San Jose. The Santa Monica victory was engineered by a broad-based tenants' organization, SMRR, which was committed above all to rent control and "human-scale" development in a city long governed by conservative forces. The SMRR slate captured five of the seven city council seats (including the mayor), two seats on the school board, and a majority on the important rent-control board. SMRR was built upon a coalition of three grassroots organizations, including CED. Derek Shearer, later appointed to head the city planning commission, was the SMRR campaign manager and chief strategist for the 1981 election. In Santa Cruz, where progressive movements (supported by a thriving counterculture) had grown rapidly since the 1960s, a leftist-dominated city council (with three out of five seats) was elected through the combined efforts of CED and the DSA. This unique convergence of new-populist and more explicitly socialist-feminist forces was made possible by the relative homogeneity of the community and, to a lesser extent, by the proximity of the University of California campus. Whereas the Santa Monica government was preoccupied with rent-control issues and only secondarily with larger urban-development concerns, in Santa Cruz progressives set out to tackle a broader panorama of objectives—women's and gay rights, establishment of a nuclear-free zone, environmental protection, and new cultural projects as well as rent control. The electoral breakthrough in Berkeley was carried out by the BCA—a coalition of tenants, students, peace activists, minority groups, gays, women, and the elderly radicalized by the historic struggles of the 1960s and 1970s—which won eight of nine seats. The result was a municipal council somewhat to the left of those in Santa Monica and Santa Cruz, with an overwhelming popular consensus behind it, and with a range of commitments even broader than that of Santa Cruz. The BCA goals included more stringent controls over landlords' power, a more equitable labor–management bargaining arrangement for city employees, promotion of community-based holistic health-care clinics, limits on further urban development, and restrictions on businesses involved in military production. Like other new-populist councils, moreover, the Berkeley government never hesitated to pass resolutions on international issues (the Middle East, Central America, the arms race) even if its capacity to influence events was minimal.

The Santa Monica experience deserves special attention because it probably best typifies the new populism and because it has been the most successful, in both organizational and electoral terms, over the longest period of time. Moreover, the seminal concept of economic democracy is most closely linked to the CED and progressive politics in Santa Monica generally. And in less than a decade this milieu has given rise to an extensive new-populist literature, as we have seen.

The 1981 electoral triumph, representing a long-awaited break with what some activists called the Growth Machine, was made possible by a mounting wave of progressivism that can be traced back to the early 1970s with the strong impact of the new left and the McGovern for President campaign. Emergent popular movements broke the political stillness of what had been a traditionally conservative beach-side community. This progressive energy, fragmented and ineffectual throughout most of the 1970s, coalesced around a rent-control movement that gained strength in a city where nearly 80 percent of the population was tenants, housing was becoming extremely scarce, and real estate profiteering pushed the cost of housing rapidly upward. Beneath this trend was an even deeper sentiment in favor of community autonomy at a time when the sprawling, haphazard urban development of the Los Angeles metropolitan region was getting out of control. These two concerns were enough to bring together elements of the new movements, liberal Democrats disenchanted with their party leadership, and tenants of greatly varying age, race, occupation, and even ideology. But it was not until the victory of a rent-control initiative in 1979 (an earlier one failed in 1978) that new-populist forces were finally able to rally around a common focus, setting the stage for the 1981 triumph.

Within a few short years the municipal public sphere in Santa Monica was to be dramatically transformed. Civil life underwent a process of renewal, political debate became more intense and open, and the dominant urban interests (landlords, developers, bankers) were challenged and put on the defensive for the first time. The formation of SMRR made possible an efficient organizing machine that could turn out hundreds of activists and supporters on short notice. The consensual base of progressive support was large, heterogeneous, and seemingly durable. All of this seemed to validate the new-populist maxim that, given the peculiarities of American political culture, a viable left-wing politics would necessarily have to be a local politics.[32]

Much like the Eurosocialists, the new populists in Santa Monica celebrated their initial year in power with a flurry of reforms and innovative activity. The popular mood was one of exhuberance and optimism. The city council implemented the most radical rent-control laws in the United States and established a large board of experts to implement them. Limits were imposed upon high-rise development and condominium conversion (part of the landlords' efforts to sidestep the effects of rent control). Affirmative-action criteria were adopted by the municipal government. In 1983 a system of task forces was set up to study, advance, and oversee various projects and, at about the same time, there was some initiative for creating a network of neighborhood councils to ensure grassroots democratization. However, neither of these efforts really got off the ground. Some activists wanted to establish a public agency to facilitate the shift toward municipal control of investment, but this, too, remained on the drawing board.

The rent-control board perhaps best epitomized new-populist values insofar as it was able to wield a good deal of authority independently of federal, state, and even local institutional restraints. Created by a popular referendum that was written into the city charter, the board was more or less free to interpret its own mandate. It was able to promote the development of what Kann calls "liberated public space." Kann suggests that "Santa Monica's Rent Control Board can be seen as a model local institution that circumvents elite control mechanisms."[33]

Political life in Santa Monica after 1981 was inspired by a language of democracy and citizen empowerment, which served to ideologically unify diverse community groups in response to participation and consumption issues. The implicit understanding was that "people come first," that community needs should be asserted over private interests.[34] Beyond the issue of tenants' rights, however, the new-populist agenda lacked coherence. Instead of a comprehensive program, there was little more than visionary statements and an issue-oriented "ad hoc radicalism" that solidified the left for a few years but then dissipated, eventually giving way to disillusionment.[35] With the rent-control struggle seemingly won—and with the vast majority of the electorate behind it —progressives began to lose their sense of forward motion and expansiveness. Public support ebbed slightly, leading to the narrow defeat of Mayor Ruth Yannatta Goldway in 1983 and then to a stunning loss of the council majority (owing to a technicality) in 1984. As we shall see, this predicament reflected an even deeper impasse: the failure to make the guiding new-populist commitment to democracy a living reality.

THE LIMITS OF DEMOCRATIC REFORM

The new populism accumulated a series of remarkable victories in the sphere of conventional politics during the early 1980s. These victories immediately inspired optimism. In the words of Carnoy and Shearer: "We are now at the stage of constructing a movement which will be rooted permanently in American communities and American experience, and not based on the needs of perceptions of foreign 'revolutionary' parties or ideologies."[36] Surely this liberation from past Marxist–Leninist orthodoxies did fulfill one necessary condition for pragmatic political success. But "liberation" from the larger Marxist vision—abolition of the profit motive, wage labor, and the social division of labor—suggests that the formula for "success" might in fact only amount to a recipe for leftist failure to carry out any thoroughgoing social transformation.

The growth of progressive tendencies can be understood in part as the reintegration of rebellious and democratizing energies—the driving force of 1960s radicalism—into the mainstream of American public life: the professions, schools, unions, businesses, media and culture, political parties, and the churches. In part, however, it is also the result of continuing struggle over the allocation of economic resources, over the control of capital. Examples of "citizen action" gains during the 1970s and 1980s include not only the electoral victories referred to above but also the appearance of anticorporate, consumer, and public interest organizations, the rise of environmental and health projects, the emergence of research institutes and foundations sympathetic to social change, a broadened interest in democratic management or worker ownership, and so forth. What all of these efforts have in common, according to Carnoy and Shearer, is an emphasis not on "nation-

alization of the means of production from the top down, but on democratization of the economy from the bottom up starting with the workplace and the community." [37]

Such a tangible goal of democratic transformation is no doubt larger
and more compelling than the lingering statism and productivism of
the Marxist-Leninist and social-democratic traditions. One advantage
is that it appears to be solidly grounded in postindustrial issues and
constituencies, as exemplified by the Santa Monica experience. Yet this
proclaimed vision of democratization is ultimately impeded or even
blocked by a strategic conception (i.e., the new-populist version of
structural reformism) that basically contradicts it. In three crucial areas
—the political system, the workplace, and internal organizational forms
—the new populism replays the dilemmas and failures of social democracy that, as I stressed in the preceding chapter, have resurfaced in the
Eurosocialist parties. The difficulties are imposing: how to reconcile
efforts to take over state bureaucracies with an emphasis on grassroots
mobilization; how to generate capital investment and business support
while subverting the logic of capital accumulation (asserting social-use
value over exchange value); how to establish a presence in the Democratic party and trade unions while at the same time appealing to the
rank and file; how to create a broad multiclass alliance while sustaining
a real oppositional dynamism. In earlier cases (German Social Democracy, for instance) the all-consuming drive for immediate political gains
served to confine the left to the boundaries of pluralist democracy. Is
the new populism, which presents itself as an alternative to corporate
capitalism and the bureaucratic state, likely to fall prey to the same
illusions? This question will be taken up first at the level of the new
populists' conceptualization of their tasks and then, in the following
section, at the level of the Santa Monica experience.

Although this model is still in its infancy, the tensions between vision
and strategy are already so pronounced as to suggest nearly insurmountable roadblocks ahead. As in the the case of Eurosocialism, populist
insurgency in the United States has restricted its activity largely to the
legitimate political-institutional sphere (party system, elections, municipal government, interest groups). New-populist organizations like
CED do, of course, have an extensive community base where grassroots mobilization takes place, but the relationship between those formations and their mass constituencies is generally little more than an
instrumental one stressing the power of the ballot box and interest-

group influence rather than autonomous popular struggles. Under such conditions, as I argue in the case of the Mediterranean Socialist parties, the logic of elite competition, alliance building, and bureaucratic strategems counters the logic of popular revolt and disruptive protest, thus setting clear boundaries to democratization.[38] By narrowing the scope of conflict, an institutionally oriented politics routes the oppositional energy of social movements into acceptable modes of participation—at least where such politics is effective. Should popular mobilization spill beyond these boundaries and get out of hand, the state (whether local, national, or some combination of the two) generally intervenes to conciliate or repress such struggles. In order to win and preserve power, therefore, new-populist formations find it necessary to accede to or collaborate with corporate interests and therefore abandon even token efforts to challenge systemic priorities. The Italian Communist party, with a strong mass presence but also with an exclusive attachment to electoral politics, has experienced this sort of institutionalizing dynamic in provinces and cities where it has administered local power continuously over a period of many years.[39] And the Santa Monica progressives, as we shall see, appear to be duplicating this pattern.

The dilemmas of new-populist strategy are perhaps nowhere so clearly visible as in the commitment to work inside the Democratic party. Proponents of this tactic argue that the American party system is uniquely open to diverse ideological currents, and this is undeniably true up to a point. Both the Republican and Democratic organizations, conducting business as they do in a dispersed federalist system and sharing more or less the same fundamental values, are inevitably forced to the moderate center. As a consequence, they become diffuse, fragmented structures lacking real identity. Compared with most Western European parties, for example, membership and participation in American parties is open, undisciplined, and undemanding. This fact, combined with the firm hegemony of the two-party system, the absence of proportional representation, and the nonpartisan character of many offices, makes left entry into the Democratic party not only possible but, some would argue, absolutely imperative. Such entry is of course least prohibitive at the grassroots level, where major party structures are decidedly weakest. Following this prescription, CED efforts to penetrate the Democratic party in the Los Angeles area and throughout California have been both serious and fruitful. By 1980 the CED had emerged as a powerful force within the left wing of the state Democratic organization. With twenty-two chapters scattered around the state, the CED helped to elect more than sixty local candidates and was the single largest voting bloc (with about 300 delegates) at the 1981 state Democratic convention. In this fashion the new-populist current had become a legitimate if still somewhat thorny presence within the political system.

Yet it is one of the unyielding facts of American political life that the two-party system remains a bastion of ruling-class interests and ideologies — a reality that no amount of party "pragmatism" or fragmentation can conceal. (Policy differences between Republicans and Democrats, which in many cases are real enough, are secondary to this reality.) So long as this is the case, the unavoidable pressures and compromises required to build leverage within the Democratic party are bound to stifle radical impulses. It is difficult to actually mobilize constituencies within this arena around any kind of transformative project.[40] For example, efforts to appeal simultaneously to business and labor (or consumers), landlords and tenants, government officials and the poor, can go only so far. Hayden's image of a "new majority governing coalition" invokes precisely this flawed premise — "a joining of several forces" including "however many enlightened bankers and industrialists can be enlisted, labor leaders (and especially the rank-and-file), minorities and women constituencies, many liberal politicians of both parties, and of course an energetic base of representatives of new movements for social change."[41] The rallying together of such totally opposed social forces might be a prescription for traditional pluralist catch-all politics, but hardly for the kind of sustained populist insurgency, or new politics, that Hayden and others claim is on the agenda. To the extent such a strategem might ever work, it would be primarily integrative rather than oppositional, statist rather than democratizing.

There is considerable irony in the new-populist desire to infiltrate and revitalize the two-party system at the very moment of that system's most acute legitimation crisis in recent times. The 1970s witnessed a steady decline in popular attachment to both major parties: voter turnout dropped below 50 percent in national elections and often fell well below that for state and local elections, while surveys reflected a sharp rise in the number of "independents." Thus we have the spectacle of an avowedly left-wing, Democratic party–oriented strategy that promises to restore faith in an ailing two-party system that remains fully within the framework of capitalist priorities and values.

As for the Democratic party itself, on both domestic and foreign-policy issues it has adopted an increasingly conservative stance in order to compete with Reaganite Republicans for the middle ground. It has retreated from even basic welfare-state programs, hedged on its previous commitments to the minority and women's movements, endorsed U.S. intervention in Central America with only minor criticisms, and has fully supported the arms race with its stratospheric military budgets. Indeed, the entire Democratic structure is integrally connected to the war economy—and thus to the very forms of domination that new populists ostensibly want to oppose. For the left to "enter"this type of party organization, which admittedly allows for some open competition at the local level, will in the long run force it to abandon its progressive identity, for the terms on which it can purchase influence will be those of ideological submergence.[42] As Stanley Aronowitz argues, the prospects for supplying an ideological direction for the social movements, of laying the groundwork for effective direct action, of confronting the power structure—that is, of forging an anticapitalist coalition—within the Democratic party must be considered nil.[43]

Only in a few limited circumstances, such as the mayoralty campaigns in Chicago, Boston, and Philadelphia during the early 1980s, has the left been able to exert even minimal influence upon party debates or ideological directions. Even where new social movements are taken seriously within electoral politics, their radical goals are generally shunned. Surely the landmark Jesse Jackson campaign in 1984 reflects as much the failure of a tactics focused on the Democratic party as its success because the sense of renewal this campaign injected into the political arena had little impact on the party itself. Where progressives have made significant advances in local politics, such advances have typically flowed from the energy of popular movements located on the periphery of the party system. An example of this was the Mel King campaign for mayor of Boston in 1983, which built its momentum on a "rainbow coalition" of movements but which also drew upon Democratic party resources. In mobilizing a variety of constituencies around the struggle of neighborhoods against downtown interests, the King campaign utilized electoral politics to empower blacks, enlarge the realm of public discourse, and unify progressive forces.[44]

New-populist efforts to penetrate the Democratic party and win positions of official power sooner or later require a generalized defense of the political system against insurgent challenges. This is not merely a function of electoralism as such, or even of institutional power objectives, but rather of a strategic approach that is so single-minded in its pursuit of these aims that it must sacrifice the possibility of retaining its grassroots character. As Robert Brenner notes, this model of politics in effect constitutes an *alternative* to mass struggle insofar as its logic of simply representing the prevailing views of the electorate is incompatible with a process of consciousness transformation directed toward structural change. The demand is for bodies and money—little more.[45] From this viewpoint the two-party system in American politics serves, more than anything else, to legitimate the larger social order.[46]

Popular revolt has its own subversive logic and rhythm—a logic and rhythm, however, that can be easily interrupted once this revolt is instrumentalized (i.e., subordinated to the needs of stable institutional politics). One illustration of this dynamic is the retreat within new-populist theory from any conception of democratic participation that goes beyond pluralist democracy or, for that matter, that questions the rationale of existing power relations. (The parallel here with both Eurocommunism and Eurosocialism is rather striking.) References to "community power," "popular democracy," and "free social spaces" are largely devoid of any concrete structural (or strategic) definition, and alternative forms such as neighborhood or community assemblies and local councils receive little if any attention. In the absence of local democratic structures, prospects for the growth of nonbureaucratic social and authority relations of the sort anticipated by new populists are exceedingly remote. The perpetual conflict between the imperatives of institutional management and the goals of local movements appear in sharpest relief. Thus Sheila Rowbotham argues, from the standpoint of feminist objectives, that broad social and cultural changes cannot be advanced within the framework of a political–institutional strategy, which favors a "politics of deferment" to the exclusion of a prefigurative approach that stresses local mobilization, direct action, small-group processes, and consciousness transformation.[47]

The new-populist approach to democratic reforms within the economic sphere goes somewhat further, but it too suffers from many of the same ambiguities and limitations. Carnoy and Shearer, for example, present a seductive view of "economic democracy": the establishment of labor banks, workers' and producers' cooperatives, community development corporations, and worker-owned industry, all leading toward expanded democratic control of investment and more egalitarian income distribution. They further envision a system of workers' self-management that borrows from the experiences of Yugoslavia, France, Sweden, and Chile under Salvador Allende.[48] Yet they seem ambivalent, at best, about extending workers' control beyond corporate exchange relations in a way that would confront the managerial hierarchy itself; their schema is really more one of "workers' participation" along lines of the West German model. Hence, restrictions that naturally arise from the choice of a political–institutional strategy reappear: hoping to secure structural reforms primarily through legislative and regulatory efforts, and hoping to attract Democratic party and trade-union leaders, Carnoy and Shearer are forced to downplay militant class conflict in the workplace. Their strategy assumes that democratic control can somehow be achieved without collective or socialized ownership—and without a process of direct confrontation building toward a transition.

This contradiction is even more pronounced in the case of both Hayden and Boyte, who offer versions of "workers' control" and the "economics of self-reliance" that are perfectly compatible with managerial discretion and control. Hayden, anxious to dispel the notion that CED is uncompromisingly antibusiness, calls for the development of more efficient and "participatory" managerial techniques, greater public accountability, and more extensive community involvement. Following the model of Japanese industrial management, Hayden's version of restructuring amounts to yet another path to economic rationalization: democratic reforms, however ambitious, ultimately leave intact the established hierarchy of capital over wage labor. What Hayden apparently has in mind is some variant of the familiar tripartite corporatist network encompassing business, labor, and the state.[49]

Boyte, meanwhile, falls back upon a very old-fashioned notion of workplace "organizing," which, for all practical purposes, amounts to little more than conventional unionization drives. Parallel citizens' movements in the community would include grassroots economic projects, publicly owned community development corporations, and occupational safety and health groups.[50] Like Shearer and Carnoy, Boyte places the main weight of new-populist strategy on the community rather than on the workplace. He finds special inspiration in community-based countercultural movements and in consumer-oriented and worker-run cooperatives, which he sees as representing a "challenge to the normal patterns of American economics."[51] For the most part, however, Boyte seems content to describe a long list of "self-help" activities as if the mere cataloguing of hundreds of local organizations, groups, and projects is enough to demonstrate the presence of oppositional movements. Lumped together as citizens' formations, these undifferentiated groups are never really analyzed with the aim of determining their transformative potential. What distinguishes such community-based efforts from similar ones that have failed in the past? What conditions are necessary to radicalize constituencies involved in struggles for limited reforms? And, given the unions' largely mediating role between labor and capital, to what extent can unionization campaigns today catalyze or feed into a broader process of social transformation? These are complicated questions with no simple answers, but they must be taken seriously. Boyte, unfortunately, chooses to sidestep them entirely.[52]

The internal structure of new-populist organizations reproduces similar tensions and difficulties. Insofar as political strategy has revolved around local government, pressures toward what Piven and Cloward call the "mass-based permanent organization model" have been understandably quite irresistible.[53] Whatever the electoral or administrative efficiency of such formations, their capacity to initiate democratization (let alone sustain it) is limited by a bureaucratic conservatism stemming from their need to compete with rival elites for mass allegiance, institutional leverage, and, of course, governmental power. The most sincere attempts to counter elitist and manipulative political styles have usually been futile under these conditions. Over time, strictly power-defined successes generally come at a high price: the abandonment of collective decision making, a decline of rank-and-file vitality, and the emergence of an insular elite stratum.[54] Once in power, formal mass organizations tend to become absorbed into the state apparatus, adopting in the process many features of classical machine politics (the exchange of patronage and favors for votes, for example). Here again the postwar evolution of the Italian Communist party, which has exercised administrative control (often in coalition with the Socialists) in virtually every major city of the country, presents an appropriate case study.[55] This phenomenon will be explored more fully in the next section.

There is no intent here to discount the reform potential of new-populist electoral movements. The crucial point is simply that power conquests along the lines of new-populist strategy will probably do little to facilitate a viable oppositional politics, and might in some cases even pose new obstacles since the strategy, tied as it is to pluralist rules of formal representation, is not likely to generate the kind of participatory culture that helps to vigorously democratize knowledge, skills, and awareness.[56] Genuine democratic transformation requires far more than structural engineering from above: it demands extensive changes in the social environment and popular consciousness—not to mention a break (ultimately) with bureaucratic politics—of the sort largely ignored by new populists.

From yet another angle, such an institutionally centered strategy would likely solidify conventional, system-sustaining political practices. As Piven and Cloward observe on the basis of several historical cases: "Organizers . . . typically acted in ways that blunted or curbed the disruptive force that lower class people were sometimes able to mobilize. In small part, this resulted from . . . organization-building activities [that] tended to draw people away from the streets and into meeting rooms. . . . But in the largest part organizers tended to work against disruption because, in their search for resources to maintain their organizations, they were driven inexorably to elites, and to the tangible and symbolic supports that elites could provide. Elites conferred these resources because they understood that it was organization-building, not disruption, that organizers were about."[57] Once again we are presented with two rather distinct approaches to social change: a political–institutional strategy requiring stability and ideological cohesion (legitimacy) defined in terms of existing power relations, and popular mobilization sustained by a milieu of upheaval, conflict, and insurgency.

SANTA MONICA: INSTITUTIONALIZATION AT THE GRASSROOTS

The limits and contradictions of new-populist governance are perhaps most clearly reflected in the Santa Monica experiment. As we have seen, roughly a decade of patient grassroots and electoral work had preceded the progressive takeover of the city council in 1981; hopes for community renewal and political change were high. But in the wake of an initial phase of reform, achieved mainly in the area of tenants' rights issues, apathy became widespread. The left was confronted with the problem of how to exercise the power it had struggled so hard to win. This dilemma was most obvious in the realm of democratic participation, which was, after all, a central theme of the new populism. The electoral triumph held out the promise of local autonomy, revitalized community life, and citizen empowerment—all presumably grounded in creative new forms of civic involvement. For Santa Monica activists, the form of politics was at least as important as its content. However, it did not take long for the structural obstacles of government to impose themselves on the progressive agenda. The inherent tension between power and participation was rather quickly resolved in the direction of the former—that is, in favor of organizational stability and the instrumentalized politics it embodies.

The left majority in Santa Monica chose from the outset to concentrate its resources largely within the legitimate public sphere, which had been historically colonized by the dominant local interests. Although many SMRR and CED leaders wanted to move ahead with far-reaching reforms that would redistribute political power and economic resources, their unwillingness to challenge the narrow scope of pluralist decision making and interest-group bargaining inevitably undercut those objectives. A form of institutional politics began to take precedence, in practice if not in theory, over community-based activity. There was a gradual but emphatic retreat from original commitments to reconstruct local political arrangements—to build neighborhood councils, to carry out political education, to ensure that leftist organizations themselves were accessible and democratic.

By 1983 these deradicalizing tendencies were already in full swing, even if they did not immediately translate into dramatic loss of public support. At this juncture the once-sporadic criticisms of SMRR and CED (and of the city council) for being heavy-handed, arrogant, and bureaucratic were becoming routine. Later electoral difficulties were only symptomatic of a deeper problem, the erosion of democratic process. The vast majority of people was increasingly remote from the debates taking place within progressive organizations, whose leaders seemed intent upon pursuing their own agenda with a minimum of disruption from below. Although several thousand Santa Monica residents made financial contributions or became involved in electoral work such as telephone banking or precinct walking, most never joined a constituent organization and therefore could rarely be much more than supporters within an amorphous mass public. In this context, and given the type of institutionally centered strategy adopted by the leadership, even the most active and committed citizens (outside the leadership stratum) could have little input into decision making, little role in debates over what programs or what candidates to endorse, and hence little sense of empowerment. And of course those more distanced from

SMRR activities were, predictably, even more alienated from the political process. As SMRR and CED leaders grew more obsessed with the urge to control and manipulate discussions, the criteria for entry into the inner circle became more rigid. As one close observer of the Santa Monica scene writes: "The SMRR groups have basically seen fit to rely on SMRR supporters as an electoral network which can be geared up to win an election and otherwise lies dormant. In terms of its own internal structure, then, it is clear that there is at best fear and naïveté and at worst disdain for participatory democracy." [58]

Although progressive delegates on the city council were generally more open to new ideas and responsive to public opinion than their conservative or liberal counterparts, mechanisms for ensuring accountability to the grassroots were simply absent. Hence, a small group of elites could easily predominate in decision making, both on the city council and within new-populist organizations as well. Soon after the 1981 election a task force was set up to explore the role of neighborhood planning and decentralized forms of authority but, in the end, such democratizing schemes were never carried forward. In its initial report to the city council, the task force called for development of neighborhood structures but urged the council to retain all power over policy formulation and implementation; the local forms, in other words, would have at best advisory functions. This approach was shared by leaders of various community organizations, who rejected the principle of neighborhood control in favor of pressure-group efforts to influence municipal government from within—for example, by packing citizen commissions and boards with their own members or by negotiating with city hall officials behind the scenes. CED, for its part, opposed the idea of the city council's sharing power with neighborhoods because the latter were expected to be overly provincial in their views, which would of course work against the formation of programmatic unity.

One result of this reversal was that crucial issues (for example, rent control and urban development) were to some extent depoliticized as they were removed from the give-and-take of community action and placed exclusively in the domain of leaders and experts. The plain reality was that, in the Santa Monica case, new-populist elites were fearful of sharing power with local constituencies and even with their own rank and file. Nor was there any serious attempt to transform popular consciousness—to set up mechanisms of political education (forums, lectures, films, discussion groups)—outside the limited circle of CED and the SMRR cadres. As for the system of task forces, by 1984 it could be said to have existed on paper only. An underlying concern of the leaders was that free-wheeling debate or expressions of direct democracy might challenge their ideological (and social) cohesion.

This problem is partly explained by SMRR's failure to expand its political reach beyond the single-issue focus of tenants' rights. Insofar as success of the left coalition revolved primarily around the rent-control movement, there was every temptation to capitalize upon discontent over housing issues to the fullest possible extent. And this focus did indeed offer tangible challenges and possibilities: the rent-control board was established, sympathetic lawyers and other experts were attracted to the cause, and most significantly a critical mass of city residents was likely to respond favorably to any rent-control campaign. By 1983 a community consensus in support of tenants' rights was firmly in place, to the degree that even some conservatives and landlords muted their hostility. But what about a range of other equally vital issues in a city whose populace had been in varying measures politicized if not radicalized: neighborhood control and direct democracy, health care, women's issues and child-care facilities, environmental control, even a broader definition of housing struggles (for example, a commitment to public, low-cost residential units)? Unfortunately, Santa Monica progressives never incorporated such demands into their agenda—even if they sometimes attached symbolic meaning to them. Whatever the long-range vision articulated by a few theorists, there was little concrete effort to arrive at a program of social transformation in which these and other issues could be linked together and further politicized. Instead, both SMRR and CED continued to place nearly exclusive emphasis on rent control long after the issue had become defused as a rallying point for progressives. When other issues were taken up, such as pier restoration in the aftermath of the 1983 storms, they were defined as technical or "nonpartisan" in character. Most of the progressives apparently wanted to refrain from any controversial or "radical" action that would undermine their newly won institutional power base. But this timid modus operandi was ultimately counterproductive.

The point here is that the governing left in Santa Monica wanted to limit the popular role in decision making since this would have posed a broader range of concerns than the leadership was prepared to confront. More specifically, grassroots involvement would have unsettled the narrow single-issue politics of SMRR and CED, which under the circumstances preferred "pseudo-participation" over actual citizen empowerment.[59] For the new populism this signaled a triumph of the formal over the substantive, the institutional over the grassroots dimensions of activity.

By 1984 it had become obvious to even the left's staunchest supporters and allies that the progressive breakthrough, however impressive in the area of rent control, was not likely to lead very far beyond the old-style liberalism it had detested.[60] Its approach was conventionally pluralist. Despite inspiration from a visionary new-populist ideology, therefore, the Santa Monica experiment rather quickly lapsed into a bureaucratic attitude toward popular movements and neighborhood concerns once power was consolidated. The distrust of direct democracy was hardly a matter of ideological myopia or tactical retreat. It was built into a strategic methodology that assigned primary and unquestioned legitimacy to pluralist institutions and that, by extension, downplayed those social forces outside them. The Santa Monica case suggests that the logic of new-populist structural reformism works against the energy of popular revolt beneath the outward appearances of a grassroots, community-based politics.

POPULAR REVOLT AND THE SEARCH FOR COMMUNITY

The lessons from Santa Monica point to a persistent tension between the instrumental bias of strategically oriented power concerns and the prefigurative thrust of social movements tied to the struggle for local autonomy. It further illuminates the complex relationship between democracy and community, and the difficult tasks that surround what might be called cultural politics. Returning to the general framework of this critique, I will discuss the extent to which new populism represents either a subversion of or adaptation to bourgeois ideological hegemony. New-populist theorists have in fact devoted considerable attention to this rather challenging problem. "Economic democracy" and "citizen empowerment" clearly demand far more than institutional engineering or legislative reforms. The assumption is that fundamental social change will occur, if at all, only on a basis of reconstituted beliefs, values, and lifestyles developed through the process of community building—of transforming civil society.

To have any reasonable chance of success, popular movements must have not only institutional outlets but also ideological space to advance their goals. Thus, democratic objectives require an attack on hierarchy and violence in every area of social life, but such objectives cannot be realized unless the various fragmenting and depoliticizing ideologies (bureaucratic rationality, privatized individualism, cynicism, and the like) are in some way subverted. Oppositional formations, even those guided by the most farsighted and critical vision, have often ended up doing more to extend than to overturn dominant beliefs and values that help to keep the power structure intact. Examples abound of parties and movements that either began as radical forces but were integrated into the larger political system (classical social democracy) or espoused a revolutionary ideology that in effect camouflaged a system-sustaining reformist strategy (Eurocommunism). Much depends, therefore, upon both the intent and capacity of leftist organizations to challenge bourgeois hegemony and, at the same time, to create a counterhegemonic presence. The vital question is: can the new populism, with its distinctive emphasis upon "building a new culture," hope to escape the dynamics of ideological reassimilation?

New-populist writers are rather unambiguous about their intentions. Hayden, for example, speaks of the need to create a new American "identity" based upon "the inner tendency to desire love, warmth, art, craft, community, knowledge." In his view, "the new era needs a new morality in the same sense that the Protestant Ethic served the rise of expansionist capitalism." If American development was historically defined by material growth, profit, and ecological destruction, the "new era" of limitations requires an ethic of inner rewards, austerity, and environmentalism—a commitment to a "simple, self-determined lifestyle with an enrichment of the meaning of labor." [61] Hayden's vision is a series of reforms that will "empower people in some way—through change in both consciousness and structure—to take greater control over their lives, and then to make still greater advances." Hayden's ideology (which remains otherwise unspecified) is anchored to "yet another expansion of the American tradition of citizenship and democracy." Convinced that profound cultural changes may already be occurring, Hayden cites survey data to show that a "quiet revolution may be taking place in our national values and aspirations." [62]

These themes are echoed throughout the work of Carnoy and Shearer and of Boyte. Each stresses the importance of citizen empowerment from the perspective that a depoliticized public, which naturally drifts toward cynicism and retreat, must be converted into a dynamic political force. Carnoy and Shearer argue that workers' struggles to democratize the economy, for example, can unleash the most powerful system-challenging energies.[63] They suggest that "workers in capitalist societies are socialized to limit their democratic ideals to the political (voting) sphere and to freedom of choice in consumption. They do not expect to participate in production decisions. Any outright worker demand for control over production transcends that socialization and the whole concept of private property." It follows that "consistency with democratic ideals should make workplace participation an important reform issue."[64] Yet in the final analysis economic democracy of this sort can only legitimate itself by winning elections and demonstrating its capacity to govern effectively.[65] And this cannot occur without the development, over time, of an active, participatory political culture extending into all spheres of public life.

Similarly, Boyte looks to the emergence of a grassroots democratic culture that could replace the "marketplace ethic" and sustain new levels of citizen activism. Democratization requires a sense of community and "roots" to nurture the skills and self-consciousness necessary to challenge elite domination. According to Boyte, the new populism has already initiated this process as it spreads through "unseen social networks" kept alive by the old populist and democratic traditions.[66] It expands on a foundation of social movements concerned with participation, cultural pluralism, self-help, and community autonomy, and employs a transformative language with a distinctively American accent. It promises to reinvigorate a political life that has long been denatured by an obsession with personalities, isolated or marginal issues, and superficial glitter.[67] In this context the renewal of community life—and with it the rediscovery of a socialized personal identity—necessarily poses the question of ideological hegemony.

Structural reforms tied to a progressive deepening of democratic and communitarian norms is clearly a new-populist innovation, in theory at least. The transition from a privatized mass consciousness to collective subjectivity is central to any radical politics, especially where corporate hegemony is strong and where "democratic" ideals are distorted for authoritarian ends. New populists sometimes refer to a *continuous* developmental process uniting the best of various currents: liberal democracy, populism, social democracy, the new left.[68] More sensitive to the role of broad social and cultural forces than the traditional left, they have recognized the need to build a counterhegemonic presence.

But the constituent elements of such a presence have yet to be posed with any political or strategic clarity. Two serious problems arise: first, the failure to spell out both the political forms and the class content of cultural transformation and, second, the absence of any real counter-hegemonic theory. Interestingly enough, the trenchant new-populist critique of corporate liberalism never questions the logic of accumu-lation itself. Moreover, one finds little effort to confront the problem of domination as it is expressed through the ideological filter of techno-logical rationality, commodified culture, patriarchy, and racism. This void might be regarded as a mere oversight by progressive leaders anxious to win immediate victories, but such an explanation ignores the decisive impact of a consciously designed structural-reformist strategy that necessarily reduces the scope of social change. By confining politics to specific institutional boundaries, new populists are forced to define what is possible in strictly instrumental (pragmatic, "realistic") terms. And by rejecting any version of socialism as an alternative to out-moded corporate liberalism, it suspends itself ideologically between two realms with no recourse but to remain within the orbit of bourgeois hegemony.[69]

New-populist strategy thus converts a commitment to democratic and cultural transformation into relatively harmless internal challenges to elite power: "workers' control" comes to mean greater trade-union or consumer involvement in the corporate structure; "community self-management" signifies little more than introduction of new adminis-trative agencies; the attack on corporate priorities takes shape as a call for public "accountability" and "responsibility"; "feminism" implies the development of new affirmative-action programs; and so forth. Though potentially significant, these reforms nonetheless fail to challenge bour-geois hegemony or even push the limits of corporate capitalism. The gulf between concept and reality is not a matter of language or even, for the most part, of proclaimed objectives. The deeper contradictions are rooted in a particular theory and strategy—a theory that is too diffuse and a strategy that is too instrumental.[70]

One example of this predicament is provided by the trajectory of the Santa Monica tenants' movement. Linked closely to CED, ten-ants' organizations helped pass stringent rent-control laws, form a rent-control board, and elect the progressive city council slate. Allan Heskin's study of tenant politics shows that, despite radical leadership expecta-tions, the vast majority of participants never went beyond the limits of interest-group consciousness. Most tenant activists were politicized only briefly, with organizing directed primarily toward the narrow "con-sumer ethic" shared by renters and homeowners in relatively affluent areas. Heskin found that housing struggles remained firmly locked into these "hegemonic boundaries" and thus could never transcend a defense of material interests embedded in capitalist property relations. Yielding to the ethic of private property, and in some cases even to the estab-lished landlord-tenant relationship, "economic democracy" in this con-text generated little support for egalitarian measures or more ambitious social priorities (e.g., low-cost public housing). Although there was a heightened sense of political efficacy, Heskin observes that this was acquired only through the long and difficult battle with landlords. Once significant reforms were won, tenant organizing appeared to lose its focus and momentum, resulting in a sharp decline of political activity.[71]

This process often takes place when progressive movements seek formal representation or legitimation within the bourgeois public sphere. In the case of the new populism, the consequences became immediately visible: social goals were instrumentalized, limits were imposed upon democratization, and political conflict was moderated even as change in specific (but limited) areas was being pursued or implemented. Hay-den as well as Carnoy and Shearer are correct to insist that democratic transformation must be grounded in American conditions and cultural values rather than in imported formulas. And many of the "Marxist-Leninist" abstractions that Boyte rejects clearly deserve to be discarded. Yet how far can such logic be pushed without relinquishing an effective strategy for radical change? At what point does adaptation to the American heritage become a synonym for adaptation to bourgeois he-gemony? New-populist theorists seem to approach such issues with cavalier indifference.

Boyte criticizes the left for its insensitivity to the "complexity of tradi-tion, the internal changes that occur within traditional communities in the course of protest, and the multi-dimensionality of social movements itself." He argues that "actual movements inevitably draw on rich buried cultural themes from the past that coexist alongside repressive ones." It follows that progressives are mistaken to disdain "old-fashioned and traditional ways and institutions that . . . appear as backwaters of cul-ture, since it is in the provinces—through associations like the church, family, and ethnic traditions—that social movements are often spawned." Boyte adds, "American society has a tradition of mass democratic revolt more organic, more culturally rooted than that of classical socialism or liberalism."[72] This outlook, part of a general romantic attachment to eroding traditions and social relations, has gained wide credibility in certain sectors of the American left as well as within the popular movements. One striking example was the emergence, in the early 1980s, of fervently "pro-family" groups that saw in the conventional nuclear family a strong counterforce to the rootless individualism, narcissism, and abdication of social responsibility that were seen as typical of the new left and even feminism. By embracing family (and, by extension, community) values, moreover, the left could more effectively combat the ideological appeals of new-right movements on their own terrain.[73]

At the most abstract level, this Rousseauian vision of rebuilding local communities in the name of progressive politics is compelling. But some difficult questions have to be asked: what are the constituent elements of "mass democratic revolt" in American history? To what extent have these traditions ever challenged the structures (and ideologies) of domination? How can we disentangle the essence of revolt from the totality of liberal politics, from the ideologies of racism and sexism, from the confining localism and individualism typical of interest-group bargaining? What criteria permit us to distinguish between the positive and negative dimensions of popular struggles over nationalism, religion, the family, and "old-fashioned" cultural values? What is to be discarded, and what reappropriated? Neither Boyte nor other new-populist theorists confront these issues very directly.[74] The problem is that most of the grassroots legacies that Boyte exalts simultaneously contain pervasive elements of racism, sexism, and of course anti-Communism. This is why the very concept of democratization needs to be spelled out more carefully. Bourgeois hegemony is reproduced in part through what Gramsci called the "ensemble of relations"—the complex of activities, beliefs, and norms deeply embedded in civil society, in everyday life. The multiple forms of domination will remain intact until this ensemble is transformed, until a new "integrated culture" evolves to replace them. Such a process, in turn, ultimately requires a fundamental rupture in the capitalist division of labor accompanied by a "general crisis of the state."[75] The new populism, so anxious to legitimate itself, has renounced this very possibility.

In relation to the struggle for ideological hegemony, therefore, the new populism represents a fairly coherent (if sometimes only implicit) strategy of adaptation and retrenchment. In effect, it disavows prospects for a "new integrated culture" that could sustain a dynamic radical politics. Despite frequent if vague references to "Gramscian" themes—building a new culture, democratizing authority relations, transforming consciousness—new-populist organizations accept a rather conformist view of politics, culture, and social life, which coincides with the emergence of a machine-based, interest-group-oriented politics mentioned above. The result is that whole expanses of civil society remain more or less undisturbed even where progressive struggles achieve some real success. To pose the transformation of civil society in this fashion is to refocus emphasis not only on the concept of "dual power" (emergent local forms of democracy in the community and at the workplace) but also on the subversion of patriarchy, racism, and various expressions of commodified culture.

The issue of feminism provides a case in point. Although new populists have been the recipients of political energy from the women's movement, and have usually striven for equal female participation in their organizations, in fact they devote only peripheral attention to feminist issues in both theory and practice. From all appearances, democratization does not fully extend to the sphere of sexual relations. Their political discourse contains scarcely any mention of patriarchy, no critique of the family, no serious effort to confront the sexual division of labor. Moreover, those grassroots struggles most closely linked to new populism (housing, the neighborhoods, toxic wastes) have often been remote from the feminist movement, which expresses many of the psychological and cultural dimensions of contemporary democratic renewal.[76] The experience so far has been that new-populist organizations take up feminist concerns—for example, affirmative action—largely to the extent such concerns can be integrated into a pragmatic electoral strategy. With only a few exceptions, the tendency has been to deemphasize issues that are central to feminism: abortion, violence against women, social services like health care, sexuality, and so forth. The thinking no doubt has been that such issues might be culturally threatening to critical sectors of the electorate—and also divisive for the leadership.

To the extent this analysis is correct, new populism can be understood as actually working against elements of a cultural and political radicalism that enter into a broadening of the public sphere. Thus, although in the immediate aftermath of the progressive electoral triumphs in Santa Monica and elsewhere there were initial glimpses of what Kann calls a "liberated public sphere" and the beginnings of "cracks in elite hegemony,"[77] this dynamic was quickly and rather systematically reversed. Insurgency was fully absorbed into the pluralist ordering of rules and norms, and then domesticated.

In conceptual terms there was little effort to redefine what is meant by nation, community, religion, and family within a transformative framework, little attempt to theorize a radical break with the forms of domination. One problem is that oppositional politics in the industrialized countries must confront a world of mobility and rapid change—a world in which social individuality is anchored more and more to novelty, modernity, the movement away from parochial local ties, the celebration of variety in relationships, cultural life, sexuality, and so forth. In great measure this entails an historical loosening of affiliations with neighborhood, family, and religion or at least a growing tolerance of those changes already well in place. It suggests an extension of secular–radical tendencies that incorporate but go beyond Enlightenment rationalism and individualist humanism. The critical consciousness without which qualitative change is impossible requires an expansion of space, autonomy, and diversity along with the freedom to rebel against established authority and conventional morality. This is the milieu within which social movements flourish. All of this is not to deny that various traditional affiliations can have, at certain times, an empowering and radicalizing impact on large numbers of people—especially as a defense against external colonizing forces.

The new-populist dilemma here reflects a larger failure of the American left to address the possibility that the notion of community itself may be rather problematic as a normative (and attainable) goal. Tightly knit local communities, as previous experiments from Puritan settlers through the myriad utopian collectives and the recent new-left counterculture have shown, can be stifling rather than liberating insofar as they tend to restrict social and cultural diversity, limit the boundaries of discourse, and instill an ideology of conformism that can produce fear and insecurity rather than the cooperation and sharing posited by communitarian ideals.[78] From this viewpoint a strong collectivist ethos can actually impede rather than facilitate emancipatory possibilities. The romanticist impulse toward preindustrial themes of mutualism, simplicity, and cohesion is confining in the sense that it assigns a certain immutability to established patterns of local cultural and political life. Such antimodernist currents—by no means uniformly shared by new populists—are completely inadequate to the requirements of analysis and strategy consonant with the complex dynamics of social movements. At the same time, it is improbable that such a mythical community setting could be recreated today on any large scale: the very material and cultural base of the old rural, small-town, and even urban neighborhoods has been eroding for some time. There are several demographic factors at work: vastly increased levels of physical or geographical mobility; the sprawl and fragmentation of social life in the large cities; the breakdown of the nuclear family as the standard domestic unit; massive shifts in culture, sexuality, and lifestyles. Dramatic changes produced by capitalism itself and secondarily by the response of popular movements have called into question some of the sacred premises of "community organizing," neighborhood autonomy, and populist cohesion—at least where these premises are shaped by traditional values and social relations.

New-populist fetishism of popular traditions and the "common person" thus blocks understanding of the way in which old forms and practices present obstacles to change. As Jim Green argues, such a model conceives of people essentially as objects and victims of history rather than as active participants in social transformation.[79] A radical alternative proceeds from a different set of assumptions, with history understood as the dialectical interplay between subversive impulses and existing traditions, between creative intervention and social immediacy, between the old and the new. It counterposes the logic of conflict and disruption—however that might be expected to unfold—to the logic of consensus and equilibrium immersed in the prevailing "ensemble of relations." In this way the crude and one-dimensional "Marxism-Leninism" that the new populists justly attack gives way to a more complex framework that corrects an equally one-sided populist spontaneism.

Finally, the very social basis of new populism—grounded in the new middle strata of professionals, white-collar workers, intellectuals, and students—may impose limitations upon its capacity to advance counterhegemonic struggles. Beneath the ideology of community and social solidarity, the middle strata typically express concern for an entirely different range of values tied to the American liberal tradition: individual choice, mobility, job autonomy, social and cultural opportunity.

As we have seen, these values enter new-populist ideology at several points. Further, they coincide with a deemphasis of "class" issues such as poverty and social equality.[80] Although these voluntaristic impulses —not to mention the abundant resources and skills of the middle strata —have been vital to the growth of progressive politics, and although libertarian strivings associated with the affluent cannot be dismissed as a mere cloak for social privilege, they do raise serious problems. There is a danger that the new populism, lacking a broad class foundation, will ultimately carry forward a type of individualism rooted in narrow self-interest, momentary personal feelings and issue concerns, and spontaneous impulses that resist efforts to forge a viable political strategy. As Robert Bellah observes, "Populist politics, in good part because of its individualist component, tends to be discontinuous, oriented to single issues, opportunistic, and therefore easily coopted, local, and anti-institutional. As a result, it is difficult to sustain pressure over time for the attainment of principled political ends."[81] In this way the new-populist alternative is readily integrated into the liberal-individualist component of bourgeois hegemony.

What this suggests is that the new populism, like the old left it set out to transcend, fails to articulate a concretely transformative politics for its own social setting. Such a predicament could have been easily anticipated, even if the difficulties of actually confronting it are well known. The reality is hard to deny: new-populist strategic preoccupation with the bourgeois public sphere forces assimilation of bourgeois forms and practices. The new populism, following the old, embellishes both an interest-group politics and a bureaucratic modus operandi beneath its rhetoric of democratization. The difficult historical task of overturning the multiple forms of domination, so essential to reclaiming the democratic heritage for the left, is replaced by a more "realistic" agenda oriented toward the "control," regulation, and rationalization of those same forms.

NEW POPULISM AND BEYOND

It would be self-deceptive to look to the new populism as a fundamentally novel break with past leftist strategies that, because of its uniquely indigenous and appealing character, could inspire a revitalized oppositional politics for the coming period. Like Eurosocialism, it combines an intriguing (and in certain respects original) post-Marxist vision of change with a conventional political strategy that conflicts with this vision and with the radical potential of new social movements. As the brief history of Santa Monica progressivism shows, the strategy gives rise to a situation in which the old Bernsteinian dictum naturally applies: "The movement is everything, the goal nothing." Indeed, whatever its distinctive American discourse and priorities, the new populism seems destined to repeat the mistakes that haunted European social democracy. From the standpoint of analyzing institutionalization, whether structural reformism has a national focus (Eurosocialism) or a local one (new populism) seems to make little difference: in each case the result is a stabilization of corporate and bureaucratic power.

In this context the prospects for radical change become immensely complicated. For example, Boyte's vision of "free social space" that would permit the growth of autonomous democratic forces is largely neutralized through a relegitimation (by the left) of established power relations. Even the most ambitious social reforms would be carried out within the logic of exchange relations, bureaucratic hierarchy, and the other spheres of domination. Viewed from yet another angle, this process can be understood as part of a struggle by the new populists to secure control (from above) over various forms of capital with the goal of redirecting investment, social priorities, and consumption while leaving intact the capitalist division of labor.[82]

Such a theoretical and strategic impasse, then, is not a function of an unwarranted emphasis on "community" over "workplace" mobilization or even of the predominant role it assigns to "alliance" politics and coalition building. It is difficult to imagine that any social movement, or grouping of movements, could achieve very much on its own, and it is equally farfetched to believe that progressive organizations could establish a dynamic public presence without some form of community-based, alliance-oriented radicalism. Moreover, it is not true that new-populist theorists have abandoned a commitment to workplace struggles, at least in principle. Nor is the problem one of pursuing an essentially localist strategy. True enough, a geographically limited focus of activity—as the Santa Monica case reflects—can easily breed elements of provincialism and perhaps the illusion of self-sufficiency; it can also give rise to a disabling cultural isolation. And of course political issues are more than ever national and even global in scope, so that local efforts to combat plant closings, environmental damage, the housing crisis, militarism, and decaying social services can never really get to the source of these problems. Still, it is necessary to take the first step: new populists believe that by winning a series of local skirmishes it is possible to build, in molecular fashion, toward societal transformation.[83] And organizations like CED and ACORN have constructed a broad network that extends to scores of towns, cities, and states. Likewise, the familiar obstacles posed by electoralism itself (many of which were discussed in Chapter 3) hardly go to the core of the matter insofar as abstentionism provides no real alternative in American society, where electoral participation, flawed as it is, remains so clearly imbued in the political culture. The question revolves more around the precise content of electoral activity (its relationship to social movements, its long-term goals, its linkage with new forms of authority, and the like). For both Eurosocialism and new populism, the fatal mistake has been to devote almost exclusive attention to electoral politics—the consequences of which have been universally deradicalizing.

The larger underlying problem is deeper and more complex. On the one hand, new-populist theory formulates no critical or transformative approach to power relations, or to domination in general. The vision of democratic structural reforms is not based upon any radical alternative to the bourgeois state—that is, it anticipates no overturning of social hierarchy, no sustained attack on the bureaucratic state apparatus, no articulation of new forms of self-management. Lacking such a dialectic, the principles of citizen empowerment and economic democracy must somehow be fitted into the matrix of the corporate power structure. New populism ends up reinforcing, more or less by default, the institutional and ideological imperatives of the entire system of domination. Hence, the stifling of grassroots activity by well-organized electoral engineering is hardly a surprising outcome. In Santa Monica, as I have argued, the signs were almost immediately visible: perpetuation of elite control, narrowing of political discourse, retreat from a commitment to transform popular consciousness, and drift toward an ideology of moderate liberalism.

In the case of CED, this drift is reflected in the adoption of a rather straightforward, mainstream liberal politics by 1985. Though formal membership was still large (roughly 12,000 statewide in California), the organization had obviously lost its grassroots dynamism of the early 1980s. With local operations in decline and with a rising mood of cynicism among its leaders, CED had evolved into little more than an electoral machine. In fact, organizational resources were devoted increasingly to Hayden's legislative work and career. Ideologically, its rightward shift involved a discarding of its critique of the corporate system, a focus on high-tech development and creative entrepreneurialism, and renewed efforts to achieve legitimate status within the Democratic party. In a 1985 position paper entitled "Going West," Hayden called for a "liberal bloc" incorporating the progressive elements of labor, business, and government and committed to a program of technology-driven economic growth. The vision of "economic democracy" was finally reduced to just another version of the corporate liberalism it had originally rejected.[84]

There can be no escaping the conclusion that the instrumentalist character of new-populist strategy functioned to reduce the space available to local movements and, ultimately, to democratization. Even where progressive coalitions were able to introduce genuine reforms, the outcome was far removed from a "new politics" grounded in a system of democratic control. There is abundant political irony in this, since new populists have done much to retrieve the themes of community, local control, and democratic participation—themes that to one degree or another will be central to any future rebirth of the American left. At issue here is not so much the themes as such but, rather, as we have seen in the Eurosocialist case, the particular manner in which political formations wind up translating them into system-reproducing strategies.[85]

5

THE GREEN ALTERNATIVE
IN WEST GERMANY

If Eurosocialism in the Mediterranean and the new populism in the United States both suggest a reversion, in different ways, to an earlier social-democratic pattern they both hoped to transcend, the emergent Green tendency—at least in West Germany—seems to promise a post-Marxist breakthrough consistent with the radical side of the new social movements. In March 1983 the Green party (Die Grünen) won enough votes to enter the national parliament (Bundestag) and thereby provide for the first time direct representation of grassroots movements that had mushroomed since the mid-1970s. In surpassing the difficult 5 percent barrier, which has destroyed the prospects of alternative parties in the past, the Greens had in less than five years grown from a small group of peace and environmental activists into a popular organization with nearly 2 million supporters (5.6 percent of the vote), 30,000 members, and twenty-seven Bundestag deputies. By 1985 they were able to build upon this success, establishing an even broader political presence in state and municipal legislatures, local movements, and the larger political culture. They achieved all of this without vast corporate resources, institutional support, or even the kind of media exposure available to the major parties—and against the sometimes hysterical opposition of the bourgeois press.

Of course this initial advance hardly signals any imminent conquest of power, much less a "Green Revolution," in West Germany or elsewhere. But it did give those movements that buttress the Greens a structural presence and ideological credibility that was lacking before. From the outset the Greens, organized around essentially new-left themes and programs, hoped not so much to build an electoral machine that could siphon off votes from rival parties as to give coherent strategic expression to popular struggles rooted in the citizens' initiatives

(*Bürgerinitiativen*), peace and ecology movements, feminism, and the large youth-based alternative culture.

Perhaps most significantly, the Greens have come to represent a rather novel approach in which there is a more dialectical relationship between party and movements, national and regional spheres of activity, electoral politics and grassroots mobilization. Within this framework they have established a more clear-cut radical identity than either the Eurosocialists or new populists, and they have opened up far more space outside the corporatist bloc of forces than either—despite common points of departure. In contrast to Eurosocialism, the Greens represent a break with social democracy and a new kind of politics embedded in the ideal of an "anti-party party." In contrast to the new populism, the Greens not only strive for a national existence but are also more skeptical of participation in the bourgeois public sphere. Unlike both, therefore, the Greens are uncomfortable with conventional politics though hardly abstentionist, insofar as one of their main goals is to politically "enfranchise" the new movements. Finally, as distinct from these other strategies, the Greens uphold a vision of a qualitatively new society that can only be realized through radically democratic styles and methods.

The Greens diverge from other post-Marxist movements in yet another way: whatever their recent advances in West Germany and elsewhere, in no country have they actually reached the point of taking over and administering governmental power, either locally or nationally. Although they do occupy some institutional space, even in West Germany they remain a minority party in every sense, which means that their brief history is more ambiguous and difficult to analyze than the other strategies. However, much like these models, the Greens can be examined in terms of their ideology and strategy, or more precisely, on the basis of the relationship between their ultimate vision and the means chosen to implement it—as well as their impact upon the social movements and of course West German politics generally. They simply cannot be judged according to their record in power.

NEW MOVEMENTS AND THE RISE OF THE GREENS

The Green insurgency must be understood in the context of rapidly multiplying social movements that found particularly fertile terrain in West Germany. More than a decade of SPD hegemony served to isolate or pacify the remnants of a once-thriving new left, breeding with-drawal and cynical alienation, especially among youth and the unem-ployed. As I point out in Chapter 3, the SPD was able to carry out a reform-oriented restructuring of German capital that did ensure a phase of economic growth and prosperity—the Modell Deutschland. Its productivist adaptation to the logic of accumulation was closely tied to a steadfast Atlanticist foreign policy along with a refinement of the corporatist state that included repressive measures against the left. The Social Democrats were cut off from progressive social forces and lost whatever legitimacy they had as a socialist party committed to an anti-capitalist alternative. As a catch-all party enmeshed in the authoritarian state, the SPD's celebrated "crisis of identity" was nothing more than the abandonment of any real leftist identity. With the ideological con-vergence of the SPD and Christian Democrats around basic domestic and international goals, debate within the public sphere narrowed so much that critical issues were largely sidestepped by the major parties. Moreover, with the decline of the welfare state itself by the late 1970s, the SPD-FDP governing coalition turned increasingly to austerity poli-cies, cutbacks in social spending, and more repression.

This milieu was ideal for the vanguardist posturing of tiny Marxist-Leninist sects and the terrorism of the Baader-Meinhof "urban guerril-las." Operating out of despair, these groups gravitated toward strategies and methods that could not possibly work, much less attract wide-spread popular support, in an advanced capitalist setting like West Germany. An insurrectionary seizure of state power by a minority was out of the question. By the end of the 1970s, however, yet another tendency with roots in new-left radicalism began to surface: the youth-defined countercultural "alternative" scene in several urban centers (notably West Berlin, Hamburg, and Frankfurt), environmental and antinuclear protests, the women's movement, the squatters' occupa-tions, and, finally, the largest and most militant peace movement in Europe. It was this "third" tendency, tied to the nascent popular move-ments and citizens' initiatives, that eventually inspired and nurtured the Greens, who championed a libertarian approach directly opposed to the theoretical and organizational premises of vanguardism.

These movements appeared on a large scale in West Germany as early as 1977, mostly outside the sphere of corporatist party politics. In Frankfurt there were the first stirrings of an alternative culture—clubs, cafés, meeting halls, journals, newspapers, bookstores, communes, service-oriented cooperatives, theater, and so forth. As such centers of popular activity spread throughout the country, they began to furnish gathering places for the hundreds of small groups and organizations that, despite their fragmentation, would give expression to a nascent oppositional politics. A driving force behind the alternative scene was the "Sponti" student and youth movement, which stressed a neo-anarchistic commitment to direct action, political subjectivity, and the struggle for a new collective consciousness. By 1979 the focal point of West German activism was the citizens' initiative groups, which took up the issues of housing, social services, the environment, women's and minority rights, and unemployment. The rapid multiplication of citizens' groups reflected the mounting crisis of the Modell Deutschland. For a brief period the axis around which the new movements congregated was the theme of environmental protection: protests against nuclear power stations in the Hamburg area, the Startbahn West airport expansion in Frankfurt, the decaying forests and urban blight throughout the country. Only seven years after the founding of the Federal Association of Environmental Citizen Initiatives (in 1972), the number of ecology groups reached into the tens of thousands, with a membership estimated at 2 million.[1] Finally, the Ecology and Peace Conference held at Kassel in October 1979 symbolized a fusion of the environmental and peace movements that would typify Green politics during 1980–83.

One of the most dramatic expressions of the Green phenomenon in this period was the erection of a *Huttendorf*, or "hut village," at the time of the Frankfurt runway protests. The camp, which stood squarely in the path of the planned runway extension that was part of NATO's plans to reconstruct the Rhein-Main air facility for military purposes, was occupied mostly by Spontis and environmentalists but with the involvement of a broad range of citizens' groups struggling against urban decay, militarism, and the erosion of political democracy. (A Frankfurt University survey revealed that nearly 80 percent of the area's residents were opposed to the airport expansion.) In late 1980 a series of demonstrations at the campsite drew as many as 20,000 people. Although police attacked protesters with water cannons on several occasions, the resulting confrontations only served to further politicize activists, who now intensified their resolve to block the project—and they succeeded in the end.[2]

In this way the explosion of popular movements touched the daily lives of millions and made deep inroads into the traditionally authoritarian and deferential German political culture—to the degree that by the early 1980s it threatened the postwar corporatist alignments. Between 1980 and 1983 large sectors of the population were activated by militant struggles against Euromissile deployment, which were driven by realization that West Germany could well become the main theater in any future nuclear conflict. The massive rallies in Bonn, Hamburg, and West Berlin were simply the most visible signs of popular mobilization. Throughout West Germany hundreds of peace groups appeared virtually overnight. They initiated creative forms of civil disobedience, rallies, marches, street theater, boycotts, and conferences publicized by a variety of newspapers and newsletters. These activities were sustained by a burgeoning grassroots subculture that supported an amazing number of local projects—reportedly 11,500 of them with a combined active membership of 80,000 already by 1980.[3] Sometimes housed in large complexes like the Meringhof Center in West Berlin, such projects included work centered on health care, child care, housing, economic conversion, publishing, psychological counseling, film, and music. They generally relied upon the skills and dedication of ordinary people who, within the scope of their chosen activity, came to value the relatively autonomous space provided by this subcultural milieu.

What the new movements shared was an emphasis on nonviolent forms of direct action; a struggle to recover community that had been destroyed by rampant urbanization; revulsion against the worst manifestations of economic modernization and the consumer society; hostility toward the party system and interest-group bargaining; and a skepticism toward conventional ideologies of whatever sort—liberalism, Marxism, Leninism, even anarchism. Those involved in grassroots struggles resisted the attraction of simple formulas, schemes, and strategies, which were associated with rigid bureaucratic models (the SPD, the Communist party, Leninist vanguard sects). This was inevitable given the movements' great diversity along with the fluidity of the political situation, not to mention the dismal results of postwar left-wing activity in West Germany.

At the same time, many local activists began to search for something new around which to construct a united but still pluralistic radical politics that could effectively contest for power. An institutional framework was needed to supply both a national presence and a political continuity without simultaneously stifling spontaneity. It was this historical void that would be filled by the Green party. The Greens' origins can be traced back to 1972, when a small group of non-Marxist progressives, most of them former SPD members unhappy with the party's growing bureaucratization and programmatic moderation but with no illusions about vanguardism, founded an association to elect representatives to the European parliament. But it was not until 1979 that the Greens finally decided to constitute themselves as a political party ready to compete in the electoral process. The founding Congress was held at Karlsruhe in January 1980. Though still numerically small and marginal, the Greens projected an image of a dynamic party of a new kind, which brought immediate and dramatic growth in both membership and popular support.[4] With little in the way of either ideological specificity or programmatic concreteness, they nonetheless managed to choose themes that spoke to the concerns of many West Germans: participatory democracy, civil rights, environmental and cultural renewal, pacifism, and anti-Americanism. The first real electoral advance came in June 1980, when the Alternative List in West Berlin (a "rainbow coalition" loosely tied to the Greens) won 7.5 percent of the vote in the municipal assembly elections. When this was followed by other regional successes, Green membership grew rapidly to a level of more than 20,000 by early 1981. Prior to the 1983 federal election the Greens would overcome the 5 percent barrier in seven of the eleven West German states, winning a combined forty-eight seats (including nine in Hamburg and eight in Hesse). In the Lower-Saxony communal elections of September 1981 they received well over 10 percent of the vote in some areas. The Greens' first failure came in the 1982 Bavarian election, where they narrowly missed getting into the state parliament, with 4.6 percent of the vote (an outcome that would be duplicated in traditionally conservative Schleswig-Holstein in March 1983). In most contests the Greens were able to attract votes from the SPD, which stood aloof from the new movements, and from the uncommitted or those voting for the first time. These local gains set the stage for the March 1983 breakthrough in the national election.

The Greens' historic achievement in 1983 was overwhelmed, at least on the surface, by the decisive mandate won by the Christian Democrats, who wound up with 244 of 498 Bundestag seats and 48.8 percent of the vote. The SPD captured 38.2 percent of the vote (a drop of 4.7 percent) with 193 seats, while the Free Democrats won 6.9 percent and 34 seats—enough to ensure their partnership with the CDU in the governing coalition. The outcome reflected a shift to the right within the general electorate, allowing for a potential new phase of CDU hegemony.[5] Yet the larger meaning of the Green breakthrough for West German politics could go far beyond this momentary electoral balance of forces. First, insofar as the Greens represent an initial step toward a "postindustrial," post-Marxist model of radical change, their significance is not reflected in electoral statistics alone. The remarkable fact that 28 percent of first-time voters cast their ballots for the Greens suggests the need for a longer-term perspective. Second, whatever the limitations of electoral politics, the appearance of such a dynamic and irreverent party in the staid Bonn parliamentary environs demonstrates that a leftist formation with roots in local movements can, given the proper congruence of issues and hard, intelligent campaigning, become a formidable popular force in a relatively short time. Above all, the Greens were able to translate radical ideas into a language intelligble to broad (and heterogeneous) strata of the population. They drew support from professionals, young workers, students and intellectuals, feminists and the unemployed, from older conservationists as well as younger Spontis, from Marxists as well as peace activists, from progressive religious elements as well as urban new leftists. The media picture of the Greens as a motley assortment of alienated youth is a serious distortion.[6] Finally, the Greens injected their subversive agenda into the national political discourse, thereby forcing at least a semblance of authentic debate over issues related to the economic crisis, the arms race, democracy, and the quality of life. From all appearances West German political culture in the 1980s was undergoing a profound transformation.

If the Greens' impact upon German society has been much deeper than electoral strength alone might suggest, their capacity to win further victories is problematic considering the novelty (and fragility) of the social forces at work. Of course there is the possibility they could slip beneath the 5 percent threshold and thus lose their momentum and presence. Yet in the two years following the 1983 election they actually broadened their support, winning 8.2 percent of the vote in the 1984 European parliamentary elections while maintaining their foothold in the state legislatures of Baden-Württemberg, West Berlin, Lower Saxony, Hesse, Hamburg, and Bremen. For the Europeanwide balloting they scored well in the major urban centers, reaching 11.8 percent in Bremen, 10.6 percent in Hanover, 10.5 percent in Munich, 10.7

percent in Hamburg, 12.2 percent in Stuttgart, 11.2 percent in Frankfurt, and 9.5 percent in Dusseldorf. Such results point to the continuing attraction of the Greens for voters who seem disillusioned with the old formulas offered by the mainstream parties. And the corresponding decline of the Free Democrats has opened up additional space for the Greens to maneuver on the edge of the party system.

In 1985 the Greens remained located precariously at the apex of a wide array of social forces, movements, and cultural tendencies. The Green ideological synthesis, to the extent one can be said to exist, reflects an unprecedented fusion of disparate traditions: ecological radicalism, Marxism, new leftism, feminism, populism, even spiritualism. This type of synthesis defies a Marxist definition of leftist politics grounded in a single coherent theory, strategy, or historical agent of change. At the same time, it also guarantees the perpetuation of sharp internal conflicts leading to divisions and factionalization that could, in the end, exert a powerful centrifugal thrust. These splits now cut a number of ways—between ecological "fundis" committed to a holistic politics, Marxists who stress class struggle, and pragmatic "realos," or reformists, anxious to achieve something tangible; between those who seek closer ties with the SPD and those who wish to preserve Green autonomy; between those who emphasize parliamentary activity and those who look primarily to grassroots movements; and so forth. There is, moreover, something of a geographical dimension to some of these divisions. For example, in Frankfurt and West Berlin, Green politics revolves around the alternative scene and ecological issues; in Baden-Württemberg the unifying focus is participatory democracy; and in Hamburg there is a strong contingent of Marxist-oriented Greens that seeks closer ties to labor and the trade unions.[7] What has served to unify all of these tendencies, factions, and regional struggles, however, is a deep and militant involvement in the peace movement—and the search for a new politics.

PARTY OF A NEW TYPE

After March 1983 the Greens were suddenly catapulted into an institutional position from which they would now be able to pursue a dual strategy linked to the simultaneous development of party and movements, electoral politics and grassroots struggles, legislative reforms and direct-action protest. True, their representation in the state parliaments had already permitted such a strategy, but in a more fragmented and limited way. As a marginal (but nonetheless highly vocal) opposition in the Bundestag, the Greens could challenge the CDU's corporatist and authoritarian politics behind the protection of constitutional legitimacy while at the same time initiating extraparliamentary actions in tandem with the popular movements. Because the Greens were struggling to create a distinct identity apart from the bourgeois public sphere, and since they are uncompromising on the issue of nuclear weapons, the freedom to "walk on two legs" was strategically indispensable. With this leverage it is much easier to resist pressures toward institutional absorption and, with the Social Democrats weakened and more hostile to the CDU, to work with elements of the SPD to build a viable local opposition, especially around disarmament issues.

Within the Bundestag itself, Green delegates were in a position to offer programmatic alternatives to the stale ideas set forth by the CDU and SPD, guided by the hope that ensuing debates would at least provide an ideological forum in which fresh ideas and new information could be put forward. Beyond that, the Greens brought a more confrontational and less deferential style to parliamentary proceedings, which were typically formal and austere. Upon their initial entry into the legislative chamber the twenty-seven Green representatives, having abandoned the customary formal black attire, appeared in their everyday clothes, each carrying a small tree or plant as a symbolic token of nature. The warning by the old party elites that the Greens would be a "disruptive" or "subversive" presence in the Bundestag turned out to be accurate enough.

The uniqueness of the West German Greens—and a vital source of their political strength—lies in their organic relationship to emergent popular struggles. Their role in parliament thus goes far beyond the conventional goal of advancing or "representing" a particular set of demands. Insofar as they form a kind of organizational synthesis of these struggles, their involvement tends to clash with the norms of pluralist democracy. Whereas the new movements often seem content with a replay of 1960s-style militancy, especially in their spontaneist rejection of large-scale organization and electoral politics, the Greens wished to translate radical goals into a strategically coherent language and action. This meant building a national organization prepared to move onto the institutional terrain without sacrificing the vitality of popular initiatives. Viewed in this way, the Greens embody neither a flight from politics nor a simple return to traditional pluralism, but a convergence of party and movements that suggests a broad redefinition of politics.

It follows that the new politics of the "anti-party party" does not fit neatly into the requirements of the traditional parliamentary system. The Green modus operandi generally insists upon a certain distancing from the other parties, including the SPD. As Petra Kelly writes, "Our illusions are dead and gone. We do not believe a word the established parties have to say any more. We shall not be carrying any more torches for them. We only trust ourselves now." [8]

As we have seen, the West German two-and-one-half party system (CDU, SPD, and Free Democrats) had evolved into a bureaucratic and corporatist apparatus that restricts political discourse and represses democratic initiatives. The ingredients of what Hirsch calls "pluralistic integration" were in place: technological rationalization, an institutionalized labor-management partnership involving "worker participation," state regulation of the economy, attacks on the left associated with the rise of the security state.[9] Its underlying premises were state control, industrial expansion, and, in the sphere of international politics, collaboration with U.S. foreign policy. This developmental path is of course hardly peculiar to West Germany—nor does it have anything remotely in common with socialism, a goal that in any case the SPD abandoned long ago. Even before the technocratic leadership of Helmut Schmidt consolidated its hold on the party, the SPD had exhausted its oppositional role in West German society. In the language of one observer, it never really built a "culture of opposition," only a type of "state consciousness tied to winning positions of institutional power." [10] While still a party of modest social reform within the boundaries of welfare-statism, with deep roots in the German labor movement, it is a righteous protector of the status quo.

The German model was ultimately bound to generate its own discontents and marginals who were not willing to go along with the imperatives of the administered society. Indeed, the corrosive effects of economic crisis, cold-war militarism, and institutional stagnation were visible throughout German society by the late 1970s. Wedded to the state system and the old technocratic solutions, the SPD was saddled with a legacy of unemployment, deteriorating urban housing, repressive laws, and of course the NATO Euromissile decision. In this context the drastic erosion of SPD electoral support in March 1983 was hardly astonishing. The Greens took advantage of this impasse to occupy an expanding space to the left of the SPD and, within it, to chart their own innovative political course.

What already emerges from the very brief Green experience is the struggle for a more comprehensive democracy—and with it a completely new understanding of state power and domination in general. On this issue àll factions of the party were in basic agreement. What inspired the Greens to construct an alternative party in the first place was a deep hostility to the corporatist state, to which the party system was viewed as a mere appendage. The entire apparatus was authoritarian, manipulative, and, as the Flick scandal of 1984 revealed, at times also corrupt. Hence they could never be content to simply "work within" state institutions along the lines prescribed by structural reformism. They do not anticipate a party that would strive to "conquer" state power (by whatever means), sensing that this would only reproduce features of the corporatist system and, in the final analysis, extend state penetration into civil society. Such a statist "solution" to the crisis of liberal capitalism would simply play into the illusions of both Leninism and social democracy.

The Green concept of politics and democracy diverges from this statist tradition in several ways. First, while hoping to advance by means of electoral politics, the Greens do not see the road to power as simply taking control of political institutions but rather as a complex process of transforming the network of social and authority relations throughout society. Democracy is viewed not as a fixed phenomenon tied to discrete institutions but as a dynamic, fluid process unfolding within a context of popular struggles on every terrain. Further, in contrast to the SPD, the Greens express a populist distrust of elites and the bureaucratic structures over which they preside. Their vision of democracy, inspired by themes of local self-management and cultural transformation, is a "direct" model in contrast to the "representative" version of corporatist pluralism. The party program is quite unambiguous on this point: "A policy of grassroots democracy means the increased realization of decentralized and direct democracy. We start from the premise that priority must always be given to the decision of the base."[11] Third, in Petra Kelly's words, social change must proceed from the energy of a "subversive counterculture" with its own community centers, printing presses, publications, stores, cooperatives, and self-help institutions.[12] These forms provide the link between daily life and political activity without which democratic participation would be impossible. Finally, through their ideal of an equal relationship between industrialized and Third World countries, their emphasis on the disbanding of military blocs, and their view of nationalism as a source of arms buildup and war, the Greens affirm (however tentatively) the logic of radical internationalism.[13]

All of this corresponds to a subversive political style—one more directly confrontational, yet more sensitive to the Green ethos of nonviolence and direct democracy. It is grounded in the holistic notion that every aspect of social existence—and of the global crisis—is intimately connected and cannot be understood in a piecemeal fashion. Indeed, the movements themselves, quite disparate on the surface, are historically joined in a complex web of interrelated social processes.[14] Politics involves much more than institutional engineering or interest representation, since, in Rudolf Bahro's language, "The problem is not to create a space for minorities but to create a new solution for the whole of society."[15]

For the Greens, then, the struggle for a liberated society cannot be reduced to changes in any one aspect of the totality (e.g., the economy), any particular set of institutions, any single constituency or agency. Social transformation is necessarily multifaceted and dispersed. From this viewpoint a new politics challenges all structures of domination: not only the power of capital over wage labor, but that of industrial civilization over nature, bureaucracy over community and the individual, men over women, and of course rich nations over poor ones. These hierarchies would be replaced by a new system of authority and meaning rooted in self-management, direct democracy, and decentralized social activity. Efforts to dismantle any single hierarchy in isolation from the others, or to reduce it to a single overarching or determining structure, cannot be sustained. The Greens' essentially post-Marxist understanding of multiple and overlapping forms of domination clashes with the Marxist emphasis on relations of production, a single dialectic of wage labor versus capital, and the primacy of working-class struggles. Bahro confronts this issue head-on: "I think it has become very doubtful that the proletariat within bourgeois society will be the bearer of the subject of the new society. At the end of this capital formation, the problem is not the abolition of the bourgeois class but the dissolution of the whole formation constituted by wage labor and capital.

However, the confrontation of wage labor and capital is not the mechanism of this dissolution."[16] Virtually every page of the Green program resonates with this understanding and spirit.

For Green politics this theoretical edifice lays the basis of a refined conception of democracy, one that is simultaneously direct, popular, and ecological. The Greens have sought, with mixed results, to construct a national organization that can coordinate and direct popular struggles while allowing for diverse inputs from below. To sustain this seems to require a constant (perhaps excessive) vigilance toward all expressions of elitism, egocentrism, and media posturing. Participation is maximized through open, decentralized assemblies in which, technically, all Greens can become active in decision making and take up leadership roles. The instrumental concern for quick, tangible results is generally subordinated to the search for "consensus" which, in turn, depends upon free debate, education, and consciousness transformation. It follows that, in certain respects, the form of any human activity is just as important as its content. Thus: "Our internal organizational life and our relationship to the people who support and vote for us is the exact opposite of that of the established parties in Bonn. They are neither able nor willing to take into account new approaches and new ideas, nor the concerns of the democratic movement. Because of this we have decided to form a new type of party organization, the basic structures of which are set up in a grassroots-democratic and decentralized way; the two things in fact cannot be separated. A party which did not have this kind of structure would never be in a position to convincingly pursue an ecological policy in the context of parliamentary democracy. The central idea in this respect is the continuous control of all office holders, delegates and institutions by the rank and file."[17]

The theoretical components of direct democracy and social ecology converge on the ideal of human-scale, grassroots structures, both within the party and in society as a whole. Part of the Greens' loose national organization is a system of coordinating and task groups, local assemblies and councils, and networking bodies integrated into the flow of popular movements. Leadership both within these party structures and the legislative assemblies is held in check by the practice of rotation, which serves to counter (in principle) the emergence of an elite stratum. Policy decisions and programmatic statements typically follow lengthy, often stormy and chaotic, periods of debate and struggle. Moreover, in cases where the Greens have been at the center of nationwide mobilizations—for example, the Bonn antinuclear rally of October 1981 and the huge protests against Euromissile deployment in late 1983 —the locus of activity has been literally thousands of small ad hoc groups and committees. Whether this model of coordination can be sustained over a longer phase of struggle remains to be seen.

Yet the Greens do not envision an unmediated process of grassroots democratization, as if the world of parliamentary politics could somehow be sidestepped or ignored. The very decision to build an electoral party in order to run candidates for all levels of office imposes constraints and compromises as well as new opportunities. In this sense the Greens are, and must be, considerably more than a party of the social movements. It may be that the label "anti-party party" is slightly misleading. Still, they have brought a spirit of imagination to the Bundestag that reflects an innovative desire to utilize parliament in a different fashion—that is, to seize upon every opportunity for expanding their institutional power while simultaneously channeling it back into the local constituencies. Within each jurisdiction—national, state, municipal, communal—the Greens hope to bring representative forms closer to the grassroots, by opening up debates, sharing material resources (e.g., through the "ecology fund"), setting up local committees to handle specific issues, and, of course, rotating leadership.[18] Thus, electoral politics is not really an end in itself but constitutes merely one component of a broader ensemble of activities. Parliament is more a vehicle for mobilizing consensus around issues than for winning immediate power, which in any case resides largely outside formal institutions. What this suggests, as one Green member put it, is a dual approach characterized by a "playing leg" in parliament and a "standing leg" outside it, combining a vocal presence in the legislative sphere with a steady base of democratic initiative in the community. Success in the electoral sphere confers upon the Greens a kind of legitimacy that can be used, though not without pitfalls, to empower and politicize local struggles. The result is a synthesis of party and movements, institutional and local activity, national and grassroots politics that has few parallels in Western Europe or elsewhere. There has been scarcely any attempt to conceptualize, let alone implement, this type of radical democracy in either the Communist or Socialist traditions. The real challenge for the Greens, in the long run, will be to maintain such a delicate balance in the wake of new electoral advances.

The Green vision of democracy—and of politics in general—probably owes more to new-left radicalism than to any other ideological current. This influence can be detected in several areas: the theme of overcoming alienation, the ideal of a countersociety, the emphasis on internal party democracy, the dynamic role of feminism, the commitment to nonviolence, an open and eclectic theoretical style.

• Insofar as the Greens uphold an emergent system of values and social relations, their concept of politics necessarily transcends the representation of specific group interests. On the contrary, it embraces a general struggle against the many forms of domination. Green politics is based upon a process of consciousness transformation extending throughout civil society and incorporating the universal affirmation of creativity, meaning, desire, and social individuality against a bureaucratic and destructive social order. This is something akin to a Gramscian counterhegemonic politics that, in this case, celebrates the value of "life" against a commodified and administered world that seems to have reached a point of no return.

• At the same time, social transformation must be grounded in an entirely new political culture, or countersociety, in which the liberation of the self takes collective shape. The Greens believe that every structure, from the family to the state, must be remolded through a process of popular mobilization in which parliamentary democracy would be transformed from within and from outside, merging ultimately with local democratic forms. Representative institutions would provide an enlarged arena for expression of social conflict. And the Greens would presumably be situated within this dialectic, not above it, as in the conventional Marxist formulas.[19]

• A new politics likewise depends upon a shift toward more egalitarian norms and practices within the party organization itself. The ideal of internal party democracy requires open meetings and assemblies, rotating leadership, protection of minorities, the accountability of deputies and electors, and the right of movement and community representatives to speak and submit resolutions.[20] Whatever the difficulties of putting such prescriptions into practice, the Green model reflects a sharp departure from hierarchical patterns typical of the mainstream (including leftist) parties. It resists an instrumental politics that favors the role of "leaders," "experts," and "technicians" as party (and state) managers who can freely deploy human and material resources. At issue is not only the problem of *embourgeoisment*, but also the very notion of "mass" politics (electoral or otherwise) in which popular constituencies appear as manipulable and objectified phenomena rather than assemblages of diverse groups and individual personalities.

• The Greens' theory of radical democracy has deep roots in the feminist movement as well: the aim of gender equality, as applied to both leadership functions and general participation, has been honored from the outset. And women have typically played a prominent role in the West German party, as spokespersons within leadership bodies, the women's council, and the larger membership. In early 1984 the women's council was able to establish, briefly, an all-female leadership ("speakers") structure for the Greens. The infusion of feminist sensibilities into Green ideology (often resisted, to be sure, by males) has not only encouraged women to become involved and to contribute in many ways, but has injected a "personal" politics into organizational life unheard of in other parties.

• For Green strategy, a cornerstone of the new politics is nonviolent methods of struggle. An environment in which coercion is the norm undercuts the entire raison d'être of the party. The transition to a new society will obviously involve disruption, confrontation, and mass mobilization, but armed insurrection is not on the agenda. Violence, even in the service of change, can only reproduce the culture of domination while also delegitimating popular insurgency itself. Thus the terrorist activity of the Baader-Meinhof group in the 1970s had a double impact: it strengthened the repressive state apparatus, and it further isolated and discredited the West German left. The Greens assume that it is possible, through the evolution of grassroots formations, to overturn the power structure in a relatively peaceful fashion, without resort to military force. Given the inseparability of methods and aims, the party program states that "humane goals cannot be achieved by inhumane means. Nonviolence should prevail between all human beings without exception, within social groups and between nations."[21] The personality attributes needed to carry out acts of violence are precisely the opposite of those required for genuine human communication—for dialogue, education, persuasion.[22]

• Finally, the Green ambience is rather hostile to rigid and all-encompassing ideological frameworks. Party leaders and intellectuals devote little attention to sacred theoretical texts, a tendency sometimes criticized as antitheoretical by Marxist and academic leftists. The writings of Marx, Lenin, Luxemburg, Gramsci, and Mao are read, respected, and discussed by many Greens, but they are rarely approached as offering the final word on contemporary problems or debates. "Theory" in Green usage therefore does not refer to a fixed body of ideas or to a certain methodology but to a living, ecumenical, always-changing conceptual framework and political vision. The assumption of a single vanguard leadership or agency of change cannot be squared with such a departure. As Daniel-Cohn Bendit suggests, from the perspective of the Frankfurt Spontis, "Traditional theories and ideologies stand little chance of success here since no one can postulate the avant-garde role of the working class as simply and as naively as in the past."[23] If there are limits to such eclecticism, the Greens argue that it is the only viable basis of a politics that has been characterized as a "gathering of movements."

Of course the Greens are much more than an umbrella organization or a clearinghouse for the new movements. They have managed to construct the edifice of a new type of party that departs from the Communist and social-democratic models. Though an official Green ideology in the customary sense does not exist, there is a tentative framework of analyses, objectives, and programs that suggest a post-Marxist radicalism—an uneasy blend of Marxism, social ecology, feminism, new leftism, and expressions of the alternative culture.[24] The prospects of a new politics are linked to a shifting equilibrium of forces within which the Greens strive to maintain a delicate balance between strategic needs and ultimate goals, electoral politics and grassroots struggles. The leitmotif of this is democratization—expanded popular participation, the attack on all types of hierarchy, the recovery of local autonomy within civil society.

AN ECOLOGICAL MODE OF DEVELOPMENT

The Greens' commitment to a new politics would be meaningless without their readiness to implement a "new economics"—that is, to transform the state-capitalist system according to a new set of economic premises and priorities. The ideals of democratic participation, workers' control, and community renewal will have little substance unless the form of production is simultaneously altered. Integral to this process is the transition from a wasteful and destructive economy tied to consumerism and arms production to one more rationally designed to meet human needs. To the extent the global crisis described in Chapter 2 persists, the methods needed to confront it will derive from a conceptual framework far more imaginative than the statist, growth-oriented system that has failed in West Germany and elsewhere. Contrary to a false image conveyed by the media, the Greens do have a clearly formulated economic analysis and program—indeed, one that is more elaborate and visionary than those of the SPD and CDU.

For West Germany, the global crisis signaled the eclipse of the *Wirtschaftswunder*—a prolonged economic miracle during which the majority of Germans had come to expect affluence and nearly full employment virtually as natural entitlements. During the 1960s and 1970s the German economy was in the forefront of capitalist dynamism and stability. Sustained economic growth, a favorable balance of trade, and technological advantage buttressed this development, which made the deutschmark one of the world's strongest currencies. By the early 1980s, however, the system entered a downward spin: unemployment rose to 10.4 percent (2.5 million workers), fiscal crisis gripped the major cities, social services began to stagnate, and the environment suffered from the effects of uncontrolled industrialism. At the same time, Keynesian techniques that had worked so well during the prosperous years—state intervention to stave off cyclical decline, expanded welfare functions— were themselves in crisis, with the phase of social-democratic growth now giving way to a more difficult period of austerity, labor controls, and cuts in social spending typical of the capitalist world as a whole.[25] But the rapidity of economic decline meant greater disruption in West Germany than elsewhere. First, the seemingly durable compact between the state, corporations, and labor unions (accepted by the CDU and SPD alike) was floundering as one of the partners, labor, grew restive under the impact of austerity and unemployment. Second, unemployment was a cause of widespread alienation among marginalized groups, and thus a source of "alternative" tendencies that furnished a haven for the new movements.

From the Greens' standpoint, the growth model engineered by the monopolies, banks, multinationals, and the state was itself bankrupt, incapable of stimulating further development without severe dysfunctions. Not only the CDU and SPD but most of the trade unions as well were attached to this model. Its guiding criteria were profits, efficiency, and material expansion linked to a vision of social progress defined in largely quantitative terms. Moreover, the Marxist solution—posed in

theoretical terms, since no mass-based Marxist (or Leninist) organization exists in West Germany—would only rearrange certain structural
features of the system without challenging the state-centered growth
economy. What was urgently needed, and had been absent from previous leftist economic strategies, was an understanding of the contradictions and limits of industrial growth itself. For example, there were
few insights into the ecological basis of development and therefore little
understanding of what decades of capitalist resource exploitation had
destroyed. There was little inclination to press for a radical shift in
forms of production and consumption, the nature of investment, the
structure of work—in the very ends of economic activity. Then, too,
there was an aloofness toward Third World problems that, in many
ways, could be attributed to European chauvinism.

The Greens' programmatic response to the crisis was an outgrowth of
intense debates between the rival party factions, so it bears the marks of
struggle and compromise. Although the CDU and SPD had not come
forth with real alternatives to the Keynesian model, except to apply a
more conservative twist to it, the Greens were at first hesitant to leap
into the ideological void. Partly this was the function of an impasse
within the Green leadership. More fundamental was the lack of a clear
theoretical outlook from which to move toward post-Keynesian initiatives. Finally, at the Sindelfingen Congress in January 1983, the party
arrived at a series of tentative proposals in a thirty-nine-page program
that brought together the views of the "ecological" and "Marxist" factions on a broad range of issues. The proposals were stated in the
form of immediate demands calling for strong measures to roll back the
power of large corporations and banks, to shift away gradually from
private ownership (of large units) toward a socialized and decentralized
economy, to broaden workers' control, to increase ecologically sound
forms of social investment, and to reduce the work week (at the same
pay levels) as one method to combat unemployment.[26] For the longer
run, the Greens looked to a society reordered on the basis of "new
forms of production," ecological equilibrium, new social priorities, and
grassroots self-management. An important theme running through
Green ideology is the commitment to a process of conversion—a transition from commodified and wasteful to socially useful forms of
production.

• The chief objective is to initiate a shift from quantitative to qualitative development, from a "mass consumption" industrialism to a self-
sustaining, nonexploitative system.[27] For the Greens it is no longer

sufficient to emphasize industrial output for its own sake without questioning the content of what is produced. Resources devoted to armaments, goods that are environmentally harmful, and wasteful private commodities should be redirected into sectors closer to collective human needs: health care, housing, transportation, urban reconstruction, culture, education. This would permit reduction in absolute levels of growth while also improving living standards, enhancing the general quality of life, and restoring the balance between economy and nature. For such a model to work, however, there would have to be a vast transformation of consciousness, with the old productivism and privatized consumerism giving way to an ecological thinking that placed human values and needs at the core of historical progress.[28]

• The Green model anticipates a democratized economy distinct from both the corporate market system and the Soviet command type of statism. The Keynesian reliance on nationalizations, state planning, and institutional manipulation is shunned, and there is ample room for market activity and private ownership within small and even medium-sized enterprises. The Greens' ultimate aim, allowing for sharp differences of emphasis among the factions, is to create a nonexploitative mixed economy that would allow for growth of a socialized network of production based in cooperative enterprises, workers' self-management, human-scale organization, and respect for regional peculiarities and ecological diversity. But here, as in other areas of Green politics, the means for accomplishing such emancipatory objectives are nowhere clearly set forth.

• Changes in the nature of production and consumption are vitally linked to the emergence of new forms of work and the overturning of hierarchical social relations. As the Green program states, "The key premise is that those people affected by any decision should make that decision themselves. What is produced, *how*, and *where*. People must be able to freely develop their various abilities and initiatives at work and at leisure."[29] The prospects for creative and meaningful work, not for a small number of professionals and artists but for the entire adult population, depend upon the full involvement of workers made possible by popular control (local committees), alternative technology, expansion of socially useful production, and more leisure time with greater cultural options. Clearly such a schema has little in common with the familiar *Mittbestimung*, or "co-determination," which for years has shaped the West German industrial structure.

• Essential to a Green-style economy is a renovated scientific and technological infrastructure that presently reinforces every prospect of hierarchy and control. Although technology contributes to economic efficiency, it has yet another reality: it can be repressive and alienating to workers, ecologically harmful, and wasteful (as in the case of nuclear power stations and weapons systems). The Greens argue for an alternative technology with emphasis on renewable (e.g., solar) sources of energy, a "democratically-controllable application of technology" within small-scale units,[30] and a system of "ecological accounting" that supplements the normal financial accounting.[31] Though vague in specifics, these proposals would give substance to the revitalization of social services. Just one example: the health-care system would abandon its reliance on technocratic and profit-based criteria—on large-scale institutions and expensive remedies—in favor of a "preventive ecological medicine [that] is based on the knowledge that the greatest part of the diseases of modern civilization are due to external—i.e., environmental and social—influences."[32] The pouring of material and technological resources into medical services corresponds to an actual decline in health conditions, as reflected in the growing cancer epidemic throughout the advanced countries. In turning toward neighborhood-centered, small-scale health-care units, the holistic approach would replace a technology-intensive with a labor-intensive system.

• Such a radical economic path must inevitably take into account the history and needs of Third World countries, whose economies and cultures have been plundered by the capitalist powers, reproducing forms of dependency that are becoming sharper. The Green developmental policy aims for a "genuine partnership" with the poor countries in order to reverse this dependency. As the party program states, however, "The industrialized states can attain a new relationship with the countries of the Third World only if they renounce their continuous industrial expansion. . . . This model of development, together with so-called development aid, leads to the Third-World countries being exploited by the industrialized countries, and robbed of their own forms of life and resources. In its place we shall try to develop jointly with the Third-World countries those new ecological practices which will preserve us from all becoming victims of the gathering world crisis."[33] To this end, the party would establish trading arrangements in which a fair price would be received for work and products, profit-based investments would be terminated, material assistance would be upgraded (e.g., for an ecologically viable agriculture), military aid would be discontinued, and so forth.[34] In this policy area, more than elsewhere, the Green position appears to be shaped by Marxist sensibilities. Thus: "What industrial society calls 'growth' is based in reality on a global competitive battle by the strong against the weak, which can only end with a general collapse. The domination of the world market by giant corporations leads to an increasing impoverishment of the Third-World countries and must end in a breakdown of the present world economic order."[35]

The Green analysis of the global economic situation is connected, as we have seen, to the problem of militarism and the renewal of cold-war international competition between the superpowers. Hence, economic transformation and the struggle for peace are inseparable goals. It can be established that the material predicament is in fact doubly linked to the arms race, since military buildups both contribute to the crisis and serve as a useful device to mask it or at least deflect attention away from it. If the Greens during their infancy were divided over how to strategically merge these issues, they have nonetheless managed to build a consensus around the assumption that they should be integrated into a unified framework of theory and practice.

The conceptual fulcrum of the dialectic between militarism and economic crisis, between the struggle for peace and the vision of ecological development, is social conversion.[36] To speak of a total societal reconstruction, as the Greens do, refers to a distant goal that can be reached only by progressively cutting away at the military sector and redirecting those resources into socially useful (and ecologically balanced) forms of production—by shifting from nuclear power and other weapons systems to housing, education, health care, the environment, public transportation, and so forth. In West Germany, where more than 3 percent of the domestic product is consumed directly by the military, conversion would mean nearly an additional $100 billion for social programs in just two or three years. For the Greens, the fight to abolish militarism takes on a material as well as moral dimension. It is grounded in concrete social and political action rather than normative appeals alone. Since nuclear weaponry (like other types of weaponry) has no autonomous logic but is the product of a specific social system, the peace movement is faced with the (ultimate) task of overturning that system if it is to achieve its most far-reaching aims such as disarmament. In the West this means that it will have to confront the realities of capitalism and imperialism, a matter less of tactics or methods than of fundamental goals. Viewed in this way, the process of conversion represents (ideally) the intersection of the struggle for peace, the other new movements, and working-class politics.

Conversion thus encompasses far more than a simple transfer of resources from one sector or another, more than another Keynesian plan for getting capitalism on the road to recovery. It differs from the narrower liberal schemes of "economic conversion" that initially appeared in the 1960s insofar as it fully challenges the corporate power structure that, in its pursuit of profit and growth, is assaulting the earth and threatening to destroy it. The radical break with social democracy could not be more obvious and total. The Green objective is nothing less than to reverse the pattern of state-capitalist accumulation. That, as Bahro insists, requires a complete "exit" from industrial civilization in its present form.[37]

There is of course ample disagreement among Greens over how far, and in what ways, to extend such an ecological vision. "Eco-socialists" like Thomas Ebermann, for example, remain attached to a more traditional workerism. They are suspicious of any attempt to subordinate class struggle to other priorities. Still, there is a strong consensus that the economy and nature are more indivisible than ever, and that even from the standpoint of immediate reforms drastic measures must be taken before the violent impact of capitalist industrialization is allowed to run its course. Thus, air and water pollution must be brought under control, atmospheric radiation must be curbed, blighted urban areas must be restored, occupational health and safety must be improved, the toxic-waste problem must be eliminated, and the health-care system must be overhauled and democratized. A more livable human space can be created by encouraging a "pro-people," environmentally sound architecture that integrates "the areas of home, work, recreation, self-education, and shopping," in a more harmonious way.[38] Overall, the Greens estimate that damages to the West German environment run at about $25–30 billion annually—damages so vast as to defy the kind of technological restructuring and cosmetic touching-up envisioned by the mainstream parties.

The political means for carrying out these reforms, even leaving aside the Greens' more ambitious and visionary objectives, calls for imaginative solutions and novel organizational forms. And of course this suggests the importance of new theoretical perspectives since "the prevailing economic rationality must be replaced by a policy guided by long-term and ecological goals."[39] The ecological premises of change involve an organic relationship between the economy, the state, and the natural environment. Each component is interrelated with the others, as part of the multiple and overlapping structures of domination, and all must be transformed if radical change is to occur. In its most extreme version—for example, Bahro's—this holistic outlook is associated with an anarchistic return to "voluntary simplicity" along with a vaguely defined spiritualism.[40] Other Greens incorporate a strong feminist dimension, or what has been called "eco-feminism," into this totality.[41] It is true that Green proposals on the economy have suffered from a certain ambiguity over what forms of ownership are most appropriate to radical ecology, so that this crucial issue has generally been sidestepped. All agree, however, on the centrality of popular control over all areas of production, work, consumption, and social life, motivated by an understanding that the economy as such does not constitute an end but rather a means to the free development of everyone according to the principles of self-activity and collective sharing.

This model, though not yet grounded in a coherent post-Keynesian theory, represents an effort to move beyond corporate-liberal, social-democratic, and Soviet-style economic strategies. Green economics challenges the productivist and statist character of both liberalism and Marxism in its recognition that the global-ecological limits of industrialism (East and West) have finally been reached, yet it does not lapse into a romantic fetishism of preindustrial values and social relations (although a good number of the Fundis do embrace something close to this).[42] Change would not depend upon the "revolutionary" intervention of a vanguard party, or party-state, but would have to be realized through broad consensual support leading to a counterhegemonic politics. In the meantime, the Greens seem to be more adept at specifying ultimate goals than at formulating the strategic and institutional mechanics for their actualization.

NEW COLD WAR AND THE PEACE MOVEMENT

The Greens can be understood as a convergence of disparate social forces and ideological tendencies, but their initial success was made possible by a single movement, the great peace mobilizations of 1980–83. The massive protests against NATO's planned deployment of the

Euromissiles (which did take place beginning in December 1983) were the most powerful catalyst behind the Greens' emergence as an organizing focus of the new movements and their electoral breakthrough in 1983. The momentum supplied by the peace movement grew out of a Europeanwide sense of urgency over escalation of the arms race, renewal of cold-war tensions, and the U.S. missile scheme that would station 108 Pershing II and cruise missiles on West German territory. In this context the antimilitarist outlook of the Greens was partly a response to the widespread German fear that the country would become the center of a nuclear battlefield. Beneath this psychological response lies a pervasive sense of disenfranchisement over the issue of nuclear weapons and foreign policy in general, since important global decisions are made in Washington and Moscow. Feelings of powerlessness are probably more acute in West Germany, which lacks even a semblance of national sovereignty or identity.

The 1979 NATO decision to "modernize" an already sophisticated nuclear arsenal in effect launched the new peace movement. As I argue in Chapter 2, this resurgence of militarism stems from the U.S. obsession with maintaining nuclear supremacy over the Soviet Union. Its underlying motive is to preserve American hegemony over Western Europe, the Middle East, and parts of the Third World. Under these conditions large sectors of the European population were convinced that U.S. policy was governed by less restraint than Soviet policy and that the West, with its more elaborate weapons systems and technological infrastructure, was continuing its role as primary instigator of the arms race. President Reagan's speech of March 8, 1983, in which he rejected the notion of a "simple-minded appeasement" of the Soviets who in their "totalitarian darkness" constitute the "focus of evil in the modern world," only reinforced long-standing European anxieties.[43] For this and other reasons, the evolving consensus within the peace movement was that only large-scale popular resistance could prevent NATO from deploying the missiles (a resistance that, although both enormous and militant, ultimately failed in its aims).

As for West Germany, the Helmut Kohl government, revitalized by the stunning CDU electoral coup, fully supported the Euromissile program, which in fact was originally advocated by the SPD under Helmut Schmidt. For Kohl, any West German decision to detach the country from U.S. global interests would inevitably "subject Germany to Soviet hegemony." He readily accepted the Carter-Reagan argument that the new missiles would be needed to counter the Soviet SS-20s already in place. And none of the other Western European governments, whatever their ideological makeup or fears of domestic upheaval, chose (before 1983) to reject the NATO plan. Thus not only West Germany, but also England, Italy, Belgium, and Holland seemed prepared, despite reservations, to accept the military planners' pleas for nuclear "modernization."

As for the peace movement, a rekindled militarism in Western Europe had begun to raise issues that went far beyond missile deployments or the endless debates over who has nuclear superiority. There is first of all the imposing fact that the arms race has devoured enormous technological, economic, and human resources that could be better used for socially productive investment. The perpetual struggle for "deterrence" furnishes a handy pretext for dismantling the welfare state, which conservatives had placed on the agenda in the United States, England, and West Germany. Each new cycle in the spiraling arms contest heightens contradictions between wasteful military spending and social progress, between nuclear development and material welfare, so that the linkage between corporate interests, militarism, and economic crisis has become more and more transparent. Second, nuclear politics has become a useful (if risky) device for reinforcing U.S. domination over Western Europe at a time when its global position is being challenged—whether from Japan, the Middle East, or areas of the Third World. And Western European elites seem content enough to gather beneath the American nuclear umbrella as a means (however illusory) of protecting their own interests.

The new cold-war atmosphere that accompanies the latest wave of militarism is profoundly centralizing and antidemocratic, as E. P. Thompson stresses.[44] Not only are epochal decisions involving "national security" made without prior knowledge and participation of the citizenry, but the nuclear dimension pushes capitalism even further along the path of concentrated state power insofar as it relishes secrecy, control, and an enlarged role for military "expertise." In this sense the culture of militarism is no longer restricted to isolated bases and missile launching sites. As Thompson argues, the nuclear weapons apparatus requires a vast institutional and ideological support system that "researches it, 'chooses' it, produces it, polices it, and maintains it in being."[45]

It follows that the new peace movement has a transformative capacity far deeper than specific protests against nuclear reactors, missiles, and arms spending—however vital and efficacious these actions. As the more politicized elements of the antinuclear campaign begin to reject the military structure in toto, they invariably encounter issues of class and power. And by opposing the general militarization of society, these struggles are forced to confront the economic crisis and the obstacles to democratic participation posed by the war economy. Because of its strongly populist character—its ability to bring millions of people from different strata into the streets—such radical implications of antimilitarism have often been overlooked. To be sure, moderate currents have typically pushed for a "nonpolitical" direction to peace activism on the premise that to inject "ideology" or "divisiveness" into the movement alienates the mainstream of likely supporters. Yet in a relatively brief period the Western European peace mobilizations profoundly disturbed the old political alignments and, notably in West Germany, inspired a renewal of left militancy. Bahro may have been exaggerating only slightly when he predicted that "the peace movement is now at the head of an entire social constellation that is rehearsing the emergence of a new epoch."[46]

For the Greens, popular struggles over disarmament were from the beginning tied to a vision of radical change, even if the precise content of that vision and the methods for achieving it were a matter of uncertainty and debate within the party. If the arms race posed the question of life and death—of survival itself—the solution was not to be found either in an alarmist moralism or an interest-group lobbying that tries to force the power structure away from its irrational, self-destructive course. The Greens see the problem as something much deeper: the opposition to militarism in the West is simultaneously opposition to the entire state-capitalist system, not merely to specific policies of that state.

The general international outlook of the Greens is rooted in the concept of an "ecological foreign policy" based upon cooperation and nonviolence, one that substitutes a "peace policy" for a military or national security policy, that calls for an end to "all forms of aggression . . . competitive armaments, and the arms madness." The moral imperative for such a global shift in foreign relations has never been greater, since "with the introduction of nuclear weapons war has reached completely new dimensions. The possibility of destroying the whole Earth several times over has turned into the pure and simple murder of nations and a crime against life in general."[47] The idea of an "ecological" foreign policy assumes that peace can be sustained only within a context of global social justice where the principles of regional diversity, mutuality, and independence hold sway. Of course, the advanced capitalist countries systematically and brutally violate these principles in the service of their own national interests. In reaction, the Greens "condemn the presumption of the industrialized countries in seeking to force on all other countries—out of their own economic interests—their uniform technical and material civilization. The policies of the industrialized countries toward the Third World has so far been predominantly geared to their own profit and must therefore be rejected."[48]

Of course such grandiose statements cannot serve as a concrete organizing platform or an immediate unifying focus. What did furnish a specific target of mobilization for the Greens was the NATO Euromissile decision: the new missiles were, after all, being installed on the European continent at a time of heightened international tension. Casual references of U.S. leaders to the possibility of waging a "limited" or "tactical" nuclear war, plans for development of the neutron bomb, and Reagan's increasingly bellicose anti-Communism only stirred this passion further. The Euromissiles became a symbol, evoking apocalyptic nightmares that moved millions of people to action. The Greens consciously situated themselves in the midst of this turbulence, with the result that their popular support spread more rapidly than anyone imagined in 1979. In West Germany the Greens were the only party to challenge cold-war mythology; and they were the only party ready to launch militant forms of civil disobedience, including blockades of nuclear sites, to resist deployment of the missiles.[49]

In her autumn 1982 public letter to SPD chairman Willy Brandt, Petra Kelly reaffirmed (for the Greens) that opposition to the Euromissiles was only the first step in a much longer process.[50] A vigorous popular movement, capable of generating political momentum over time, could not be built upon negative sentiments only. Through massive civil disobedience, as well as relentless political education, progress toward a rational society would have to continue, whether or not the missiles were deployed. "What we are talking about," she wrote, "is a decisive movement of the people against the experts and bureaucrats, optimists against pessimists and cynics, of the grassroots against the repressive state, of dreamers against crude manipulators." Reflecting the Greens' official position, Kelly characterized the superpower game of nuclear one-upsmanship as a ridiculous but macabre charade and urged commitment to the seemingly forgotten "peace" statute (*Friedens-gebot*) of the West German constitution.

Proceeding from these assumptions, the Greens called for a bloc-free Europe that would coincide with a "nuclear-free zone stretching from Portugal to Poland," the cessation of all exports of arms and nuclear reactors, and the initiation of worldwide disarmament negotiations.[51] Their "peace policy" was designed to overturn the very raison d'être of NATO, stimulate reversal of the arms race, and, ultimately, to dismantle the entire military apparatus beginning with West Germany. What all of this portends, according to the Greens' Rainer Trampert, is a continuous process of mass mobilization somewhat along the lines of a "peaceful civil war."[52]

When the Greens first began to outline the elements of their radical foreign policy in 1981–82, the SPD was still a governing party tied closely to NATO and the ideals of Atlanticism. The gulf separating the two parties could not have been wider.[53] After the SPD's fall from power in 1982, however, and especially after their electoral debacle of 1983, the Social Democrats adopted a more critical stance toward the Euromissiles (and West German foreign policy in general) from their oppositional presence in the Bundestag. Still, the gap remains formidable—and the deep skepticism that most Greens express toward the SPD has diminished little even where the SPD chose to pursue "green" issues (as in the Saarland candidacy of Oscar Lafontaine in early 1985). The majority of Greens felt that, despite its leftward shift in foreign policy, the SPD would remain thoroughly attached to American interests and would, if it ever regained its governing role, revert to its uncritical pro-NATO posture without missing a step. So long as the SPD is viewed as an integral part of the security state, cooperation between the Greens and the SPD on peace issues is improbable. In any event, the SPD strategem—on this as on other issues—is to create broad coalitions for very limited objectives, whereas the Greens look to grassroots mobilization around more radical goals. Those Greens most hostile to the SPD, like Bahro, Kelly, and Roland Vogt, argue that it should be the historical task of the Greens to supersede the SPD on the left, especially given the urgency of the peace struggle. Bahro's optimism on this point derives from his conclusion that "the paradigm of the workers' movement, this hundred year-old social democracy, is nearing its end."[54]

Since faith in elite initiative produces few results, the Greens insist that disarmament must begin with local movements through a series of unilateral steps. Unilateralism of some sort is not only thinkable but probably unavoidable because of NATO's long record of belligerency —its rigid anti-Communism and cynical manipulation of the Soviet "peril," its unwillingness to renounce first-use of nuclear weapons, and of course its deep attachment to the Euromissile scheme. Although the Greens were hardly naive about the Soviet role in the arms race, they concluded (after much heated internal debate) that the main danger to Western Europe comes from NATO rather than the Warsaw Pact countries, since NATO formulates policies based upon "rhetorical abstraction, distortions, and lies" concerning the need for high-level military vigilance. The "peace manifesto" drawn up at the Sindelfingen Congress goes even further, suggesting that the Reagan administration is anxious to "arm the Soviet Union to the death" for the purpose of exacerbating contradictions within Soviet society. Whatever the validity of such analysis, the Greens—convinced that the cycle of arms buildup is rapidly getting out of control—are willing to take risks. The implicit assumption is that, once the dynamic of arms production and deployment is unraveled in the West, Soviet leaders will be unable to resist similar pressures for disarmament within their own sphere. As the party program states, "Disarmament must begin in one's own country, designed to induce other countries to disarm as well. Unilateral disarmament should seek to strengthen the peace movement in order to assist a breakthrough to worldwide disarmament, particularly by the USA and USSR."[55]

Yet the prolonged divisions among Greens on such issues reflect a continued ambiguity toward the reality of Soviet power. At the outset the dominant tendency was to hold each superpower bloc more or less equally responsible for global tensions: mobilizations in support of the Nicaraguan Sandinistas were balanced by those endorsing Polish Solidarity, for example. With the imminent deployment of the Euromissiles, however, this balance began to tilt toward a more emphatic anti-NATO posture, as seen in the Sindelfingen "peace manifesto." At the same time, none of the Greens confused this shift with a readiness to identify with Soviet foreign policy much less any Soviet "model" of socialism; the real issue was the nature of the Soviet international presence and its degree of culpability for the arms race.

While increasingly on the fringes of the party, it was Bahro (owing in great measure to his East German background and his book *The Alternative*) who spoke most coherently for the Green majority on this issue. Bahro's main point was that the Soviet Union has neither the motivation nor the capacity to carry out a truly expansionist foreign policy. Thus: "The Soviet leadership is fundamentally conservative— there is no Western politician who is as conservative as Brezhnev was. If we look at the famous Soviet 'totalitarian' threat, what we see is something as old and ill and weak as Brezhnev was and Andropov is. The Soviet system was never able to achieve its historical aims. The original concept was to catch up with and overtake the industrial development of countries like the U.S. and West Germany. The whole idea of peaceful competition starting in the 1930s has really broken down. The economy, beginning with agriculture, did not work and doesn't work the way it was supposed to work. The extreme efforts needed to even reach a near-parity in the military sector vis-à-vis the U.S. reveals weakness rather than strength." He added that the Soviet predicament is compounded by the difficulties of maintaining hegemony over Eastern Europe—most recently Poland, which it wants to maintain as a "buffer zone" rather than as a "socialist" client-state. In Bahro's opinion, "the Soviet leaders would be absolutely mad to look for some new conquest, which would simply create more problems and contradictions. We always hear that the Soviets are ready to come West, but they cannot. They are not about to enter Western Europe." [56]

This outlook—along with the willingness to pursue a unilateralist policy—calls for an alternative nonmilitarist foreign and defense policy. For the Greens, the answer lies in the concept of social defense, which gives meaning to the general aims of an ecological foreign relations: total disarmament, social conversion, nonviolence, an end to military blocs. The essence of social defense, as theoretically elaborated in the work of Gene Sharp,[57] is the development of extensive networks, firmly rooted in civil society, that could mobilize broad civilian resistance to any imperial incursion from outside. The assumption is that massive collective solidarity in defense of threatened communities would count more heavily than any assemblage of infantry units, tanks, and missiles —or at least that the price paid by an occupying force would not be worth the terrain conquered. The threat of civil disobedience on a large scale—boycotts, work stoppages, mass demonstrations, blockades— would in the long run offer the most viable form of security. Social defense thus finds its rationale in ecological, feminist, and pacifist principles that affirm a non-negotiable respect for all human life and nature —and in the view that any use of military force, however justified, will be antithetical to the struggle for a new society. Yet the fact that the theme of social defense receives only passing attention in the Green program indicates that the party had not arrived at a unified conceptualization of this problem, or at least one that met with broad agreement.[58] Indeed, the internal divisions over this issue mirror the perpetual debates over the larger question of nonviolence.

Although the Greens are commonly viewed as a pacifist party, and although there is an obvious consensus in favor of nonviolence as an ultimate goal, conflicts over the definition and application of these principles have been intense and, for the most part, unresolved. On the one side are those who argued (Kelly, Vogt) for an unwavering commitment to nonviolence in the Gandhian tradition—not merely as a political method but as an overall "defense" policy, a moral vision, a way of life. They believe that even limited acts of violence for the noblest of "peace" objectives (as in the stoning of Vice-President Bush's car at Krefeld in 1983) will only "corrupt" those involved and undermine their participatory style; their credibility as opponents of a violent order would be eroded. Politics, as Kelly insists, must involve a unity of ends and means.[59] On the other side are those (mainly "red" Greens like Trampert and Ebermann) who were more sympathetic to the Marxist position on the role of violence in social change. They argue that any effective assault on the power structure, with its control of military, policy, and administrative coercion, cannot be peaceful because elites will be forced to defend the system by violent methods. Thus violence is less a moral choice than a political imperative, the necessary side-effect of radical change. Although pacifist ideas ought to be adopted where possible, they do not exhaust the full range of methods to be employed even in the industrialized countries, where ideological hegemony may be more critical to sustaining the power structure than physical coercion. The sense of urgency instilled by the threat of nuclear war would seem to validate the latter tendency. But the reality has been just the opposite: the "pacifists" have been in the majority presumably because their outlook appears to be most at odds with the omnipresent realities of the war economy.

The reasons for the peculiar strength of the peace movement in West Germany go far beyond the Euromissile issue. A deeper factor is the continued postwar division of the Germanies, whereby neither region has national sovereignty or input into foreign-policy decisions. For the West Germans, U.S. economic, military, and cultural domination is a festering source of anger and resentment, and this feeds the pacifism of the present generation. The German struggle for a recovery of national identity, however defined, cannot be underestimated in any attempt to explain the Green phenomenon. Inevitably, this poses the familiar theme of German nationalism, which some critics of the Greens argue contains frightening parallels with earlier periods of German history. The Greens respond that they are a party *sui generis*, located squarely in the 1980s, with commitments and values so far removed from those of fascism or right-wing nationalism that any comparison is absurd.

On this question the Greens are correct, as any familiarity with their literature, party programs, and political work will immediately reveal. Unlike the fascists (and the present-day mainstream parties), they reject the very idea of a militarized nation-state or bloc of states, and they advocate a "partnership" with Third World countries that would reverse the historic European drive toward hegemony. In this they stand for a unique version of radical internationalism. In the words of the party program, "We want all countries and all peoples to decide for themselves on their road of development. . . . We are against all forms of tutelage, interference, occupation, and pillage, whether political, military, or cultural, especially in the Third-World countries but also in relation to all states, nationalities, and minorities."[60] Further, some Greens envision a decomposition of the nation-state itself into smaller, self-determining regional entities—utopian, perhaps, but hardly a reversion to traditional Prussian nationalism. Finally, the political style of the Greens differs greatly from that of earlier patriotic movements insofar as its leadership structure, ideological symbols, and political culture all reflect a self-conscious departure from the past. The critique of militarism, along with the challenge to U.S.-NATO domination of West Germany, suggests less a return to a romantic (and authoritarian) nationalism than a forward-looking attachment to radical change. The reality is that both the CDU and SPD—and emphatically not the Greens—have an affinity for a bureaucratic and militarized German state.[61]

With the first installation of the Euromissiles in December 1983, and the realization by most Europeans that no amount of active resistance was likely to block them, the peace movement entered a phase of demoralization and decline. During 1984 peace actions were more infrequent, with a smaller number of people involved. The apocalyptic feeling that the struggle over the missiles was a matter of life and death, of imminent confrontation with the war machine, had ebbed. The Greens, too, experienced a reversal of their upward momentum, especially in the first half of 1984. Pessimism drove many activists into retreat, while others chose to regroup by simply analyzing and reflecting upon the predicament. General Gert Bastion, a Green leader influential on foreign-policy issues, left the parliamentary caucus in early 1984 out of frustration with the party's internal dissension. Meanwhile, the SPD's leftward tilt brought it in closer contact with the peace movement, undercutting Green strength in this area.

Yet the predictions of a disastrous "crisis" of Green politics turned out to be premature. Whatever the dilemmas and obstacles posed by the new situation, the party's oppositional presence was actually deepened in 1984–85 with the persistence of international tensions. The threat of the arms race was still salient for a majority of Germans (70 percent favoring removal of the missiles even after deployment had started). In fact, the Greens' standing in the polls rose substantially between 1983 and early 1985, from roughly 8 percent to nearly 15 percent according to some surveys. Judging from these and other indicators, the national mood had changed little even if the level of organized mass activity was declining. Despite the viscissitudes of the peace movement, the Greens were still a durable although internally divided force with a loyal and growing popular base.

THE GREEN PREDICAMENT

A specific congruence of events and issues permitted the Greens, despite their numerically limited support, to build a genuine oppositional party in West Germany on a scale that even the most optimistic partisans would not have anticipated as late as 1982. The Green entry into several *Land* (state) parliaments, and ultimately the Bundestag, not only legitimated the radical demands of previously existing social movements; it also gave added impetus to those movements by empowering the citizens' initiatives that were localized and dispersed. Ideologically, the Greens tapped the roots of a revitalized moral idealism, pacifism, and anti-authoritarianism that signaled a momentous break with the German past—a basic shift in the political culture that extended to foreign policy, the economy, the state, the natural environment, and social life in general.[62] In all these areas they were able to present a deeper analysis of the issues than any of their competitors. While dis-avowing vanguard-style civil insurrection, the Greens advanced a com-prehensive, or holistic, model of radical change that also challenged the limits of structural reformism. They introduced a spirit of political ori-ginality largely because they were able to create, or help create, a dy-namic intellectual and cultural milieu around which many local forces could congregate.

Politically, Green entry into the legitimate political system provided new space within which long-repressed issues could be posed and de-bated, the power structure could be more directly confronted, and of course valuable knowledge about the workings of the system could be gained. For example, the well-publicized Flick scandal of 1984–85 gave the Greens a forum for making progress on each front. The huge Flick conglomerate had been implicated in payoffs to leading West German politicians over several years—an instance of corruption the Greens helped to investigate and publicize through their aggressive parliamen-tary initiatives. Otto Schily, a lawyer and Green deputy, interrogated Chancellor Helmut Kohl in the Bundestag for seven hours, in the pro-cess forcing him to confess to the CDU's illegal campaign financing linked to the Flick affair.[63] By means of such confrontations, as well as a vigilant presence in legislative assemblies, the Greens were able to impose some modest restraints upon the Kohl government. Their popu-list challenge succeeded in penetrating the rigid institutional armor of the state. The old equilibrium was in some measure disturbed, perhaps irreversibly undermined.

Yet any discussion of Green politics must explore the difficulties that will inevitably accompany the party's electoral and organizational growth—for example, concerning how to sustain popular mobilization around "survival" issues; what strategy to adopt vis-à-vis the SPD, trade unions, and labor in general; how to articulate a viable radicalism while resolving ideological conflicts over the issues of spiritualism, pacifism, and direct democracy; and, finally, how to cope with the chronic pres-sures toward political integration which, in the Greens' case, means sustaining a delicate balance between electoralism and grassroots move-ments. The capacity of the Green leadership to confront these diffi-culties, theoretically and practically, could well determine the party's future.

A perplexing short-term dilemma concerns the possibility that U.S.–NATO efforts to defuse the peace issue—for example, by securing an arms limitation agreement with the Soviet Union—turn out to be fruitful. Since the NATO nuclear decision was the main catalyst of Europeanwide peace activism, any downplaying of the arms issue would probably impede expansion of both the social movements and the Greens, at least temporarily. Even a cosmetic treaty (such as a "freeze" on nuclear arms production and deployment), in which the superpowers appear to be reversing the arms race, could have a negative effect. Another possible scenario is a shift in NATO's strategic emphasis from nuclear to conventional weapons. Given the scope of popular hostility to the very idea of nuclear weaponry, particularly in West Germany, some military planners have weighed the merits of adopting a more conventional deterrence force relying upon sophisticated computer-based weapons that are far in advance of what the Warsaw Pact countries can hope to possess for some time. One such strategy, called Airland Battle 2000, calls for deployment of "smart weapons" using electronic guidance systems more accurate than those of tactical nuclear weapons. In late 1982 NATO commander General Bernard Rogers indicated that NATO could dispense with at least 6,000 short-range nuclear missiles if such a plan goes into effect. An obvious question that emerges from this picture is: since the peace movement has been so preoccupied with the danger of nuclear warfare, where does the deadly threat of conventional military combat enter into calculations? This question is all the more salient given the seemingly relaxed inhibitions, both East and West, concerning the more traditional forms of military warfare.

Even if the nuclear threat is not diminished in the popular consciousness, however, the peace movement—and by extension the Greens—will be left vulnerable so long as a comprehensive antimilitarist strategy is lacking. True enough, the Green vision of nonviolent civil defense is a step in this direction, but it raises more questions than it solves, as we shall see. More significant, this concept falls largely into the category of ultimate goal, which for most Europeans has little concrete relevance. As a general ideal "social defense" may or may not have promise, but far more pressing for the Greens is the question of whether very many people can be mobilized around such a distant and seemingly utopian vision. In immediate terms, what the Greens need is a transitional program on defense and foreign relations that can be reasonably attractive in the struggle to reverse NATO's cold-war direction. The theme of social conversion contributes to an imaginative domestic strategy, but it will never constitute an alternative paradigm for inter-national politics. Various components of the Green program—total disarmament, a bloc-free Europe, equilibrium with the Third World—do suggest the outlines of a reconstituted foreign policy, but again these are essentially general objectives rather than prescriptions for change. The problem of how to reach these objectives, and through what inter-mediate stages, is never fully addressed. Here as elsewhere the Greens make themselves vulnerable to charges of utopianism, which naturally damages the party's capacity to sustain a militant oppositional chal-lenge on foreign policy issues.

In this vein, the Greens will continue to be attacked, especially by the older generation of Germans, for espousing a unilateralism that might be regarded as naïve in its failure to adequately confront the Soviet role in the arms race and the "totalitarian" menace it represents. However valid such opinions might be, they do reflect fears that are pervasive in the West—fears that the Greens do not really confront. So far they have proceeded, very tentatively because of strong internal disagree-ments, from a number of basic assumptions: that militarism cannot be contained or abolished strictly by means of elite-sponsored superpower negotiations; that a militarily "defenseless" West would not actually have to worry about Soviet aggression, or that social-defense networks could adequately resist any incursions; that internal opposition to Soviet and Eastern European regimes will be encouraged by the success of peace campaigns in the West; and that, in the final analysis, antinuclear initiatives must begin somewhere and soon, before the logic of exter-minism finally wins out—whatever the global intentions of Soviet leaders.[64] But none of these premises has been spelled out, theoretically or politically. The Greens have no approach to the Soviet bloc that goes beyond either an impressionistic silhouette or blind faith.

A second problem area—long the focus of debates within the party—revolves around the Greens' relationship to the SPD and the labor movement. If the Green role in the national parliament is marginal, their growing strength in communal and state elections poses a chal-lenge to the Social Democrats, especially where the SPD has already been thrown on the defensive by the CDU. The leadership of both parties is faced with the dilemma of deciding whether, and under what conditions, some kind of "red-green" alliance might be established. On the whole the SPD has tried to keep its distance by largely ignoring the Greens, or by responding to their overtures with the contemptuous disdain of a more developed and mature party. As the Greens expanded, however, the SPD chose a different set of tactics: it would try to coopt "green" issues and Green support, but without entering into a real working coalition with the party itself. The Lafontaine campaign in the Saarland, based on such a motif, demonstrated the potential of this second alternative.

As for real party-to-party collaboration, even at the local level, the obstacles seem to be overwhelming. Tensions between the parties run deep—a psychological gulf widened by the fact that many Green activists chose to leave the SPD and have no interest in returning, even within the context of an alliance. Of greater significance, the parties' modus operandi differ so fundamentally that efforts to achieve political unity would surely be strained from the outset. Whereas the SPD looks almost exclusively to the state, political elites, and the existing public sphere, the Greens favor grassroots extraparliamentary activity. Whereas the SPD's productivism makes it fearful of programs that might scare off capital, the Greens uphold the qualitative demands of the new movements whatever their presumed economic "costs." And, finally, the Greens are less compromising and "pragmatic" on peace issues than the SPD. Of course some kind of alliance with the SPD, especially one leading to a coalition government, might confer upon the Greens a certain short-term legitimacy. However, such legitimacy would surely be purchased at the price of absorption, given the political constraints that would result. In actuality there have been only a few concrete steps in the direction of a Green-SPD coalition anywhere during the Greens' first five years of existence. In Hamburg, where the Greens held eight seats in the city-state legislature, prolonged negotiations on collaboration ultimately broke down. In the Hesse parliament, a tense and fragile "toleration agreement" was reached in June 1984; finally, in the fall of 1985, the Greens entered the state government as the junior partner of the SPD—thereby giving them their first real (if limited) administrative experience. For several years members of the Alternative List in West Berlin debated this issue, but nothing was resolved.[65]

There is a strong minority sentiment within the Greens against any form of collaboration with the SPD. The Fundi ("fundamentalist") wing, for example, fears that any entanglement would stifle the Greens' maturation during the delicate phase of identity formation; the party needs autonomy to expand within its own sphere of activity, in accordance with its own peculiar style, interests, and goals. Bahro, among others, was convinced that the SPD era of opposition was finished and that it is now the historical task of the Greens to replace it. From this viewpoint, cooperation would be harmful because it would undermine the Greens' own political mission. This outlook was reiterated at the party Congress in Hamburg in December 1984 by many speakers, including Trampert, who insisted that ongoing cooperation with the SPD would limit the party's maneuverability. For Trampert, fundamental opposition to the system can never be kept alive within the sphere of SPD politics.[66]

The dominant opinion, however, favors an SPD-Green coalition that would enable the Greens to avoid isolation and impotence, especially if they can become part of a governing majority in one of the states. This strategem still allows the Greens adequate space for pressing their own concerns within national politics. Schily, for example, has argued that the Greens cannot hope to win enough votes to govern alone in the near future, so that their only hope for popular credibility is to work with the SPD (simultaneously protecting their own ideological coherence and identity). This "realist" or (Realos) position, however, has rarely been pushed to the extent of disavowing extensive linkages with the popular movements. Quite often, the differences are presented as a matter of slight emphasis or of tactical methods.[67] In general, the mass base of the Greens has been more predisposed than the leadership to political bargaining.[68] But this debate, too, is far from resolved.

In national politics, so long as there is a strong CDU government, the Greens can defer making a decision on this issue. But at the local level there have been elements within both the SPD and the Greens pushing for alliance with the aim of building left majorities. Of course there are risks either way—of absorption in the case of alliance, of isolation and perhaps sectarian decline where autonomy is too jealously guarded. Whatever the circumstances, this dilemma will never disappear. On the one hand, to the degree the Greens improve their electoral fortunes, the temptations of an instrumentalist reform politics—and of working with the SPD—will be more difficult to resist. On the other hand, as Wolf-Dieter Narr argues, the very effort to preserve an oppositional identity (and thus minority status) can easily render ineffectual the various programmatic aims, which, in turn, would diminish Green popular support over time.[69]

A related problem for the Greens has been how to establish relations with, and a base of support in, the labor movement. Only on rare occasions has the party even briefly collaborated with the main trade-union confederation (the DGB), a source of much discomfort and anxiety among party members. Until their January 1983 party congress the Greens, immersed in peace and environmental issues, did not seriously address working-class issues such as contractual bargaining, unemployment, union democracy, and even social welfare. The SPD, in its 1982 Scharting Report, criticized the Greens for "anti-labor" sentiments and for sometimes sounding like neoconservatives in their attack on the welfare state.[70] And in fact three Green city councilors in Bremen, who were later expelled from the party, voted with the CDU on issues of social spending, presumably their way of protesting the SPD's outmoded Keynesianism. Beneath all this was a conviction that the era of "ecological" politics was now superseding that of class struggle, which many Greens considered a relic of earlier capitalist development. From this viewpoint, the truly significant movements of the future will be those concerning qualitative issues, including self-management at the workplace.[71]

But the Greens, while affirming their primary commitment to the local movements, set out to correct this deficiency in 1983, beginning with their thirty-nine-page economic statement at Sindelfingen. It merged the views of both the "reds" and the "ecologists." At the same time the Greens were cooperating with DGB leaders to work out a preliminary program for social conversion, and they later offered support to a number of unions in their militant struggle for a thirty-five-hour week. Still, the earlier charges contained enough validity to leave the Greens with an anti–working-class image that would be difficult to erase. Throughout their first years they had failed to sink roots in any labor constituency, a result not merely of the Greens' programmatic inadequacy but of most workers' perceptions that the goals of the new movements, if realized, would mean a reduction of jobs and a decline in living standards. And the labor movement, for its part, remained aloof from new-movement issues—with the notable exception of the metalworkers, who joined in the struggles of environmentalists and peace activists.

By 1985, therefore, the Greens' capacity not only to confront the economic crisis but to expand their popular base depended upon their linkages with labor. And the crisis presented new political opportunities as the postwar corporatist framework began to unravel with the onset of high unemployment and austerity. During 1984 the DGB initiated a wave of strikes in support of the thirty-five-hour week, culminating in partial victory. The diffusion of new priorities within the labor movement (e.g., concerning "control" issues) suggested at least the possibility of convergence with the new movements—for example, in the areas of social conversion, occupational safety and health, public sector cutbacks, and of course democratic participation. This intricate connection of themes and issues is at the heart of Green politics and will clearly be the key to the party's future success. Yet the problem is more complex. Unresolved is whether the Greens should establish direct ties with the trade-union structure or with the rank and file, whether qualitative demands should take precedence over quantitative ones, and so forth. Progress along these lines, both conceptually and practically, has been very slow in developing.

A third realm of problems is the potential demobilizing impact of three ideological strains—direct democracy, spiritualism, and commitment to nonviolence. The Greens have upheld the norms of democratic participation in order to differentiate themselves from the mainstream parties. In part this was a reaction against the strong authoritarian impulses of German political culture, in part an expression of feminist and ecological sensibilities. However, the ethos of direct democracy and minimal leadership, when pushed to its extremes, could easily harm the Greens' capacity to carry out effective political action, inside or outside legislative bodies. The *form* of activity (excessive attention to "process," interminable debates over organizational matters, harsh attacks on any form of leadership) might ultimately prevail over its substance.

Soon after the Greens' entry into the Bundestag some leaders expressed resentment over limitations imposed by strict participatory edicts and by persistent chafing criticisms from the base. Starting in 1983, therefore, party rules that embraced rotating leadership and the imperative mandate came under increasing attack, leading to explosive internal divisions and, ultimately, to a suspension of efforts to frame a unified statement. By 1984 the pendulum appeared to swing to the other end: the leadership stratum gathered new strength, ties between the national organization and the regions became more tenuous, and the parliamentary group gradually set itself off from the party structure as a whole. The chief difficulty is that abstract endorsements of direct democracy are bound to generate one of two possible extremes—political impotence resulting from lack of leadership and coordination, or ascendancy of a bureaucratic leadership in the absence of concrete mediating forms or institutional restraints. On the whole, the Greens have suffered most from the first of these maladies. As Eberhard, Trampert, Thea Bock, and others have argued, wide-open, unstructured debates have often degenerated into chaos, blocking prospects for ideological direction and political unity. The constant rotating of leaders, moreover, militates against both competence in tasks and continuity of goals within the party. To help solve these problems, Joschka Fisher proposed what for Green ideology had been unthinkable—the introduction of a corps of full-time, paid functionaries to provide a coherent steering mechanism for the organization.[72] A related problem is that making a fetish of direct democracy can easily reinforce a doctrinal purism at the base, whereby leaders who are politically successful or culturally prominent can be denounced as compromisers or renegades. When taken too seriously, these sentiments give rise to an isolated culture of protest in which virtually any form of concrete action becomes impossible.[73]

To avoid letting such tendencies get out of control, the Greens will need a more structurally concise concept of democracy that balances the poles of leadership and mass participation, centralized organization and local autonomy, the process and substance of political action. This requires a fuller strategic understanding of the relationship between party and civil society, party and state, without which the Green vision of a "new politics" will never be more than an abstract utopian ideal.

The "spiritual" dimension of Green politics raises equally troublesome issues. As we have seen, many party activists—mainly within the Fundi wing—call attention to the humanistic and even mystical component of the struggle for social transformation. Besides Bahro's frequent references to religious experience and to the idea of a "reconstruction of God" as a driving element in contemporary radicalism, we have Kelly's call for harmony between the intellectual, physical, and spiritual sides of life, for a return to the "religious character of love."[74] This type of spiritual emphasis can be traced, at least in part, to a powerful Green naturalist or romantic opposition to the rational-legal culture spawned by industrialism and bureaucracy. It reflects the drive to overcome alienation by recapturing a collective sense of meaning and purpose destroyed by a materialist civilization. More than that, it seek to reunite humans with nature by reproducing a "mode of consciousness in which the individual feels connected to the cosmos as a whole."[75] In this way religion, broadly defined, negates and transcends the secular character of modern life.

Even though a majority of Greens do not share this outlook, it is widespread enough to be the source of intense controversy at times. One problem is that the presumed content of spiritualism—for example, in references to the "reconstruction of God"—is never clearly spelled out in any of the Green literature. What do religious values, however construed, add to a radical ideology that is already well developed to cover a comprehensive range of issues? Second, insofar as such values have been historically linked to the notion of totality and to all-inclusive belief systems with their cults, gurus, and absolutist visions, their totalitarian implications cannot be easily dismissed. The recent appearance of absolutist religious sects in the industrialized countries suggests that these dangers are very much alive. Third, there is a profoundly escapist tendency in the search for other-worldly spheres of meaning insofar as the flight from material or productivist values can easily lead to an antimodernist retreat from efforts to change real exploitative economic and social relations. To be sure, this has hardly been the main direction of Green activity through 1986, but the awkward presence of mystical tendencies could sharpen party divisions and, should they become stronger, block the growth of radicalism within the party.[76] A religious consciousness tied to a mystical other-worldliness can offer only illusory panaceas for the crisis of legitimacy.

Finally, there is the complex and emotionally laden issue of nonviolence. With few exceptions, the Greens adhere to some general and vague notion of pacifism, to a Gandhian style of nonviolent politics. As I have suggested, this attachment goes far beyond the adoption of specific methods; it embraces an entirely new way of life that would subvert, by its powerful force of example, a bourgeois civilization that is violent to its core. For the Greens, violence in the service of any end is morally wrong, especially where that violence is directed against human (as opposed to material) targets, and they have generally followed such precepts in practice. However, a principled commitment to nonviolence opens the door to a number of ambiguities the Greens have never seriously confronted.

The crucial question is whether distinctly transformative goals—those that lead to an overturning of the structures of domination—can be realized without the employment of some violent or coercive tactics. The goal of a nonviolent society is one thing; the unwavering, absolute dedication to pacifist values in the context of a violent social order, something else. The power structure, today more than ever, is controlled by relatively small groups of elites willing to mobilize whatever force is necessary to protect their interests. Although oppositional movements can incorporate some pacifist themes (as in the attack on militarism and the arms race), the future radicalization of these movements will require a more flexible approach than can be supplied by a morally rigid pacifism. In political warfare the reduction of options inevitably provides the enemy with enormous tactical advantages. Moreover, it can be argued that pacifist submission to violence (in the broadest sense) will never effectively counter violence but in the end only perpetuate it. Since coercion of all types is an integral and daily part of the bourgeois system, especially where the war economy is strong, even the most militant expressions of peaceful civil disobedience will fall short of producing fundamental changes in the class structure and state system. Many Green and peace-movement activists argue just the opposite—that widespread nonviolent disruption can generate real change as part of an expanding pacifist culture of resistance, and they cite the studies of Sharp and others to demonstrate how nonviolence has led to positive historical results. But the evidence is not as conclusive as is typically claimed.

The Gandhian example that the Greens are fond of citing would seem to contradict rather than support the efficacy of pacifist methods. Though Gandhi did lead a mass-based movement inspired by a nonviolent strategy, and though that movement did succeed (with considerable help) in throwing the British out of India, it clearly did not produce any basic changes in the class structure or social system, nor did it effectively combat the chronic ills of Indian society: repression, disease, hunger, and poverty.[77] Gandhi was tied so closely to indigenous ruling-class interests—indeed, to the struggle for hegemony of a national bourgeoisie—that he could not possibly have encouraged a wholesale social revolution. Pacifism in this context therefore corresponded to the efforts (on the part of both Gandhi and the Indian bourgeoisie) to channel mass energy into a system-sustaining politics. More than that, much of Gandhi's nonviolent philosophy was connected to a romanticization of poverty and tradition along with mystical illusions fed by a rhetoric of moral renewal, populist enfranchisement, and cosmic oneness of humanity. Thus, in the Indian as in other cases, pacifist forms of opposition gave the appearance of total rejection although in fact they were fully prepared to coexist with the old power structure. The Gandhian example, in other words, proves quite the opposite of what the advocates of nonviolent methods contend. It is worth pondering whether the Green version of pacifism would have similar implications for West German politics in the 1980s and beyond.

The last range of obstacles that could impede Green radical advances is one familiar to the experience of any party immersed in electoral politics, that of possible integration into the bourgeois public sphere and, with it, deradicalization. The Greens discuss this danger often, given their obsession with identity and autonomy. The challenge is rather imposing: how to avoid those domesticating forces that overwhelmed, first, European social democracy and then, in the postwar period, the Communist parties of the industrialized West. There is little reason to believe that, in the 1980s, the Michelsian dilemma of institutionalization is any less ominous for leftist parties than it was earlier in the twentieth century.[78]

Yet the Greens remain a party sui generis, and there are factors operating in their case that might resist the Michelsian pattern. Thus, the novel effort to articulate a new politics grounded in a balance between electoral activity and grassroots mobilization obviously distinguishes the Greens from parties that have devoted the bulk of their resources to parliamentary and interest-group politics. The Green program—in the attention it lavishes on participatory democracy, qualitative change, and cultural radicalism—is designed to subvert pressures toward assimilation. Green political style has been altogether different from the instrumentalism typical of the Social Democrats and Communists. For the present, moreover, the Greens are a small party lacking the kind of mass membership (still only 35,000 in 1985), entrenched leadership, and institutional position of the conventional leftist parties. They have a license to pursue an independent path because structural reformism is not yet a realistic option. There is, finally, the strong pull of the social movements toward local, extra-institutional initiatives, even if this influence on the Greens was already in decline by 1985.

Still, a steady Green electoral advance could favor assimilationist tendencies that even the most determined leadership and dynamic local struggles might not be able to resist completely. Green participation in the Bundestag has already encouraged a structural adaptation that would likely be accelerated if the Realos faction is able to establish broader control over the party organization.[79] Without doubt the Greens were, by 1986, fully integrated into the parliamentary arena, both locally and nationally. Whatever their initial ambivalence toward electoralism, they accepted their legislative tasks with cheerful enthusiasm (for instance, by joining all of the Bundestag committees in the first year). The cooptative dynamic inherent in this situation seems obvious enough: the West German parliamentary milieu is one of extremely competitive social relations, elitism, and patriarchal norms—all at odds with the alternative style of work championed by the Greens. This type of setting reproduces a pragmatic organizational style, not to mention a separation between legislative sphere and local base, which the media reinforces through its focus on leaders as celebrities.

On this terrain the Green experience through 1985 has been emphatically mixed. First, the party has not (and probably could not) become an institutionalized fixture of the bourgeois state; its deep presence in the new movements, even if reduced in scope, would at the very least retard this process. At the same time, it cannot be denied that some kind of adaptive momentum has been set in motion since the party's entry into the Bundestag. Seen in the context of the familiar German contrast between *Machtkontrolle*, "restraint of power," and *Machterweb*, "pursuit of power," the Greens more and more find themselves giving priority to the latter: they are willing to compromise their new politics in the sense that the struggle for institutional power is no longer regarded as making a pact with the devil. To be sure, many Greens (again, mostly Fundis) hold out against this drift, but as the logic of parliamentarism and alliance politics clashes with the logic of democratic radicalism, integrative tendencies are difficult to block entirely. The party's resistance to the pull of "old" politics has in some measure broken down. Some sympathetic observers even argue that the Green parliamentary faction has already become divorced and insulated from its popular base, that excessive attention devoted to electoral activity has begun to demobilize the social movements, and that the organization has become steadily more dependent upon the state for financial support and access to mass media.[80] Others have gone further, suggesting that the Greens have become "functional" to the West German system by virtue of their ongoing involvement in the bourgeois state.[81] Of course, it is still too early to establish such generalizations with any certainty.

At the same time, integrative tendencies have been serious enough to produce a mood of vigilance within the Green orbit. Debates throughout 1984–85 revolved around how much energy should be devoted to electoral campaigns—on the assumption (of many) that the equilibrium between party and movements, electoralism and grassroots activism, has tilted too far in the former direction. Conventional politics can be an important source of jobs, money, and influence, but it is primarily within civil society that the Greens will have to build a counterhegemonic identity that could sustain a broad-based radical opposition. This implies not only a harnessing of new-movement energy but an infusion of "green" themes and priorities. To this end, some have pointed to a strategy of creating "local majorities" with emphasis on local and regional activity that would unite the two realms of change. Others have urged concentrating on specific strategic issues instead of trying to incorporate a totality of concerns or cater to numerous clientele groups. An example of such a focus might be the struggle for an alternative (Green) industrial policy.[82] The outcome of debates over these issues, as well as over how to confront the SPD and labor, will help decide the party's evolution.

For the present, however, the gulf between the Greens and the dominant party structure is too vast for absorption to be imminent. The originality of Green politics, which speaks a language of "break" or "rupture" with the past (but not of revolution in the classical sense), remains essentially intact.[83] More pressing is how to translate new-movement goals into a coherent programmatic alternative without losing sight of complex material and class issues. For example, the Greens have yet to articulate a strategy for transforming capital, one that specifies the mechanisms whereby the system of production can be effectively socialized.

Perhaps because of their proximity to the new movements and their qualitative concerns, the Greens have avoided wrestling with complex economic issues: above all, they have never specified the material dimensions of a transitional system that would anticipate the principles of an alternative ecological model. The party program does seem to anticipate an entirely new framework of accumulation with different forms of ownership, planning, and labor process, but such questions remain theoretically unexplored. The Greens tend to sidestep critical issues of political economy that have occupied Marxists for more than a century: the relationship between ownership and control, market and plan, micro (local) and macro (societal) levels of development. More specifically, there is a failure to address the problem of who owns the instruments of capital accumulation, thus perpetuating the fallacy that popular control can be exercised without socializing the means of production. Green economics does point toward a transcendence of both the Keynesian welfare state and Soviet-style state socialism—toward something akin to a democratic socialism with an ecological overlay—but nowhere are its constituent elements clearly defined. Much like the early utopian socialists, the Greens devote sparse attention to the strategic linkages between present and future, between existing material reality and ultimate vision, although Werner Hülsberg's contention that "the program slides into a utopian vision of social harmony" is greatly exaggerated. Still, Hülsberg offers a valid critique when he notes, "There is no mention of social classes, the struggle between them, or of the bourgeois state that presides over capitalist society."[84] True enough, this flaw can be attributed in part to programmatic compromises needed to satisfy the different Green tendencies. Nonetheless, in the absence of clear formulations it will be difficult for the party to resist the pull of social-democratic reformism, which of course would leave the capitalist system intact; such logic would prevail more or less by default. Some Green intellectuals, conscious of this predicament, have sought to lay the groundwork for a more explicit anticapitalist, "eco-socialist" alternative, but such views do not command anything close to a majority.[85]

Beyond such theoretical issues, there are some immediate psychological concerns: pessimism and even apathy began to overcome many Green activists after mid-1985, in the aftermath of electoral defeats in the Saarland and in North Rheinland-Westphalia.[86] Party members often expressed boredom over interminable ideological debates as well as frustration with internal factionalism that showed no signs of disappearing. (In some cases debates became vitriolic and led to harsh personal exchanges in violation of the spirit of Green democracy.) Moreover, the period of fascination with the Green upsurge between 1980 and 1983 seemed to have crested. An increasing number of members and supporters could be heard complaining that being a Green was no longer so exciting. The phase of relatively easy and quick breakthroughs on the basis of widespread moral protest soon yielded to a period of soul-searching, even doubt.[87]

Still, the fact that the Greens have been subjected to ideological assaults of the sort that the SPD has not encountered since before World War I suggests that they are perceived as a threat, even if not an insurrectionary one, to the West German power structure. They have been repudiated as "enemies of parliamentary democracy," "opponents of economic progress," and romantic nationalists looking for the return to an idyllic preindustrial order. And of course they have been scorned as hopeless "utopians." Yet, whatever the assorted dilemmas and road-blocks encountered by the Greens—and they are many, as we have seen—criticisms of this sort add little to serious discourse or analysis.

THE DIFFUSION OF GREEN POLITICS

The immense ideological energy and political originality brought for-ward by the Greens inspired a pervasive optimism about the "global promise" of a new phase of radicalism for the industrialized countries. Yet the Green phenomenon has taken root as a popular force only in West Germany. This raises the question as to whether, and in what ways, Green politics is so unique to the German context that initiatives elsewhere are likely to be problematic. The historical and geographical specificity of the Green model would seem to be evident. In the words of one hostile observer, the Greens represent a "Utopian idealism, political romanticism, an overreaction to the Nazi past, a kind of adolescent rebellion against stepfather America: all this comes through in the voices of German intellectuals—voices which sound a strange, high note of apocalyptic alarm."[88] Leaving aside the harsh oversimplification of such attacks, it is still true that the Greens' appeal has been made possible by a unique convergence of developments and issues: the absence of Ger-man national sovereignty, a growing concentration of nuclear weapons in central Europe, intensive urbanization, the legacy of fascism and the conflict of generations, and closure of the West German party system.

But the Green metaphor for a postliberal and post-Marxist radicalism —reflected in a mosaic of tendencies, groups, networks, and themes— does have significance beyond German boundaries. Surely, the circum-stances underlying the Green success in West Germany, including the arms race, economic crisis, decline of the party system, and personal alienation, are universal in their scope if not in their political impact. Popular struggles for peace, social equality, democratization, preserva-tion of the environment, racial and sexual equality are hardly specific to German politics, even if they have converged in a uniquely explosive fashion there.

It is perhaps accurate to say that the West German Greens lie at the center of an emergent tradition that is being diffused elsewhere—though not precisely along the lines of any global model. Green-oriented movements and parties of diverse types have appeared throughout the advanced capitalist world—for example, in Holland, Belgium, England, Ireland, France, Italy, Canada, and the United States—since 1980. The first European Congress of Greens, held at Liège, Belgium, in April 1984, attracted delegates from eight European countries interested in establishing a broad network of communications (but not an ideological or programmatic consensus).[89] Competing in the 1984 European parliamentary elections, a Green-style Progressive Alliance won two seats while furnishing a pole of attraction for pacifists, feminists, ecologists, the unemployed, and other elements of the left. The small British Ecology party has sought to model itself after the West German Greens.[90] In the United States, an initial effort toward a unified Green alternative took place in August 1984, when at St. Paul, Minnesota, hundreds of activists gathered for a Greens Committee of Correspondence meeting. Here again, divisions over how to define (and carry out) Green politics stood in the way of cohesive ideological or organizational statements. In both Western Europe and North America a new politics has grown out of the energy of new social movements and has received additional impetus from the dissemination of literature on "green" concerns— holism, deep ecology, pacifism, feminism, and so forth. The political context, moreover, is typically one of generalized disillusionment with the traditional parties (including the Socialists and Communists).

Still, these developments—whether self-consciously Green or not— quite often depart from the West German example. Thus, in most countries there is nothing resembling a coherent Green party, with its own ideological and organizational identity as well as a mass presence in the political system. Not only do Green tendencies elsewhere lack the radical articulation of the German party, they tend to be more hostile to leftist and working-class politics. The very amorphousness of Green activity in other countries seems more compatible with either a "new-age" populism or a libertarian communalism tied to the revolt against modernism. To what degree the relative lack of popular support for a Green alternative outside West Germany accounts for this type of "soft" or countercultural definition remains unclear.

The customary American translation of Green politics fits this pattern rather neatly: its promise is to progressively build upon the American heritage of civic participation, decentralization, and local self-help, with the hope of rising above the conventional views of left and right that have chronically stood in the way of fresh departures.[91] From this standpoint, new-age ideology unites a remarkably broad range of movements and groups with a holistic vision of transformation rooted in continuity and respect for established customs and cultural motifs. "Green" in this sense is defined as antithetical to the entire European leftist tradition, which is dismissed as hopelessly obsolete, enmeshed as it is in the paradigm of industrial civilization and bureaucratic politics.

The very breadth and eclecticism of Green ideology, however, obstructs the development of a theory and practice of radical change. It tends to sidestep what needs to be confronted directly—namely, the issues of capital accumulation and political power. The result is often little more than an old-fashioned liberal-populist critique of socialism that looks to an illusory solution attached to the limited reality of small-scale communities.[92] The meaningless slogan "neither left nor right" in fact amounts to either a form of escapism or an endorsement of the status quo (modified slightly to accommodate more local autonomy)—or both. The call for decentralization and citizen empowerment lacks substance because it ignores the structural and material sources of domination that lie at the heart of those crises that new-age theorists bemoan. There is, simultaneously, a peculiarly moral character to the Americanized version of Green politics in its fascination with social bonding, mutuality, and trust—all elements of the Rousseauian concept of community and themes that strike a deep chord in American history. Ironically, this species of moralism breeds precisely those qualities of dogmatism, sectarianism, and vanguardism that many Green theorists are so eager to attack in the Marxist or socialist left. These flaws are similar to those of spiritualism: the flight from conflict toward a commitment to moral (or spiritual) regeneration has absolutist and antidemocratic implications, which inevitably undermine the ideal of grassroots participation so central to the Green vision.

If some form of Green politics is to gain ascendancy in the West, it will almost certainly have to dispense with most of this new-age outlook. Success will probably depend on a convergence, rather than polarization, of the radical (or democratic-socialist) left and deep-ecology thematics, not a jettisoning of the former. Holism can have a truly subversive meaning only when aligned with a class-based socialist ideology, not against it. Hence the symbols *red* and *green* do not emerge as polar opposites but as complementary strains within a broader leftist tradition, assuming that by *red* we mean an outlook that is no longer narrowly conceived as workerist or vanguardist, as Leninist or social democratic. There can be no real "exit" from either industrial society or an authoritarian state system—only the potential to reshape these destructive realities by democratizing and socializing those global economic and political structures that actually exist, and this requires a balanced political strategy of the sort outlined above. The West German Greens, during their brief existence, have at least posed such an alternative in realistic and yet visionary terms. They have, despite their myriad shortcomings, laid the basis of a renewed public sphere in which democratic-radical change can be more openly advanced.

6

SOCIAL MOVEMENTS
AND RADICAL CHANGE

The diverse social movements explored in this book have all developed in accordance with their peculiar rhythms or cycles since the 1960s: their ideological and political impact has varied greatly from setting to setting, from moment to moment, not following a unilinear logic or flow. Yet the persistent social dynamism underlying these movements—not to mention the structural contradictions they express—indicate that they will remain a vital source of political opposition in the industrialized world. Popular movements linked to the demands of antinuclear activists, ecologists, urban communities, women, minorities, and youth correspond to changing economic realities, social and cultural forces, and political constellations that are only beginning to coalesce and that, in time, promise to reshape class and social conflict. These new phenomena amount to an emergent social bloc that would revitalize civil society against incursions of the bureaucratic state, commodity production, the spiraling arms race—against bourgeois hegemony in general. The very multiplicity of struggles reflects their penetration into every sphere of human existence; social conflict is more pluralistic and dispersed than ever. Perhaps more than anything else, the new movements have introduced a legacy of political discourse that challenges myths of the "end of ideology," "one-dimensionality," and welfare-state prosperity along with the deadening formulas of the traditional left.

In leading toward a renewal of the public sphere, this new phase of struggle poses a broad challenge to the dominant modes of discourse in economics, culture, the family, sexuality, and political life itself.[1] It captures the strong democratizing and modernizing trends at work in the West throughout the postwar years. Despite the continued governance of right-wing forces in a number of countries (the United States,

Britain, West Germany), the overall direction of change has been toward disintegration of many traditional institutions and values. Throughout the industrialized world conservative regimes were destroyed (fascism, the military dictatorships) or were thrown on the defensive (Gaullism in France, Christian Democracy in other parts of the Mediterranean). Mass participation in its infinite varieties has increased incrementally, and sometimes dramatically, though largely outside formal party systems and state structures. Appearing as the antithesis of corporatist integration, social pluralism and localism are gathering strength. Not only popular consciousness, but public policy, has been altered significantly as an outgrowth of progressive struggles on many fronts: civil and minority rights, the role of women, cultural tolerance, the environment, and so forth.[2] The new movements appear simultaneously as cause and effect: though democratization is in some sense an outgrowth of these movements, at the same time it provides enlarged space for their further growth.

A major premise of the foregoing chapters, however, is that the new movements possess no necessary or intrinsic ideological content, radical or otherwise. Their historical meaning has depended upon, and will continue to depend upon, their relationship to one or another political formation shaped by particular visions and strategies. I have analyzed three such formations (Eurosocialism, new populism, the Greens), each with its own promises, dilemmas, and contradictions. The post-Marxist character of these formations hardly guarantees any radical or even progressive outcome, as I have tried to demonstrate. On the contrary, the complex political mediations between new movements and the state have more often than not generated integrative tendencies very similar to those identified by Michels and other theorists in their studies of social democracy. Among these three alternatives, only the Greens seem to have posed (in theoretical terms) a clear radical or counterhegemonic challenge to the general system of domination. But the Greens, too, have run up against their share of difficulties, as we have seen.

The purpose of this chapter is to explore the potential consequences of new-movement activity for the development of a radical-democratic phase of change in the West—admittedly on the basis of a brief historical span. What obstacles and dilemmas do the different post-Marxist formations confront in the industrialized world? What are the constituent elements of a radical-democratic "model" against which these efforts might be measured? What are the general prospects for a transformative politics grounded in the experiences of the new movements? Although no conclusive answers to such questions are now possible, it might be fruitful to address them within a conceptual framework that focuses attention on four areas of analysis: the global economic and military situation; the economy and class forces; the state and the general problem of social organization; and the struggle for ideological hegemony.

THE GLOBAL DIMENSION

Insofar as the workings of the international economy give rise to intense forms of national competition, the policymaking of all Western governments is bound to be shaped by the priorities of capital. The task of managing perpetual crisis sets definite boundaries to what economic solutions can be realistically advanced or implemented. Even where the left is in power, the goal seems to be a dynamic and competitive domestic economy that can weather the capricious turns and pressures of the world market. Any program that hinders a fluid process of capital accumulation will predictably be jettisoned, even if this means a worsening of unemployment, renewed labor strife, and austerity measures.

Even though Social Democratic parties have typically followed this pattern, adapting to the logic of capital in countries where they were able to win state power, they were rarely forced along the path of austerity owing to the much stronger growth potential of their economies. Global pressures constituted a lesser impediment to material expansion. Yet, though the choice today between a status quo politics and a radical, anticapitalist alternative may have more far-reaching implications than before, and though unimaginative system-sustaining programs are more difficult to justify on socialist grounds, when faced with this set of options leftist governments regularly carry out policies designed to administer the capitalist system (and the bureaucratic state) more efficiently. The imperatives of economic rationalization are both more universal and more controlling than in the past. Further, as I have argued in Chapter 2, the productivist side of Marxism converges perfectly with these imperatives. Not only social democrats but Eurocommunists, too, were ready to introduce restructuring and austerity programs with the aim of restoring a semblance of economic stability and competitive dynamism. And the Eurosocialists, whatever their protests to the contrary, have in the space of only a few years fallen into the same morass. By 1985 the policies of Mitterrand, Gonzales, and Papandreou (not to mention those of Craxi and Mário Soares) were undeniably tied to the needs of capital accumulation—to the securing of national advantage within the world market. And the outcome has been predictable enough. Rationalizing goals have been justified by the claim that economic stability, technological progress, and labor productivity are vital to sustained growth, without which the transition to socialism could never be initiated. However, the long experience of social-democratic governments reveals the fallacy of this premise, since the reconsolidation of capital only serves to repress and distort rather than actualize socialist possibilities. Put another way, rationalizing programs do more to reproduce than to subvert the structures of domination.

The new populism, on the other hand, seeks to bypass these dilemmas by pursuing an essentially localist strategy. To win and exercise local power does not require any serious or immediate intervention in the global crisis. The most pressing concern is to chart a new path of community development stressing manageable local issues. Of course the reality of the international (and national) industrial and financial systems cannot be ignored entirely, but new populists are confident that quintessentially urban issues of rent control, tax reform, social services, and land-use patterns can be confronted without the need for a comprehensive economic plan. They are convinced that people can be more easily mobilized around themes close to everyday life, that neighborhood autonomy and human-scale development must therefore take precedence over classical growth objectives. In fact, however, such localist emphasis merely defers coming to grips with the global crisis until a later period when, presumably, the cumulative impact of small-scale political successes will add up to a national presence, with its new opportunities and choices. Here one finds little in either theory or practice—aside from general references to "limits of growth"—to indicate that the new populists can avoid those pitfalls that overwhelmed Eurosocialism. Neither has outlined a plan for reconstructing the economy along different lines, and neither has offered a radically insightful approach to state power.

Of the three strategies, only the Greens confront these problems head-on within a qualitatively new framework: the concepts of deep ecology, ecological development, social conversion, and demilitarization, though never fully worked out in the Green literature, do suggest a model of political economy (or social ecology) that subverts the logic of capital accumulation insofar as it questions the "requirements" of enhanced productivity, technological restructuring, military production, and the frantic search for new sources of investment. This is not so much a question of "exiting" from industrial society as of subordinating the economy, with all of its technological achievements, to the domain of social needs. Of course, the abolition of military-related production— not really a priority for the Eurosocialists—would free vast amounts of human and physical resources that are presently wasted. To the extent that Green economics could reverse tendencies toward irrational competition within the global market, further rationalizing processes would lose their ideological justification.

Perhaps the Greens are much too cavalier about the difficulties of reversing this global economic pattern. They seem to have largely ignored the problems of capital flight and technological stagnation that would probably accompany any drastic effort to break with the imperatives of capital. The ecological model, at least in its present form, lacks a transitional character. The Greens' developmental project is devoid of the strategic concreteness needed to counter the effects of an internationalized capitalist system in which the centers of economic power are impervious to national control mechanisms. Decisions made by national governments can be subverted by the greater mobility of capital, by the capacity of a relatively small nucleus of industrial, financial, and managerial elites to control the deployment of resources. By the same token, popular victories in one setting are readily nullified by a rapid shift of capital to yet another setting.[3] Moreover, as Castells argues, the formation of an increasingly unified worldwide production network has a dual outcome: it allows for the centralization and coordination of capital flows, but it simultaneously fragments markets, work processes, and social control functions. In this context local movements can be seen as attempts to recover meaning and autonomy in a world where real decision making has shifted to the transnational arena—but without disturbing the larger global structures.[4] Such a dualism may well be at work in West Germany. Still, even if the Greens have not fully grasped that dialectic, they have at least begun to theorize the foundations of an alternative path.

If global economic forces tend to favor the capitalist rationalizing impulses of specific nation-states, the other side of the international situation—the arms race, nuclear politics, cold-war rivalry—reinforces superpower domination in the deepest ideological and psychological sense, as a clear expression of bourgeois hegemony. More than that: economic and military conditions alike function to repress or domesticate popular movements in every region of the world—developing countries, the Soviet bloc, the West.

As George Konrad observes, the military balance of power established in the aftermath of World War II has determined the political status quo, rather than vice versa. Those power structures that deploy the most missiles, bombs, and tanks decisively influence the overall character of social systems.[5] Today, the nuclear arms race permits great-power interests and nationalism (or bloc identity) to shape politics, especially in Europe, far more than in the past. Under such conditions it is difficult if not impossible for "organic" social and political forces to assert themselves fully. The nuclear umbrella allows both the United States and the Soviet Union, through NATO and the Warsaw Pact, to strengthen the prevailing international order. Konrad suggests that the arms race functions more to preserve superpower control than to defend particular values or beliefs (liberal democracy, socialism, and the like), which are cynically manipulated for purposes of legitimation. One result is the disenfranchisement of citizens in both spheres of control. Thus, struggles for local autonomy (Polish Solidarity, the European peace movement) have been denied complete expression since great-power hegemony has restricted the space for maneuver. Nuclear politics thereby assists in the triumph of state over civil society, characterized by the erosion of an active and lively political culture, both East and West. The "reasonable" options—either U.S. capitalism or Soviet Communism—are ultimately false ones that can be transcended only through a large-scale refusal to cooperate with the statist imperatives of global competition, by an affirmation of what Konrad calls "anti-politics."[6]

In the West this predicament is connected to a double mythology—that of Soviet military supremacy, and that of a Soviet totalitarianism bent on relentless military expansion and conquest. During the Reagan years such mythology has reached entirely new proportions. Mindless anti-Soviet hysteria obscures the fact that the NATO countries have enjoyed a huge (if diminishing) technological and military superiority over Warsaw Pact countries throughout the postwar years, and that the United States exercises much greater international leverage than the Soviets owing to its leading role in the world capitalist economy and its commanding military presence.[7] More to the point, obsession with the Soviet Union inevitably distorts analysis of, and undermines support for, virtually any type of left-wing opposition (including some of the new movements). Antinuclear campaigns, for example, are often discredited because of their presumed naïveté concerning Soviet intentions and their own role in objectively weakening NATO's capacity to defend against Soviet aggression. So long as the Soviets are effectively portrayed as a dangerous enemy of freedom and democracy, cold-war patriotism will remain an integral part of the political culture (notably in the United States)—and radical goals will be forced outside this nationalist consensus. There is every temptation, even within some sectors of the left, to subordinate all concerns to the more urgent priority of containing Soviet power. In the United States this state of affairs has had a chilling influence on the development of critical thought and radical politics insofar as it ideologically marginalizes those forces that seek even a modest reversal of the arms race.[8] The very shape of political discourse in the West, then, where it revolves around the themes of national security, the Communist threat, and terrorism, tends to stifle the growth of a mass-based opposition.

The Eurosocialist parties came to power as firm if ambivalent opponents of Western militarism, including NATO's decision to install the Euromissiles. Party leaders expressed discomfort over bloc-oriented politics—specifically over the U.S. military presence in their countries. Moreover, they were (and continue to be) critical of American policies in the Third World, notably in Central America. Yet, for a variety of reasons, the Eurosocialists (with the partial exception of PASOK in Greece) rather quickly withdrew to familiar social-democratic ground: dedication to Atlanticism, cold-war politics, endorsement (however qualified) of American global aims. As we have seen, in the period from 1981 to 1985 the Mediterranean Socialists turned back from their earlier promises and, in the process, entered into a tense relationship with the peace movement. This shift can be attributed to three major factors: a residual anti-Sovietism inherited from their social-democratic predecessors, U.S. economic and political pressures, and the absence of a programmatic alternative to conventional bloc-style foreign relations.

The new populism, for its part, managed on the strength of its localist politics to essentially sidestep foreign-policy issues in much the same way it was able to avoid directly confronting global economic problems. Given the overwhelming emphasis upon community-defined issues, debates over international politics were bound to be viewed as unnecessary distractions at best, potentially divisive intrusions at worst. On occasion, progressive city councils passed resolutions in support of foreign-policy positions, from endorsement of anti-apartheid struggles in South Africa to calls for U.S. disengagement from Central America, but such actions demanded little commitment of political resources or real programmatic initiatives. Although social-service demands are a driving force behind the new populism, and although massive public-sector cutbacks result in part from astronomical increases in military spending, little attention was devoted to the arms race itself as the underlying basis (and rationale) of such lopsided, irrational economic priorities. Since efforts to revitalize social programs cannot be divorced from the budgetary effects of military spending, new-populist localism is caught in an impasse. Unless this connection is made, not only the resources but the very political mechanisms needed to spur new modes of community development will be lacking. And resolutions endorsing peace and nonintervention, however well intentioned and symbolically valuable, can never be the vehicle of concrete struggles against militarism.

The Greens, on the other hand, have chosen to tackle the global political situation more or less directly—indeed, this is one of their hallmarks. They have consistently denounced bloc politics, whatever its ideological rationale, and of course they helped to coordinate the European-wide campaign against the Euromissiles. They have no illusions about the ideological claims of either NATO or Soviet-bloc countries: each side is viewed as a threat to world peace, if for entirely different reasons. The Greens' exceptionally strong peace commitments allow them to retain a close (if always tense) linkage with peace organizations, a relationship never really developed within Eurosocialism (again, except for PASOK) or the new populism. Perhaps most significant, the Green political style (openness of discourse, decentralization, personal politics, direct action) rather closely corresponds to that of the antinuclear movement. At the same time, a number of critical problems remain. There is above all no real consensus within the Greens about how to strategically counter the military apparatus or the bloc system, or how to approach the Soviet Union—admittedly thorny problems but ones requiring far more depth of analysis than the Greens have provided to date. Intense divisions over such issues have already led to a breakdown in personal relations among some Green activists. Moreover, the critical themes posed by Konrad could become more salient with time. Specifically, in a Germany still divided between East and West, and where anti-Soviet feelings run deep in the West, the obstacles to subverting U.S.-NATO hegemony in its claim to be a bulwark against Soviet power are not likely to disappear.[9] The decline of the West German peace movement after 1983 reveals the great difficulties in restoring "organic political processes" in a cold-war milieu, despite the important breakthroughs of the early 1980s. Here as elsewhere the capacity of national parties (or governments), acting alone, to challenge omnipresent global restraints is certain to be minimal.

A NEW PHASE OF CLASS POLITICS

A second order of strategic dilemmas that any radical opposition will encounter involves the convergence of three factors—the economic crisis, class forces, and the new movements. Put another way, social transformation in the West will require a confluence of labor struggles and popular movements, quantitative and qualitative demands, within a unified theoretical and strategic perspective. Innovation has taken shape slowly, in part because there has been so much antagonism between the two realms: organized trade-union activity versus grassroots mobilization, immediate reforms versus universal goals, "old" versus "new" left ideologies. Of course fundamentally new departures would be impossible without the reconstitution of both labor and the new movements in their present form, a prospect never envisioned by the post-Marxist formations explored in this book.

Perhaps the most fertile terrain for such an historic merger of interests and priorities is the permanent war economy, which links the concerns of antimilitarism, material well-being, and social needs—potentially bringing together the energies of labor, the peace movement, and other popular struggles—within a common outlook. Viewed from this angle, militarism represents something beyond the problem of the arms race narrowly defined. It must be understood within the context of a political economy designed to mobilize vast amounts of resources devoted to wasteful and destructive ends. The results, even in the absence of large-scale military confrontation, are visible enough: a civilian economy that is drained, social services and programs that are gutted, an environment that is being ruined, the fanning of patriotic sentiments, and a strengthening of the bureaucratic state. For many industrialized nations the military–industrial infrastructure plays a more decisive role than ever in shaping development. With the United States far in the lead, countries throughout the world currently spend roughly $600 billion a year for armaments and their support systems, of which about $100 billion is consumed by the West European members of NATO. Between 1946 and 1980 the Pentagon spent $2,000 billion, an amount that probably will have doubled between 1981 and 1986. In the United States, the Soviet Union, and several European countries technological progress is keyed to the military sector, with devastating consequences for "civilian" production. This type of growth pattern creates not only excessive taxpayer burdens and depleted social programs but further aggravates unemployment, especially among women and minorities. Estimates are (for the United States) that with every $1 billion increase in the military budget 9,000 jobs are eliminated, owing to the capital-intensive nature of arms production.[10] Although increases in military spending are often justified as a source of industrial growth and job creation, the reality has been quite different: arms production might be functional to capitalism, within certain economic parameters, but it is obviously harmful to social progress (even minimally defined).[11]

The dynamic process through which a merger of new movements and class forces might occur is the transition from a militarized economy to a socialized, democratically controlled system of production geared to meeting social needs. A conversion project of this sort—viewed as part of a larger struggle against the multiple forms of domination— suggests more than reversal of the arms race as such, more than a commitment to peace objectives, to a nonviolent future, or even to full employment. It means nothing less than a novel path of development grounded in a drastic reordering of values and priorities. At the most general level, conversion entails a mediating process between societal commitments and concrete everyday struggles, between institutional politics and grassroots activism, between class interests and broad social change.

Conversion does not require for its actualization civil insurrection but rather a gradual shift toward socially useful production—that is, toward a revitalization of health care, education, housing, the environment, and public transportation along democratic and ecological lines. The enormous freeing of resources made possible by a reduction of the military apparatus would permit greater reliance upon alternative or "appropriate" forms of technology. Moreover, conversion of this sort would renew the job structure by substituting labor-intensive areas of development for the old capital-intensive areas subordinated to the military. Not only would this generate more jobs, but employment would be closer to human needs, less routinized, and surely more interesting. Third, for conversion to be fully implemented, technocratic institutions would have to be overturned, giving way to a decentralized system in which the entire range of popular interests would be expressed: labor, community groups, minorities, women, consumers, and so forth. A basic redirection of investment policies would be undertaken within the framework of a democratized state and economy. Fourth, conversion would begin to counteract the effects of militarism itself by eroding the very material (and presumably ideological) foundations of the arms race and the cold war. A radical alternative would specify that military spending is to be justified only for minimal defense needs, such as protecting national borders and waterways—a corollary being removal of all armed forces from the soil of foreign countries. Finally, it should be evident that rather diverse social groupings have an intrinsic vested interest in conversion, given the material and cultural benefits they are bound to receive from it. In other words, conversion is the potential unifying thread of a counterhegemonic bloc.

As part of a radical-democratic strategy, this variant of social conversion is characterized by a transformative dialectic that differs profoundly from the conventional liberal model, which involves simply a limited transfer of resources from one sector to another without challenging systemic priorities or the legitimacy of the arms race. Many earlier projects grew out of the combined initiatives of government and trade unions (with occasional community input). They demanded an increase in civilian-sector jobs along with some new social programs, but little else. The implicit ideal was that of a more benign, human-spirited capitalism.

The radical model calls not only for collaboration of labor and new movements dedicated to a unified economic program, but also a redefinition of both trade-union activity and social struggles as they have currently evolved. On the labor side, this means a questioning of the corporatist attachment to jobs, productivity, and growth within a capitalist framework and acceptance of the qualitative themes posed by the new movements.[12] To the degree that working-class movements merge with other popular forces to work for disarmament, the environment, democratic control, social equality, and women's and minority rights, the old-fashioned notion of labor "interests" gives way to a more universalistic praxis with its nonbureaucratic style, attention to society-wide issues, and multiplicity of aims—that is, to an entirely new language of politics.[13] In turn, this indicates a shift away from emphasis on the manufacturing sectors toward a view of the work force as a diversified totality, from sectoral interest-group action to a vision of the common good, from a strict demand for more jobs or full employment to a focus on what and how goods are being produced, from a defensive protection of corporatist status to an active mobilization for structural change. This means, too, that labor must confront its own legacy of racism, sexism, and national chauvinism. Surely the familiar assumption that the interests of labor are simultaneously those of society as a whole—shared by many trade unionists as well as Marxists—can no longer be sustained. The complex relationship between labor and social movements, class and politics—not to mention the recomposition of the work force itself—invalidates any schema that assigns to labor a hegemonic or privileged role in social transformation.

On the side of the new movements, conversion imposes a more balanced strategy that takes into account a realm of factors typically ignored or downplayed: the economy, class forces, material demands. It is hard to deny that even the most militant disarmament campaigns have been one-dimensional in the largely "moral" character of their protest, their extremely diffuse objectives, and their frequent detachment from other struggles and issues. This singular focus is typically justified by the sense of urgency conveyed by the antinuclear mobilizations and their sometimes apocalyptic definition of politics. Peace claims, therefore, can often be expected to supersede the claims of more "mundane" struggles. The problem with this approach is that it overlooks the structural basis of the arms race and the strategic imperatives for reversing it. Conversion has the potential of injecting an element of historical realism and political leverage into the popular revolt against militarism and the nuclear threat. It is an antidote to the extreme subjectivism, moralism, and spontaneism—along with the strong antilabor bias—that permeate many new-movement organizations and constituencies. As such, it lends a more concrete definition to emergent forms of radical opposition while offering a point of convergence with labor movements.

Conversion efforts of one sort or another have proliferated in many countries since the 1970s, but few have come close to the pattern outlined above. State-sponsored programs, usually introduced by left-wing governments, have generally sought little more than to reorder budgetary allocations so as to favor particular social programs. Only rarely are they concerned with the sphere of foreign or military policy. For governing bodies and trade unions in countries like England, West Germany, Sweden, and Holland, the main task has been to finance new social services, retrain workers for the civilian economy, and establish markets for nonmilitary goods. On occasion, as during the militant West German union struggles of 1984, the demand for a shortened work-week is linked to the broader aim of expanded labor-intensive forms of production. Some conversion projects that grew out of or were aligned with popular movements enlisted the participation of community groups as well as the unions. Probably the most sustained (and visionary) conversion effort was the ten-year campaign at Lucas Aerospace in England, where the Labour-dominated Greater London Council played a vital role in bringing together elements of both the labor and peace movements. In this, as in most other cases, the impetus was the (largely defensive) fight against layoffs in technologically advanced military-related industries like Lucas.[14] Similar organizing initiatives in the United States, along the lines of the McDonnell-Douglas Project, have also united diverse community and labor groups, but they have rarely questioned the general structural features of the system or the legitimating rationale of the war economy. Several factors operate to block a more radical expression of such initiatives, including the deeply ingrained corporatism of trade unions, the patriotic ideology that infuses much of working-class life, and the preoccupation with restrictive ideological themes among elements of the local movements.

In what ways, then, do the three post-Marxist strategies fit into this picture? The Eurosocialists, as we have seen, successfully mobilized diverse social groupings; they alone were able to unite labor and new-movement constituencies under a more or less unified structural reformist program. This was accomplished, however, through the medium of a catch-all party that eventually absorbed the premises of cold-war ideology and the logic of capital accumulation. Since catch-all politics rules out any radical assault on the power structure, it would have been unthinkable for the Mediterranean Socialists to vigorously pursue the variant of conversion discussed above. The reality is that their ambitious restructuring projects have only worsened the unemployment situation and further burdened the social-service sector. Moreover, although the southern European countries do not have what amounts to permanent war economies, their level of military spending has risen, while the French Socialists in particular are committed to extended development of the nuclear *force de frappe.* The Eurosocialist retreat to an unambiguous pro-NATO position has simply reinforced these trends. Hence, the coming together of labor and other strata occurs within rather conventional political boundaries, thus negating the possibility of a transformative conversion process.

The new populism runs into an entirely different set of problems. From the outset, this strategy was more clearly situated in the new movements and therefore stood more distant from the labor tradition (even if much new-populist literature does present an analysis of working-class issues). Given their limited experience with the labor milieu in practice —not to mention their relative lack of interest in foreign or military policy—new populists could not be expected to enthusiastically take up the thematic of conversion politics. Yet those cities where new populists achieved their most dramatic successes (Santa Monica, Burlington, Santa Cruz, Berkeley) are uniformly small and nonindustrial; they hardly form the core of the military-industrial complex or urban working-class struggles. Not surprisingly, local progressive governments in the United States have rarely undertaken conversion projects of any sort, although Jobs with Peace measures outlining a transitional economy have been passed in nearly eighty cities since the early 1980s.

At the same time, new-populist groups have occasionally contributed to embryonic conversion programs in urban areas where military-related production is an important part of the local economy. In Los Angeles, for example, the Jobs with Peace campaign has established a dynamic presence built on the energy of diverse constituencies: minorities, trade unions, the peace movement, religious groups, community organizations.[15] A Jobs with Peace initiative—the first popular measure to reach the Los Angeles ballot since 1939—was endorsed by 61 percent of the voters in 1984. It requires the city council to set in motion an alternative budgetary structure whereby funds from military-related enterprises would be gradually channeled into new public projects, and to publish an annual fiscal report outlining these efforts.[16] Since Los Angeles has a massive volume of military contracts, the Jobs with Peace proposals, though still limited, could become a watershed effort for future conversion programs. An outgrowth of local struggles rather than governmental directives, the campaign is situated at the center of a multiplicity of issues: taxation, public spending, plant closings, unemployment, social services, and, of course, militarism and the arms race. How far Jobs with Peace can go in reversing corporate and state priorities—that is, in helping to create a viable post-Marxist tendency—remains to be seen. Among many difficulties is the lack of a coherent strategy for challenging the mechanisms of capital accumulation and bureaucratic integration that stand in the way of basic structural change.

Finally, the Greens—as I indicated in Chapter 5—did arrive at a theory of conversion linked to a vision of radical insurgency. The main inspiration came from the peace movement (a larger and more politicized force in Western Europe than in the United States), from the Greens' uncompromising rejection of militarism, and above all from the desire to find a more concrete and effective axis of mobilization than mass protests alone. There is indeed a sense in which conversion can be viewed as the cornerstone of Green politics, at least in theory. In practical terms, however, little progress has been made, for the actual commitment to conversion lacks substance. The problem stems not merely from the Greens' lack of real governmental leverage, since popular efforts behind conversion can be launched without state intervention, at least in the initial stages—especially in West Germany, where extra-institutional citizens' groups already have a strong legacy. A more immediate obstacle is the Greens' remoteness from the labor movement, not so much in their ideology as in their general image and their intimate association with new-movement themes. This predicament is partly a function of the Green aversion to "productivist" or growth commitments, which shapes their distinctive post-Marxist identity. The problem is not simply the Greens' imputed failure to adequately "reach out" to labor; there is also a deep antagonism to the Greens in the trade unions, or, more precisely, to the qualitative demands of new-movement constituencies that support the Greens. In any event, until this ideological barrier is overcome, the imaginative conversion schema of the Greens will never be translated into action.

Whatever the short-term fate of conversion projects in the West, the capacity of organizations rooted in the new movements—that is, in a post-Marxist paradigm—to generate a truly radical opposition will ultimately depend upon the extent of their linkage with class forces. The class dimension of domination must be taken into account without a blindness to the other forms (bureaucratic, patriarchal, racial, cultural) that compose the totality. Because the relationship between class and politics is today more complex and refracted, the key theoretical and strategic task is to develop a new conception of class struggle. Nothing is gained by sidestepping this imperative for the sake of a postindustrial or new-age radicalism. What this suggests is nothing less than new ways of understanding the formulation of collective interests in the struggle to transform the workplace, community, and state.

STATE POWER AND POLITICAL STRATEGY

A dominant motif of this book is the central role of the state in the playing out of social conflict—and the corresponding importance of political strategy in that process. The emergence of new forms of opposition, as part of the transition to a new society, poses a series of related issues: the character of state power, the struggle for democratization, the structural components of self-management. A debilitating feature of Marxism, as I have argued, is the absence of any systematic theory of the state, of the relationship between class or social forces and politics upon which the actual forms of democratic socialism could be articulated. Unfortunately, this flaw persists within the post-Marxist currents as well, at least where the new movements uphold the ideal of an unmediated civil society outside of and against the political-institutional sphere, and where, in contrast, the strategic formations revert toward statism. In either case, the various post-Marxist expressions, whatever their democratic commitments, have all fallen short of developing a workable alternative conception of the state and of participatory democracy.

It seems equally clear, however, that the new-movement thematic explored in Chapters 2 and 5 does suggest a point of departure for a transformative theory and practice that can overcome the extreme polarities of the traditional models. That a completely original conception, necessary for a nonstatist process of radical change, has yet to be delineated reveals, among other things, that real political opportunities have been minimal. Of course, the nucleus of such a conception is already present in the work of some theorists (e.g., Poulantzas, Offe, and Bobbio) and in the appearance of post-Marxist formations like the Greens.[17] Twentieth-century leftist movements and parties have typically pursued one of three strategic alternatives: the *social-democratic*, which seeks to expand and further democratize the liberal-pluralist tradition; the *Leninist*, which envisions an assault on the state fortress, civil insurrection, and the construction of a "dictatorship of the proletariat"; and the *anarchist*, which stresses prefigurative activity within local autonomous forms, directed against the multiple forms of domination.

At the risk of oversimplification, the radical model rests upon a synthesis of the social-democratic and anarchist strategies. It shares little in common with the Leninist conception, since it departs significantly from any cataclysmic rupture or "overthrow" scenario as well as from bureaucratic centralism. It represents a novel attempt, not yet concretized, to integrate the two distinct levels: state and civil society, party and movements, parliament and local forms, electoral politics and grassroots mobilization. Leftist politics seems always to have been drawn to one pole or the other, as reflected in the highly charged "either-or" character of debates that go back to the famous Marx–Bakunin exchanges more than a century ago. A radical strategy entails the broadening of representative institutions, processes, and norms rather than their abolition. At the same time, it allows for the dynamic contribution of popular movements that (ideally) give rise to local forms of authority such as factory and neighborhood committees, which permit a remaking of the national state on foundations of self-management. The goal is a socialized political system relatively free of corporate and bureaucratic control and accessible to the broad strata—in other words, a state that is no longer alienated from, and superimposed upon, civil society.

As Claus Offe argues, the potential for radical-democratic initiatives is already present within the very social turbulence produced by the crisis of the Keynesian welfare state.[18] The convergence of the fiscal crisis of the state and the spread of new movements serves to break down the formal barriers of pluralist politics. The result is a weakened party system that allows for greater expression of new social forces both within and outside the legitimate state institutions. In Offe's view, this establishes the basis of a new public sphere characterized by a merging of the social and political realms. Diversification within both civil society and the state opens up a new phase of opposition which, depending upon the scope of popular struggles, can encourage mass-based counterhegemonic formations. State institutions become more vulnerable to processes of decomposition and democratization as new centers of local power begin to proliferate. If radical change cannot occur without the utilization of state power, the obverse is equally true: an egalitarian, self-managed society cannot be built strictly upon the terrain of state power. Offe sums up the new context thus: "At a time when capitalist societies themselves, under the pressure of social and economic crises, are forced to give up their own fundamental distinction of state and civil society, the insistence upon statist strategies of socialist transformation is rendered both unrealistic and anachronistic." [19]

From this viewpoint, there can be little doubt that both Eurosocialism and the new populism, two variants of structural reformist strategy, have been reabsorbed into the classical social-democratic pattern. If structural reformism embraces a participatory ideal, its conception of democracy nonetheless fully respects the borders of bourgeois pluralism. It offers no transformative vision of the state and political strategy. Although Eurosocialism gravitates toward the national state apparatus in contrast to the essentially localist emphasis of new populism, both follow social democracy in their obsession with established, legitimate forms of participation. Both adhere to a primacy of electoral politics, centralized modes of mobilization, and instrumental styles of action. The logic of electoralism, moreover, when sustained as a primary commitment over time, encourages those features of institutionalization that, in the end, erode oppositional identity. The brief history of both strategic types already reveals clear signs of structural and ideological absorption into the matrix of bourgeois power relations—a phenomenon that the leaders themselves have begun to concede.

The Greens, however, represent yet another story: their new politics consciously sets out to overcome the historical dualism of state and civil society, which enables them to arrive at a strategy that most closely approximates the radical model. Tied more closely than the others to the constituencies and above all the qualitative themes of the new movements, the Greens foresee a transitional process that unfolds on two fronts, with democratization introduced and nourished only through the rich variety of popular initiatives. Structural reformism paves the way to a seductive but fatal trap whereby parliamentarism in some ways actually reinforces statism, so that the myriad pressures toward institutionalization remain unchecked. Yet while Green politics obviously supersedes this model, a good number of dilemmas persist—at least judging from the West German experience to date. I have already pointed to some of the difficulties associated with the strong neoromantic, antimodernist strains that enter into the Greens' commitment to direct democracy, nonviolence, deep ecology, and spiritualism. Such ideological strains can generate immobilizing tendencies quite the opposite from the effects of institutionalization: sectarianism, isolation, and political impotence.

Equally problematic is the Greens' failure to specify the conditions for a transformation of the state that can give structural leverage to radical politics. Their approach, in West Germany as elsewhere, has been rather impressionistic. The strategic prescription of "standing on two legs" has not been infused with the substance that could be furnished by a more adequate theoretical understanding of the state. A vague radical conception is merely implicit in the Green program and in the ideas of a few theorists and leaders. Thus, it is never clear to what extent the Greens in fact aim for a socialization of state functions as the precondition for democratized authority relations: there is little theorization of what a reconstituted state would look like, what forms the local movements might assume, what mechanisms would be needed to counter bureaucracy and lend concreteness to a nonstatist strategy. The overall political methodology whereby existing state institutions might be broken down and transformed remains unclear in Green thinking. Even the critique of bureaucracy, like the celebration of direct democracy, takes on the features of a moralistic crusade rather than a calculated series of political interventions. Absent is any real organizational specificity that links struggles within civil society and those within the state proper. A related problem is the paucity of theorizing about how the stranglehold of capital over the state can be effectively broken. Might such an enormous task be achieved without a comprehensive socialization of capital? Do the Greens actually have in mind, somewhere in the deepest interstices of their ideological framework, a qualitative transformation of both state and economy? Questions of this sort are rarely addressed in Green literature, and probably will not be until a more elaborate radical-democratic theory of the state is forthcoming. Perhaps the Greens' timidity is a tactical response due to party leaders' fears of alienating more moderate supporters by using too radical language—or even by spelling out Green radical objectives too clearly. Such language, however, does permeate other areas of Green politics— for example, their vision of social ecology. More likely, this ideological ambiguity is the product of genuine confusion and unresolved debates among the Greens themselves. Their capacity to deal with conceptual limitations of this type will go far in determining whether a Green-inspired radical alternative can ever gain wide acceptance or, more to the point, achieve fundamental change.

These strategic deficiencies are further revealed in the area of internal organization, leadership, and process, as part of the relationship between large-scale formations and the state as well as the social movements. Indeed, this historic tension between the flow and energy of popular struggles and the imperatives of organizational power represents still another guiding motif of this book. As Piven and Cloward observe, the conflict between the innately disruptive character of local movements and the instrumentalizing pressures of large-scale organization are seemingly universal. The "mass-based permanent organization" typical of leftist parties (whether social-democratic, Leninist, or even populist) has predictably led to institutionalization and, ultimately, to the erosion of radical commitments. This is not so much a result of electoral participation itself, or of narrow interest-group efforts to influence state power from within—or even of the role played by organizational forms alone —as a function of bureaucratic detachment from the very rhythm of mass struggles. Piven and Cloward conclude that most conventional organizing efforts have in fact blocked rather than enlarged radical opportunities.[20] Of the four strategic variants mentioned above, only the radical-democratic type appears to be consonant with systematic attempts to resist institutionalization. Interestingly enough, each of the others falls short of even posing this issue in theoretical or political terms. The social-democratic model fully internalizes the norms and rules of pluralist democracy. Leninism offers a simplistic elite-centered solution that reduces the idea of democracy to a smooth functioning of a single-party state, and the anarchist variant resolves this difficulty abstractly, by more or less avoiding the reality of state power, by assuming that the cumulative impact of local movements and forms will eventually render superfluous any centralized state. The radical approach alone anticipates a thoroughly democratized system of power that combines the two realms of change within a unified strategic conception.

Eurosocialism, as we have seen, fits the mass-based organizational pattern in virtually every respect. Party structure is hierarchical, leadership is professionalized, and electoral campaigns provide the major source of mass participation. The ethos of decentralization, which does help to counter some elitist excesses, is largely negated by the commanding position of individual leaders and the concentration of political initiative within a central bureaucracy. Even though the new populism projects a more grassroots image, its internal dynamics are in reality close to those of Eurosocialism. Most of the same operational features are intact, typically including a strong, personalized leadership. At the same time, two conditions set it apart from its Socialist counterparts: its "machine" character and a relatively delimited scope of activity which, taken together, allow for a more fluid give-and-take organizational style and greater access for community groups. Neither strategy, however, seems compatible with the mobilization functions that radical theorists regard as indispensable to fundamental change. The Greens, on the other hand, have undertaken perhaps the first realistic and sustained challenge to the old organizational premises. In contrast to the hierarchical model, theirs is based upon direct democracy, rotating leadership, and a merger of the personal and the political. Such a strategy necessarily moves both on the terrain of electoral and parliamentary politics and grassroots activism. It is much too early to determine whether the Green project, in its present form, will be a viable one. Intense divisions between Greens over how to conceptualize, and apply, the ideal of direct democracy have generated more turbulence than clarity, resulting in an impasse that, if allowed to continue for long, could destroy the party. Moreover, the ascendancy of the legislative faction over "base" elements in the wake of electoral successes reflects once again that the Greens are hardly immune to bureaucratic pressures. But the party's proximity to the popular movements (though loosened), along with a firm hostility to old-style politics, has already given it a unique identity within the European left tradition. It is probably along these lines, whatever the immediate successes or failures of the West German Greens, that a full-blown radical-democratic opposition will eventually blossom.

HEGEMONY AND COUNTERHEGEMONY

Any analysis of post-Marxist formations would be incomplete without a discussion of ideological hegemony, which draws our attention to the role of ideas, consciousness, and social relations in the unfolding of a subversive political culture. The new movements, as I argue in Chapter

2, give expression to this subversive potential in many ways. As agencies in the transformation of civil society, they constitute what Gramsci referred to as a "war of position," the prelude to changes in the structure of state power. Elements of a new radicalism are predicated upon the confluence of social bloc, democratization, and war of position in a counterhegemonic process. Viewed in this way, the struggle for ideological hegemony embodies not only an attack on the dominant ideas, values, and beliefs but also a change in lived social relations consonant with a noneconomistic, nonstatist transition of the sort emphasized throughout this volume. Implicit in the notion of hegemony is the vision of a democratized state shaped by new modes of consciousness and political culture. To say that the new movements have a counterhegemonic potential is also to suggest that they have emerged in opposition (at least partially) to those ideologies that legitimate the power structure: technological rationality, nationalism, competitive individualism, traditionalism, and, of course, racism and sexism.

The future success of a counterhegemonic politics depends upon a gradual shift toward a new (participatory, egalitarian) political culture. The old crisis scenario, involving a sudden and dramatic rupture with the social order, is incompatible with such a strategy. Radical change in the West is most likely to occur through a dialectical interweaving of state and civil society instead of the "triumph" of one over the other. It further suggests that bourgeois hegemony is never absolute or global in scope since, as the experience of the new movements reveals, ample space exists for the growth of resistance, revolt, and opposition, however partial and distorted. The forms of conflict are infinitely more complex, and the system of domination more fragile, than some rigid theories of one-dimensional society would permit. (Surely Gramsci himself never understood hegemony as a metaphor for a totally administered society.) The immense diffusion of popular struggles over the past two decades attests to the vitality of an insurgent collective consciousness within civil society. At the same time, a concern with the problem of hegemony as a mediating element in social conflict opens up a more realistic analysis of the precise content of post-Marxist formations, since their ideological direction is indeterminate and irreducible to their social base. There is no simple relationship between class or social forces and the specific political character of movements and parties.

The reverse of this generalization is equally true: counterhegemonic struggles can have a powerful impact outside of formal organizations, as agencies for transforming political culture within civil society. In-deed, changes of this sort have often prefigured epochal historical events (e.g., the French and Russian revolutions) over many decades and even generations. Accordingly, the sweeping ideological changes expressed through the new movements cannot be grasped strictly with reference to their organizational presence. The concept of hegemony directs our attention toward diffuse but nonetheless far-reaching extra-institutional forces of change. Abundant historical evidence points to a rather dra-matic shift in popular consciousness of basic life experiences (work, authority, culture, the family, sexuality) in many industrialized coun-tries since the 1960s. What Ronald Inglehart calls the transition to a "post-materialist" phase of awareness has already reshaped the contours of social and political life in the West so extensively that it amounts to "silent revolution."[21] However overstated such conclusions might be, there is no denying that popular attitudes have changed greatly or that these changes, in large measure, occur beneath the surface of institu-tional life. The rapid spread of feminist values into even the remotest areas of human activity—only secondarily the work of political orga-nizing as such—is perhaps the best example of this dynamic.

A further measure of the silent revolution is the emergence of a widespread ecological consciousness rooted in a holistic, organic out-look that spills beyond the boundaries of the environmental movement as such. Ecologism demands a critical, noninstrumental discourse: it posits a qualitatively different approach to economic development, de-mocracy, and the relationship between humans and nature. Its con-ceptual basis is interdependence and diversity, the limits of material growth, self-regulation over administrative control, and universalistic over interest-based criteria. Insofar as balance and equilibrium (as part of an egalitarian social order) supersede domination and uneven devel-opment, the ecological model requires a generalized system of self-management because no single structure or set of interests can stand above the totality.[22] Ecologism is post-Marxist precisely in the sense that it goes beyond the productivist, hierarchical, and elitist features of the Marxist political tradition.[23]

This ecological framework, moreover, is counterhegemonic to the degree that it fits the premise of a long series of ideological and cultural transformations that precede and coincide with institutional politics. Political activity cannot be reduced to the realm of methods, procedures, and tactics—or to a process of institution-building—since formal practices have little meaning outside the consciousness that permeates them. Form and content are dialectically wedded.[24] Counterhegemonic politics thus refers not only to substantive action but to a participatory ethos rooted in a changing "ensemble of relations," that is, in a revitalized political culture. The organizational barriers analyzed first by Michels and later by Piven and Cloward can be effectively confronted only through such a dialectical schema that links structures and consciousness, organization and ideology, methods and process. From this viewpoint, the state no longer stands "above" the social totality as a bureaucratic imposition but is submerged within it so that its functions become diffused and (ideally) democratized. As Laclau and Mouffe observe, "The State is not a homogeneous medium separated from civil society by a ditch, but an uneven set of branches and functions only relatively integrated by the hegemonic practices which take place within it."[25] Against this strategy the very concept of a "war of movement" (maneuvers at the level of state power), with its emphasis upon cataclysmic crises, armed insurrection, and state engineering, seems anachronistic.

The thematic of counterhegemonic politics is congruent with the reality of a multiplicity of social forces and modes of discourse that enter into the universe of the new movements, thereby calling into question the imputed primacy of any single group or class agency.[26] As I have argued, the new movements are governed by no universal laws, no single formulas, no vanguardist principles. If social change follows diverse paths, this is less a matter of normative preferences than of the plural, cross-cutting cleavages (and broad awareness of these cleavages) that typify the industrialized societies. It is possible to identify the coincidence of three phenomena—a theory that calls attention to multiple forms of domination, a counterhegemonic strategy, and the historical (if somewhat idealized) appearance of the new movements.

Of course, even the most visionary post-Marxist initiatives cannot be expected to achieve deep counterhegemonic penetration in a context where, as in the West, oppositional politics remains feeble and marginalized. For some time radical efforts will necessarily be tentative, confined to the fringes of social conflict and political decision making. Still, a few generalizations are in order.

For Eurosocialism, the general absence of a counterhegemonic strategy can be explained by two factors: rationalizing pressures imposed by the global economy, and institutionalizing processes resulting in part from electoralism. Both factors converge to reproduce elements of social-democratic ideology. Within the recent Mediterranean version of structural reformism, elements of social bloc, war of position, and democratization are incorporated into a catch-all framework that stresses moderation over activism, interest-group bargaining over popular initiative, institutional politics over local struggles. Consequently, although Socialist governance has introduced social and labor reforms along with some measure of decentralization—thus opening new space for debate and change—the public sphere remains narrow enough to block any significant radicalization of the new movements. One might even say that Eurosocialism represents a closure of the public sphere from the viewpoint of popular insurgency and the diffusion of subversive ideologies.

The new populism follows roughly the same pattern: the logic of electoralism and machine politics, operating through an institutionally centered strategy, serves to reinforce the functions of legitimation. In the pursuit of single-issue reforms, the new populists are forced to defer to systemic norms and practices, despite their rhetoric of citizen "empowerment." Their instrumentalism (or "pragmatism"), moreover, corresponds to the emphasis on adaptation to national and cultural traditions that have shaped American political life. Hence, the primary goal of electoral mobilization is to *reflect* rather than transform popular beliefs and opinions; its essence is hegemonic rather than counterhegemonic. The result, as I suggested in Chapter 4, is an increasingly harmonious if somewhat ambivalent coexistence with the power structure. For the new populism, as for Eurosocialism, there is a marked lack of interest in any form of political education or ideological discourse. Once again, this hegemonic pattern of thought and action is a matter of the fundamental direction of change rather than of its pace or timing.

Turning to the Greens, however, one finds clear rudiments of a counterhegemonic politics in the themes of deep ecology, direct democracy, cultural renewal, and a nonmilitarist foreign policy—along with practical commitments that question the efficacy of a strictly institutional strategy. The very term *alternative*, as applied to most all of social existence, runs through Green theory and practice, even if its conceptual basis remains poorly developed. Indeed, of the three post-Marxist models, only the Greens present an image of modern industrial society as an inherently wasteful, destructive, and exploitative system that must be completely overhauled. The Greens' unique sensitivity to the requisites of a subversive political culture might well anticipate a new kind of counterhegemonic politics in the West. Still, the Greens are struggling to resolve internal divisions over ideological strains that could disrupt this potential: spiritualism, neoromanticism, and antimodernism amount to an escape rather than an engagement with the explosive goals and cleavages expressed through the new movements. This tension, which is far more complex than the debates between Fundis and Realos would indicate, will surely undermine the Greens' strategic coherence so long as they persist.

TOWARD A POST-MARXIST RADICALISM

If the new social movements depart from long-established patterns of oppositional activity in the industrialized world, there is still no guarantee that these movements will form the nucleus of a new phase of radical-democratic politics. Their historical meaning will depend upon the nature of their strategic translation, which itself is a function of variable conditions and mediations (including political choice). There is no linear developmental process that governs this translation, no necessary relationship between the existence of popular struggles and their ultimate ideological direction. It is no more predictable that new-movement constituencies will become radicalized than was the case when Marx was analyzing working-class struggles in the nineteenth century. The post-Marxist formations explored in this book have been profoundly shaped by their social and institutional context. As we have seen, they are just as vulnerable to a range of cooptative and integrative pressures as their social-democratic, reformist precursors.

The appearance of post-Marxist formations in the 1970s and 1980s is hardly a fortuitous event, for it illuminates the worsening predicament of the Western European and North American left. Vital as the new social forces and movements have been in broadening the public sphere, they lack the properties to carry out a transformative project on their own. Social movements are by their very nature dispersed, provincial, and ambiguous, so it is not surprising to find that they are generally devoid of the organizational and strategic presence needed to carry out effective political intervention, especially on any broad scale.[27] Local (or even national) movements based in community, feminist, peace, and environmental constituencies have typically failed to win much in the way of concrete political victories. Most successes have been local or symbolic, or both. Grassroots struggles in the United States, moreover, have encountered peculiar difficulties since, as Margit Mayer shows, the political system itself is extremely fragmented, thus pushing movements either into neocorporatist forms of representation or toward localist disintegration.[28] Peace movements, in whatever geographical setting, have exhibited perhaps the most extreme tendencies toward disaggregation and marginalization, despite the immense appeal of their themes.[29]

The socialist tradition, meanwhile, appears to have exhausted its potential, for reasons that have been spelled out in this book and elsewhere. Quite possibly the long era of socialist hegemony within leftist politics is drawing to a close. Perhaps, as Raymond Williams notes, the familiar "crisis of socialism" can be understood as the increasingly visible failure of rigid ideological definitions and singular models to explain social reality or generate compelling alternatives. The traditional conceptions of socialism have lost sight of the immense complexity of human needs, demands, and activities.[30] Yet the problem goes much deeper, as our analysis of Eurosocialism reveals: social democracy, whatever its degree of ideological bankruptcy from a radical standpoint, is still deeply embedded within working-class culture and commands the support—in Western Europe at least—of the vast majority of trade unionists. Leo Panitch argues that social-democratic mediations give rise to a class identity quite inseparable from the capitalist system, and that a break with these powerful mediations is needed to end the "impasse" of working-class politics in the West.[31] It is worth adding here that without such a rupture in social-democratic consensus a post-Marxist synthesis is unthinkable since it, too, depends upon a revitalized labor movement.

Still, whatever the leftist predicament, the appropriate conclusion might be that the Green alternative—or something like it—offers the best hope for a radical-democratic breakthrough. If Eurosocialism and the new populism have lapsed into the institutional logic of social democracy, then the Greens (at least in West Germany) do sustain something of a counterhegemonic presence. Alone among post-Marxist formations, the Greens have struggled to overcome the uneasy strategic dualism of state and civil society, party and local movements, electoral politics and grassroots activism—with mixed results. The Greens alone recognize the centrality of direct action as a means of channeling personal and social struggles into new forms of political empowerment.[32]

And this demands nothing less than a redefinition of politics. Whether distinctly "green" or not, a radical-democratic model will challenge the old dichotomous choice between vanguardism and structural reformism, which in the end is a choice between sectarian isolation and gradual assimilation. This strategy anticipates a complex process of insurgent struggles against multiple forms of domination, leading to fundamental changes in social relations and culture, the economy, and the state. In modern parlance, such an alternative might best be characterized as "red-green" in its inspiration.

What are the prospects for the actual diffusion of such a synthesis in the West? Surely the historical conditions for a "red-green" breakthrough of some sort are present throughout the industrialized world. The explosive crises and contradictions discussed in Chapter 2 show no signs of disappearing; traditional belief-systems and modes of legitimation are in eclipse; there is a steady growth in participatory skills and experiences among populations; and, above all, the new social movements remain a vital force—despite vacillating levels of politicization. Scarcely impregnable, the structures of domination will probably come under increasing attack. Yet the content of these attacks cannot be predicted by any theory. Whether the post-Marxist paradigm of social conflict, popular forces, and ideological themes can give support to a viable counterhegemonic politics will depend, in the final analysis, upon essentially subjective factors: intellectual resources, strategic choice, the capacity of disparate groups to unite in a common outlook, and the success of activists in making concrete—making alive—issues that can attract the vast majority of people to the ideal of a democratic, egalitarian, nonviolent world.

NOTES

CHAPTER 1

1. Alain Touraine, *The Voice and the Eye: An Analysis of Social Movements* (Cambridge, England: Cambridge University Press, 1981), pp. 13, 29.

2. C. B. Macpherson, *The Life and Times of Liberal Democracy* (New York: Oxford University Press, 1977), ch. 2.

3. For an overview of American economic decline see Paul Blumberg, *Inequality in an Age of Decline* (New York: Oxford University Press, 1980), chs. 3–5.

4. Morris Janowitz, *The Last Half-Century: Societal Change and Politics in America* (Chicago: University of Chicago Press, 1978), ch. 2.

5. See, for example, Richard Falk, "Liberalism and Foreign Policy," in Walter Truett Anderson, ed., *Rethinking Liberalism* (New York: Avon Books, 1983).

6. See Adam Przeworski, "Social Democracy as an Historical Phenomenon," *New Left Review* 122 (July–Aug. 1980).

7. Carl Boggs, "The Intellectuals and Social Movements: Some Reflections on Academic Marxism," *Humanities and Society* 6, nos. 2–3 (Spring–Summer 1983).

8. On this aspect of the celebrated "crisis of Marxism," see Stanley Aronowitz, *The Crisis in Historical Materialism* (New York: Praeger, 1981), ch. 1; and Isaac Balbus, *Marxism and Domination* (Princeton, N.J.: Princeton University Press, 1982), introduction and ch. 1.

9. André Gorz, *Ecology as Politics* (Boston: South End Press, 1980), p. ii.

10. This analysis is developed further in my "Marxism, Prefigurative Communism, and the Problem of Workers' Control," *Radical America* 2, no. 5 (1977).

11. There is, of course, a distinct right-wing populism that has taken root throughout the advanced capitalist world, and especially in the United States with the emergence of the Moral Majority, the right-to-life movement, and the appeals of Reaganism to the traditional virtues of family, religion, and patriotism. But these new movements, needless to say, emphasize completely different themes and social priorities concerned with resisting rather than advancing change.

12. On this point see Stanley Aronowitz, "The Making of the American Left—II," *Socialist Review* 69 (May–June 1983): esp. 7–9.

13. See Jonathan Schell, *The Fate of the Earth* (New York: Avon Books, 1982), and Helen Caldicott, *Missile Envy* (New York: Morrow, 1984) for examples of the latter. Both hope for a universal leap in collective consciousness that could lead to abandonment of an irrational arms race by Soviet and American leaders alike.

14. For example, see Christopher Lasch, *The Culture of Narcissism* (New York: Norton, 1978); and Daniel Bell, *The Cultural Contradictions of Capitalism* (New York: Basic Books, 1976).

15. This dualism has been applied to the experience of the American new left by

Wini Breines in *The Great Refusal: Community and Organization in the New Left, 1962–1968* (New York: Praeger, 1983), conclusion.

16. Touraine, *Voice and the Eye*, p. 137.

17. Murray Bookchin, *Toward an Ecological Society* (Montreal: Black Rose Books, 1980), p. 214.

18. For an extended critique of this economistic mode of reasoning in the context of postindustrial development, see Hazel Henderson, *The Politics of the Solar Age* (New York: Doubleday, 1981).

19. Aronowitz, *The Crisis in Historical Materialism*; Balbus, *Marxism and Domination*; Jean Cohen, *Class and Civil Society* (Amherst: University of Massachusetts Press, 1983); Jürgen Habermas, "New Social Movements," *Telos* 49 (Fall 1981).

20. Michael Albert and Robin Hahnel, *Marxism and Socialist Theory* (Boston: South End Press, 1981); Zygmunt Baumann, *Memories of Class* (London: Routledge & Kegan Paul, 1982); André Gorz, *Farewell to the Working Class* (London: Pluto Press, 1982); Touraine, *Voice and the Eye*.

21. Manuel Castells, *The City and the Grassroots* (Berkeley: University of California Press, 1984); Ernesto Laclau and Chantal Mouffe, *Hegemony and Socialist Strategy* (London: Verso, 1985); Touraine, *Voice and the Eye*.

22. Castells, *City and the Grassroots*, and *City, Class, and Power* (London: Macmillan, 1978); Joaquim Hirsch, "The Fordist Security State and the New Social Movements," *Kapitalistate* 10–11 (1983).

23. Frances Fox Piven and Richard Cloward, *Poor People's Movements* (New York: Vintage, 1979), introduction.

24. Murray Bookchin, *The Ecology of Freedom* (Palo Alto, Calif.: Chesire Books, 1982); Breines, *The Great Refusal*; Richard Gombin, *The Radical Tradition* (New York: St. Martin's Press, 1979); Sheila Rowbotham, et al., *Beyond the Fragments* (London: Merlin Press, 1979); Kirkpatrick Sale, *Human Scale* (New York: Doubleday, 1982).

25. Sara Evans, *Personal Politics* (New York: Vintage, 1980); Kathy E. Ferguson, *The Feminist Case against Bureaucracy* (Philadelphia: Temple University Press, 1984); Nancy Hartsock, "Feminism and Revolutionary Strategy," in Zillah Eisenstein, ed., *Capitalist Patriarchy and the Case for Socialist Feminism* (New York: Knopf, 1979); Rowbotham, *Beyond the Fragments*. See also the contributions to Lydia Sargent, ed., *Women and Revolution* (Boston: South End Press, 1981).

26. Rudolf Bahro, *Socialism and Survival* (London: Heretic Books, 1982); Bookchin, *Toward an Ecological Society*; Gorz, *Ecology as Politics*; William Ophuls, *Ecology and the Politics of Scarcity* (San Francisco: W. H. Freeman, 1979).

27. Bahro, *Socialism and Survival*, and *From Red to Green* (London: New Left Books, 1984); Mary Kaldor, *The Baroque Arsenal* (New York: Hill & Wang, 1982); E. P. Thompson, "Notes on Exterminism: The Last Stage of Civilization," in E. P. Thompson, ed., *Exterminism and the Cold War* (London: New Left Books, 1982).

28. David Dickson, *The Politics of Alternative Technology* (Glasgow: William Collins, 1974); Henderson, *Politics of the Solar Age*; Ivan Illich, *Tools for Conviviality* (New York: Harper & Row, 1973) and *Medical Nemesis* (London: Calder, 1975); Theodore Roszak, *Person/Planet* (New York: Doubleday, 1978).

CHAPTER 2

1. C. B. Macpherson, *The Life and Times of Liberal Democracy* (New York: Oxford University Press, 1977), ch. 4.

2. Joaquim Hirsch, "The Fordist Security State and New Social Movements," *Kapitalistate* 10–11 (1983): 81–82.

3. Claus Offe, "The Attribution of Public Status to Interest Groups," in Suzanne Berger, ed., *Organizing Interests in Western Europe* (London: Cambridge University Press, 1981), p. 142.

4. On the convergence of major parties, see Luigi Graziano, "On Political Compromise: Italy after the 1979 Elections," *Government and Opposition* (Spring 1980); and Carl Boggs, *The Impasse of European Communism* (Boulder, Colo.: Westview Press, 1982), pp. 84–91.

5. This closure of the political system and the corresponding decline of popular participation in Western societies contradicts the thesis of T. H. Marshall, who argues that with industrialization the democratic revolution brought newer strata into the political arena. Marshall was obviously correct to a point, since liberal democracy did in fact make "citizens" of workers, minorities, women, and other previously disenfranchised groups by the early and middle parts of this century. Since then, however, as I have suggested, this process has been reversed even while formal citizenship remains more or less universal. For Marshall's argument, see his *Class, Citizenship, and Power* (London: Cambridge University Press, 1950).

6. See Morris Janowitz, *The Last Half-Century* (Chicago: University of Chicago Press, 1978), pp. 90–103, and Alessandro Pizzorno, "Interests and Parties in Pluralism," in Berger, *Organizing Interests in Western Europe*, pp. 253–55. For a more general discussion see Martin Carnoy, *The State and Political Theory* (Princeton, N.J.: Princeton University Press, 1984), pp. 39–42.

7. Offe, "Public Status to Interest Groups," p. 136.

8. For a similar typology of corporatist systems see Giovanni Arrighi, "A Crisis of Hegemony," in Samir Amin, et al., eds., *Dynamics of Global Crisis* (New York: Monthly Review Press, 1982), p.101. As I have argued elsewhere, the corporatist solution to labor-management struggles was part of recent Eurocommunist ideology, which here as in other respects has a close affinity with the social-democratic model—that is, where left-wing parties with a significant working-class base are able to establish political hegemony. See *The Impasse of European Communism*, pp. 76–84.

9. For an excellent discussion of this trend toward working-class fragmentation, see Richard Edwards, *The Contested Terrain: The Transformation of the Workplace in the Twentieth Century* (New York: Basic Books, 1979), esp. chs. 10, 11. Implicit in Edwards' analysis of class relations is the thesis that consciousness is shaped by a wide range of mediating factors (e.g., community, region, race, gender, culture) that lie outside the mode of production.

10. Frank Hearn, "The Corporatist Mood in the United States," *Telos* 56 (Summer 1983): 43.

11. As Gorz argues, social groups are marginalized precisely to the extent they lack job security and therefore cannot hope to join the labor "aristocracy." See André Gorz,

Farewell to the Working Class (London: Pluto Press, 1982), p. 73. One of the major benefits that corporatism bestows upon partners in the social contract is precisely this element of security. Yet in many countries massive plant closings involving autos, steel, and appliances have threatened millions of workers whose tenure was once secure. This is merely one of the many fissures in the corporatist solution.

12. Ibid., ch. 5.

13. Philippe C. Schmitter, "Interest Intermediation and Regime Governability," in Berger, *Organizing Interests in Western Europe*, pp. 319, 321.

14. Ibid., p. 332.

15. See Jürgen Habermas, *Legitimation Crisis* (Boston: Beacon Press, 1973), part II.

16. Peter Berger, Brigitte Berger, and Hansfried Kellner, *The Homeless Mind* (New York: Vintage Books, 1974), ch. 3. See also Janowitz, *The Last Half-Century*, ch. 8.

17. Barry Bluestone and Bennett Harrison, *The Deindustrialization of America* (New York: Basic Books, 1982), esp. chs. 1–3. Bluestone and Harrison estimate that layoffs in the United States during the 1970s cost as many as 38 million jobs (p. 35). Of course, some occupational loss was absorbed by the public sector and elsewhere in the private economy, but not nearly enough to compensate fully. Bluestone and Harrison estimate that for every 110 jobs lost in this fashion only 100 new ones were created. On the general decline of American capitalism, see Paul Blumberg, *Inequality in an Age of Decline* (New York: Oxford University Press, 1980), and Robert B. Reich, *The Next American Frontier* (New York: Penguin Books, 1983). On the global crisis of capitalism, see Amin, et al., in *The Dynamics of Global Crisis*.

18. Barry Commoner, *The Closing Circle* (New York: Bantam, 1971).

19. For a discussion of ecological imbalance in the capitalist economy, see ibid.; André Gorz, *Ecology as Politics* (Boston: South End Press, 1980), pp. 20–28; and Murray Bookchin, *Toward an Ecological Society* (Montreal: Black Rose Books, 1980), pp. 155–71. On the implications of a "limits of growth" stage for political policy and strategy, see Hazel Henderson, *The Politics of the Solar Age* (New York: Doubleday, 1981), ch. 1; Roger Benjamin, *The Limits of Politics* (Chicago: University of Chicago Press, 1980); William Ophuls, *Ecology and the Politics of Scarcity* (San Francisco: W. H. Freeman, 1979); Kirkpatrick Sale, *Human Scale* (New York: Doubleday, 1982), ch. 1; Tom Hayden, *America's Future* (Boston: South End Press, 1981); and Alan Wolfe, *America's Impasse* (New York: Pantheon, 1981).

20. The thesis that technology itself, as an integral component of industrialism, is so deeply embedded in the logic of domination that it cannot presently be utilized to overcome those problems is most thoughtfully argued by Langdon Winner in *Autonomous Technology* (Cambridge: MIT Press, 1977). Presumably Winner's definition of technology here does *not* extend to the sphere of "alternative" or "human-scale" technology.

21. Seymour Melman, *The Permanent War Economy: American Capitalism in Decline* (New York: Simon & Schuster, 1974). Melman argues that military and aerospace priorities have done irreparable harm to the U.S. consumer electronics industry, for example (p. 83). What has traditionally been true of the United States has not been so for other industrialized countries, which have been able to devote a greater percentage of resources to the civilian economy. But this has been changing markedly over

the past decade, as the Japanese and Western Europeans begin to develop their own weapons systems and expand their own armed forces.

22. This point is forcefully argued in David Dickson, *The New Politics of Science* (New York: Pantheon Books, 1984). For the decade 1970-80, U.S. government spending on research and development amounted to $153 billion on military and space priorities compared with $79 billion on civilian production. Ruth Leger Sivard, *World Military and Social Expenditures, 1981* (Washington: World Priorities Inc., 1981), p. 17.

23. It has been estimated that every billion dollars spent on missile production generates 29,400 jobs, while the same investment provides 30,900 jobs in housing, 38,200 in public utilities, 38,600 in solar energy and conservation, or 45,400 in mass transit. The source for these figures is David Gold, et al., *Misguided Expenditures: An Analysis of the Proposed MX Missile System* (New York: Council on Economic Priorities, 1981), p. 157.

24. E. P. Thompson "Notes on Exterminism: The Last Stage of Civilization," in E. P. Thompson, ed., *Exterminism and the Cold War* (London: New Left Books, 1982), p. 17.

25. George Konrad, *Antipolitics* (London: New Left Books, 1984).

26. Mary Kaldor, "Beyond the Blocs," in *World Policy* (Fall 1983): 11.

27. On the eclipse of democracy both East and West in the era of nuclear politics, see Alan Wolfe, "Perverse Politics and the Cold War," in Thompson, ed., *Exterminism and the Cold War*, pp. 250-53.

28. Opinion surveys conducted in several European countries before and during U.S. deployment of Pershing II and cruise missiles in 1983 showed that between 60 and 70 percent of the populations in West Germany, Italy, England, Holland, and Belgium were opposed to deployment.

29. Noam Chomsky argues that it is the Middle East which provides the frightfully optimum combination of ingredients for such a nuclear scenario. See *The Fateful Triangle: The U.S., Israel and the Palestinians* (Boston: South End Press, 1983).

30. E. P. Thompson, "Notes on Exterminism," p. 21.

31. For a documentation and analysis of this pattern of U.S. initiative and Soviet counterresponse, see Robert Aldrich, *First Strike* (Boston: South End Press, 1982), ch. 10.

32. Ernest Mandel, "The Threat of Nuclear War and the Struggle for Socialism," *New Left Review* 141 (Sept.-Oct. 1983): 20.

33. Emphasis on the North-South dimension of the arms race is central to Mike Davis' response to E. P. Thompson's thesis of exterminism. See "Nuclear Imperialism and Extended Deterrence," in Thompson, ed., *Exterminism and Cold War*, esp. pp. 42-43.

34. This shift is reflected in much survey research, which shows a marked loss of positive orientation toward the United States, a decline of negative attitudes toward the Soviet Union, and a general increase in neutralist sentiments. See Bruce Russett and Donald R. Deluca, "Theater Nuclear Forces: Public Opinion in Western Europe," *Political Science Quarterly* (Summer 1983). The authors conclude on the basis of their data that NATO is facing its most serious crisis (p. 194).

35. For a general discussion of this problem see John H. Schaar, *Legitimacy in the Modern State* (New Brunswick, N.J.: Transaction Books, 1981), pp. 15–51. On the breakdown of socialization patterns in the contemporary American context, see Daniel Yankelovich, *New Rules* (New York: Random House, 1981), preface and ch. 1.

36. Manuel Castells, *The City and the Grassroots* (Berkeley: University of California Press, 1984), introduction and ch. 6.

37. Ibid., chs. 12 and 14.

38. On the historical development of urban popular movements in the United States, see Frances Fox Piven and Richard Cloward, *Poor People's Movements* (New York: Vintage, 1979).

39. Probably the best examples of this radical dimension in ecology are Murray Bookchin, *The Ecology of Freedom* (Palo Alto, Calif.: Chesire Books, 1982); Gorz, *Ecology as Politics*; David Dickson, *The Politics of Alternative Technology* (William Collins, 1974); Ophuls, *Ecology and the Politics of Scarcity*; and Sale, *Human Scale*. See also Rudolf Bahro, *Socialism and Survival* (London: Heretic Books, 1982), for a brief and fragmentary but still powerful statement along these lines.

40. Dave Elliott, *The Politics of Nuclear Power* (London: Pluto Press, 1978), ch. 9.

41. For a good overview of this development see Jim O'Brien, "Environmentalism as a Mass Movement," *Radical America* (March–June 1983).

42. Sheila Rowbotham, et al., *Beyond the Fragments* (London: Merlin Press, 1979), esp. the essay by Rowbotham. See also Sara Evans, *Personal Politics* (New York: Vintage, 1979), and Nancy Hartsock, "Feminism and Revolutionary Strategy," in Zillah Eisenstein, ed., *Capitalist Patriarchy and the Case for Socialist Feminism* (New York: Knopf, 1979).

43. Castells, *City and the Grassroots*, ch. 14. See also Dennis Altman, *The Homosexualization of America* (Boston: Beacon, 1982), ch. 5.

44. On the emergence of the West European peace movement, see Diana Johnstone, *The Politics of Euromissiles* (London: Verso, 1984).

45. The theoretical possibility of such a convergence of issues is spelled out by the contributors to Michael Albert and David Dellinger, eds., *Beyond Survival* (Boston: South End Press, 1983).

46. See Alice Cook and Gwyn Kirk, *Greenham Women Everywhere* (Boston: South End Press, 1983). For a parallel but much more short-lived American experience, see Lois Hayes, "Separatism and Disobedience: The Seneca Peace Encampment," *Radical America* (July–Aug. 1983).

47. Perhaps the best early treatment of youth-based radicalism is Theodore Roszak, *The Making of a Counterculture* (Garden City, N.Y.: Anchor Books, 1969). See also Kenneth Keniston, *Young Radicals* (New York: Harcourt, Brace and World, 1968), and Edgar Z. Friedenberg, *Coming of Age in America* (New York: Random House, 1965).

48. On the May Revolt in France see Daniel Singer, *Prelude to Revolution* (New York: Hill & Wang, 1969), and Daniel Cohn-Bendit, *Obsolete Communism: The Left-Wing Alternative* (New York: McGraw-Hill, 1969); on the Italian events see Giuseppe Veltori, ed., *La Sinistra Extraparlamentare in Italia* (Rome: Newton Comptor Editor, 1975); on the American developments see Kirkpatrick Sale, *SDS* (New York: Vintage,

1973), and Wini Breines, *The Great Refusal: Community and Organization in the New Left, 1962–1968* (New York: Praeger, 1983).

49. On the resurgence of a West German counterculture see Sylvere Lotringer, ed., *The German Issue* (New York: Semiotext, 1983), part III.

50. See, for example, Bahro, *Socialism and Survival*, p. 129.

51. Agnes Heller and Ferenc Feher, "From Red to Green," *Telos* 59 (Spring 1984): 43.

52. Alvin W. Gouldner, *The Future of Intellectuals and the Rise of the New Class* (New York: Seabury, 1979). See also John Suler, "The Role of Ideology in Self-Help Groups," *Social Policy* (Winter 1984), and Richard Weiner, "Collective Identity Formation and Social Movements," *Psychology and Social Theory* 3 (1982).

53. Raymond Williams, *Marxism and Literature* (London: Oxford University Press, 1977), ch. 3.

54. Heller and Feher, "From Red to Green," p. 36.

55. Yankelovich, *New Rules*, pp. 3–9. See also Evans, *Personal Politics*, where the notion of an emergent social space is linked to the expression of radical feminist values (pp. 219–20).

56. Castells, *City and the Grassroots*, p. 53, and Alain Touraine, *The Voice and the Eye: An Analysis of Social Movements* (Cambridge, England: Cambridge University Press, 1981), pp. 85–87. This perspective clearly differs from that of Hobsbawm, who sees in the prepolitical phase of ideological and organizational dispersion a "primitivism" that renders social movements impotent. See E. J. Hobsbawm, *Primitive Rebels* (New York: Norton, 1959), introduction. The problem with Hobsbawm's analysis is that his choice of romantic movements tied to a preindustrial vision (millenarians, urban-mobs, social bandits) rules out any real parallels with the type of modern popular movements under discussion here.

57. Piven and Cloward, *Poor People's Movements*, esp. pp. xvi–xxi. This neo-Michelsian thesis of institutionalization can clearly be pushed too far. Rather than seeing local movements in their pure self-activity inevitably confronting institutions as an "external" form of repression and cooptation, it would be more fruitful to approach these two spheres dialectically, as part of a tense and conflicted relationship. This point will be taken up in Chapter 6.

58. Perhaps the best articulation of this theme is Harry C. Boyte's *The Backyard Revolution: Understanding the New Citizen Movement* (Philadelphia, Temple University Press, 1980). Boyte, however, stresses the more traditional side of community (family, religion, liberalism, national traditions), which, as I argue in Chapter 4, can easily work against the transformative potential of social movements.

59. Dolores Hayden, "Capitalism, Socialism, and the Built Environment," in Steve Rosskamm Shalom, ed., *Socialist Visions* (Boston: South End Press, 1983), p. 69. Hayden explores the forms of women's spatial oppression that accompany the division between public and private in bourgeois society.

60. The most comprehensive historical overview of this Rousseauian (and Greek) legacy is Bookchin's *Ecology of Freedom*, esp. chs. 1, 2, and 12.

61. See John Buell, "Community Without Coercion," *The Progressive* (May 1984): 14–15.

62. Castells, *City and the Grassroots*, p. 222.

63. On the struggle to revitalize political participation against the authoritarian closure of the corporatist bloc, see Peter Bachrach, "Democracy and Class Struggle," in Mark E. Kann, ed., *The Future of American Democracy: View from the Left* (Philadelphia: Temple University Press, 1983), pp. 245–50.

64. It is sometimes forgotten that primary social structures like the family do much to shape the overall character of democracy, in one way or another, since early socialization patterns obviously influence the development of political culture. On this relationship see Jane Flax, "Tragedy or Emancipation: On the Decline of Contemporary American Families," in Kann, *The Future of American Democracy*, pp. 102–6.

65. The need for tolerance of ideological diversity and ambiguity is stressed by Robin Morgan in *The Anatomy of Freedom* (New York: Doubleday, 1983).

66. Bookchin, *Ecology of Freedom*, p. 9. See also Isaac Balbus, *Marxism and Domination* (Princeton, N.J.: Princeton University Press, 1982), introduction.

67. This typology broadly parallels the one formulated by Michael Albert and Robin Hahnel in *Unorthodox Marxism* (Boston: South End Press, 1979), ch. 1.

68. Rudolf Bahro refers to "multiple and overlapping structures of domination" that cannot be reduced to their class dimension in the context of Eastern Europe. See *The Alternative in Eastern Europe* (London: New Left Books, 1977), ch. 8.

69. This theme is stressed by Balbus in his conclusion to *Marxism and Domination*. See also Gorz, *Ecology as Politics*, pp. 64–69.

70. Such a redefinition of public welfare implicit in the critique of productivism (and technological rationality) is visible, for example, in efforts to explore the possibilities of a holistic medicine and health-care system that would replace the existing technologically intensive and bureaucratized health-industrial complex that flourishes in the United States. See Ivan Illich, *Medical Nemesis* (New York: Bantam Books, 1976).

71. Castells, *City and the Grassroots*, p. 94.

72. Alison Jagger's treatment of feminism restores the concept of alienation to the realm of social and sexual relations, within a framework that defines it as a dialectical lynchpin of change. The implications of this view of alienation for an understanding of popular movements are far-reaching. See *Feminist Politics and Human Nature* (Sussex, England: Rowman and Allenheld, 1983), pp. 307–17.

73. On the historical antagonisms between women and male "experts" in the area of medicine and health care, see Barbara Ehrenreich and Deirdre English, *For Her Own Good* (New York: Doubleday, 1980).

74. The familiar critique of new-left and feminist tendencies for their celebration of the personal quest for fulfillment over concrete political action is only superficially valid in that it overlooks the larger developmental context (and potential) of new social movements. Christopher Lasch's critique in *The Culture of Narcissism* (New York: Norton, 1978) is already well known. See also Peter Clecak, *America's Quest for an Ideal Self* (New York: Oxford University Press, 1983).

75. Yankelovich, *New Rules*, esp. chs. 21–24.

76. Altman, *The Homosexualization of America*, p. 160, and Castells, *City and the Grassroots*, pp. 167–69.

77. Cook and Kirk, *Greenham Women Everywhere*, p. 127.

78. E. P. Thompson, "Notes on Exterminism," p. 24.

79. Perhaps the most developed theoretical effort in this vein is Sharp's concept of

social defense. See Gene Sharp, *The Politics of Nonviolent Action*, 3 vols. (Boston: Porter Sargent, 1973).

80. See, for example, Leslie Cagan, "Feminism and Militarism," in Albert and Dellinger, eds., *Beyond Survival*, pp. 81–118.

81. Cook and Kirk, *Greenham Women Everywhere*, pp. 76–77.

82. Touraine, *Voice and the Eye*, pp. 83–85.

83. Rowbotham, et al., *Beyond the Fragments*, pp. 132–46.

84. On the development of a prefigurative model of social change in the American new left see Breines, *The Great Refusal*, pp. 32–33.

85. Lucien Goldmann, *Cultural Creation* (St. Louis: Telos Press, 1976), ch. 1.

86. Perhaps the most systematic attempt to specify theoretically the convergence of new movements can be found in Balbus, *Marxism and Domination*, conclusion.

87. Castells, *City and the Grassroots*, p. 296.

88. Ibid., p. 299.

89. For a comprehensive overview of such efforts see Jagger, *Feminist Politics and Human Nature*, chs. 7–9. Many of the contributors to the volume *Women and Revolution*, edited by Lydia Sargent (Boston: South End Press, 1982), wrestle with this problem, but no real synthesis is ever furnished. The same tension is reflected in Batya Weinbaum, *The Curious Courtship of Women's Liberation and Socialism* (Boston: South End Press, 1979).

90. On this Jacobin dimension of Marxism (and not simply Leninism), see Richard Gombin, *The Radical Tradition* (New York: St. Martin's Press, 1979), ch. 2.

91. Karl Korsch, *Marxism and Philosophy* (New York: Monthly Review Press, 1970), pp. 58, 64, 87.

92. These words are from E. P. Thompson, who is describing the impact of structuralist Marxism. See *The Poverty of Theory* (New York: Monthly Review Press, 1978), p. 186. Italics in the original.

93. Jean Baudrillard, *The Mirror of Production* (St. Louis: Telos Press, 1975).

94. Gorz, *Farewell to the Working Class*, p. 15.

95. Immanuel Wallerstein, *Historical Capitalism* (London: Verso, 1983), p. 107.

96. As Mancur Olson notes, Marxism shares with liberalism a rationalist psychology that takes the form of strict economic self-interest—grounded in classes for Marxism, in organized interest groups for liberalism. See *The Logic of Collective Action* (Cambridge: Harvard University Press, 1965), ch. 5.

97. On the fallacy of identifying popular ideologies with specific class forces, see George Rude, *Ideology and Popular Protest* (New York: Pantheon, 1980), pp. 28–35.

98. Bookchin, *Toward an Ecological Society*, p. 206.

99. Balbus, after an extensive discussion of neo-Marxist efforts to correct this productivist one-dimensionality, drew precisely the same conclusion. See *Marxism and Domination*, part II. Not all tendencies within Marxism, of course, share the same degree of productivist bias. Yet what ultimately distinguishes Marxist from non-Marxist theories is the theoretical centrality of class structure and class struggle in the former.

100. Jagger, *Feminist Politics and Human Nature*, p. 236.

101. Critiques of Leninism from a variety of leftist perspectives are far too numerous to mention here. Some examples include Lucio Magri, "The Marxist Theory of the Revolutionary Party," *New Left Review* 60 (March–April 1970); Alvin W. Gouldner,

"The Revolutionary Intellectuals," *Telos* (Winter 1975–76); Gombin, *The Radical Tradition*, ch. 2; Carl Boggs, "Revolutionary Process, Marxist Strategy, and the Dilemma of Political Power," *Theory and Society* 4, no. 3 (Fall 1977): 364–71; Piven and Cloward, *Poor People's Movements*, ch. 1; Mihailo Markovic, *From Affluence to Praxis* (Ann Arbor: University of Michigan Press, 1972); and Roy Medvedev, *Leninism and Western Socialism* (London: Verso, 1981).

102. The best feminist critique of Leninism is Rowbotham's in *Beyond the Fragments*. See also Jagger, *Feminist Politics and Human Nature*, pp. 228–36.

103. Stanley Aronowitz, *The Crisis in Historical Materialism* (New York: Praeger, 1981), pp. 124–30.

104. I elaborate upon this argument in *The Impasse of European Communism*, chs. 2–4. See also Ernest Mandel, *From Stalinism to Eurocommunism* (London: New Left Books, 1978), and Henri Weber, "Eurocommunism, Socialism and Democracy," *New Left Review* 110 (July–Aug. 1978).

105. See, for example, Louise Beaulieu and Jonathan Cloud, "Political Ecology and the Limits of the Communist Vision," in Carl Boggs and David Plotke, eds., *The Politics of Eurocommunism* (Boston: South End Press, 1980).

106. For a discussion of the PCF decline see Bruno Buongiovanni, "The French Communist Party in the 1970s," *Telos* (Spring 1983); George Ross, "The Dilemmas of Communism in Mitterrand's France," *New Political Science* 12 (1984); Cornelius Castoriadis, "The French Communist Party: A Critical Anatomy," *Dissent* (Summer 1979); and Daniel Singer, "The French Communist Party: On the Way Out?" *The Nation* (Sept. 1, 1984).

107. Temma Kaplan, "Democracy and the Mass Politics of the PCF," in Boggs and Plotke, eds., *Politics of Eurocommunism*.

108. These Leninist "residues" finally came to the surface in 1984 when dissident PCE members set up an orthodox pro-Soviet party led by Ignacio Gallegos. It claimed 25,000 members, compared with 80,000 for the PCE.

109. Maurizio Marcelloni, "Urban Movements and Political Struggles in Italy," *International Journal of Urban and Regional Research* (June 1979): 263. See also Eddy Cherki, Dominique Mehl, and Anne-Marie Metailke, "Urban Protest in Western Europe," in Colin Crouch and Alessandro Pizzorno, eds., *The Resurgence of Class Conflict in Western Europe Since 1968* (New York: Holmes and Meier, 1978); and Marzio Barbagli and Piergiorgio Corbetta, "The Italian Communist Party and the Social Movements, 1968–1976," in Maurice Zeitlin, ed., *Social Theory and Political Power* (Greenwich, Conn.: JAI Press, 1980).

110. Annarita Buttafuoco, "Italy: The Feminist Challenge," in Boggs and Plotke, eds., *Politics of Eurocommunism*, pp. 214–16. In part the PCI's timidity and ambivalence regarding feminist politics can be explained by the continued pervasive influence of Catholicism in Italy. See also Judith Adler Hellman, "The Italian Communists, the Women's Question, and the Challenge of Feminism," *Studies in Political Economy* (Spring 1984); Carla Ravaioli, *La questione femministe: Intervista col PCI* (Milan: Bompiani, 1976); and Biancamaria Frabotta, ed., *La Politica del Femminismo* (Rome: Savelli, 1978).

111. To argue that the PCI has become institutionalized is not to deny the party's extensive grassroots presence — which compares favorably with other Italian parties —

nor its relatively open and participatory style in contrast to the Leninist model of organization. For a more favorable assessment of the PCI's approach to democracy, see Max Jaggi, et al., *Red Bologna* (London: Writers and Readers, 1977), pp. 7–42; and Carl Marzani, *The Promise of Eurocommunism* (Westport, Conn.: Lawrence Hill, 1980).

112. Boggs, *The Impasse of European Communism*, pp. 57–63.

113. On the peculiarly strong Leninist component of the Italian new left, see Stephen Hellman, "The New Left in Italy," in Martin Kolinsky and William E. Paterson, eds., *Social and Political Movements in Western Europe* (London: Croom Helm, 1976), pp. 256–62.

114. To be sure, these parallels are not exact and the historical context presents a range of different problems for the parties to confront. For further elaboration of this argument see Boggs, *The Impasse of European Communism*, ch. 5.

115. André Gunder Frank, "Crisis of Ideology and Ideology in Crisis," in Amin, et al., *Dynamics of Global Crisis*, p. 148.

116. Wallerstein, *Historical Capitalism*, pp. 85–92.

117. See, for example, Ash's commentary on the failure of social movements in the United States to move beyond their own localism without being absorbed into the "central institutions." Roberta Ash, *Social Movements in America* (Chicago: Markham, 1972), pp. 229–33.

118. Castells, *City and the Grassroots*, p. 328.

119. Ibid, pp. 167–69.

120. Nancy Hartsock, *Money, Sex, and Power: Toward a Feminist Historical Materialism* (Boston: Northeastern University Press, 1985), pp. 138–39.

121. Ibid., pp. 254, 261.

122. Kathy E. Ferguson, *The Feminist Case against Bureaucracy* (Philadelphia: Temple University Press, 1984), pp. 20–29, 180–82.

123. Ibid., p. 23.

124. Nicos Poulantzas, *State, Power, Socialism* (London: New Left Books, 1978), pp. 123–60.

125. William A. Gamson, *The Strategy of Social Protest* (Homewood, Ill.: Dorsey Press, 1975), ch. 7. See also Gordon Smith, "Social Movements and Party Systems in Western Europe," in Kolinsky and Paterson, eds., *Social and Political Movements*, pp. 331–50.

CHAPTER 3

1. Adam Przeworski, "Social Democracy as an Historical Phenomenon," *New Left Review* (July–Aug. 1980): 42–44.

2. Frank Parkin, *Class Inequality and Political Order* (New York: Holt, Rinehart and Winston, 1971), ch. 4.

3. The concept of the security state is developed by Joaquim Hirsch in his *Der Sicherheitstaat* (Frankfurt: Europaische Verlangsanstalt, 1980). See also his "Fordist Security State and New Social Movements," *Kapitalistate* 10–11 (1983).

4. Gerard Braunthal, *The West German Social Democrats, 1969–1982* (Boulder, Colo.: Westview Press, 1983), pp. 262–63. On the limited nature of these reforms see Manfred G. Schmidt, "The Politics of Domestic Reform in the Federal Republic of Germany," *Politics and Society* no. 2 (1978): 174–75. Both Braunthal and Schmidt observe that the Free Democrats undercut efforts toward substantial social reforms. However, this does not alter the fact that the SPD's own reform vision was linked to capitalist modernization.

5. Rudolf Bahro, "The SPD and the Peace Movement," *New Left Review* 112 (Jan.–Feb. 1982).

6. Norman Birnbaum, "The Crisis of the Social Democrats," *The Nation*, June 12, 1982. The "crisis of identity" theme was first spelled out by Richard Lowenthal in "Identität und Zukunft," *Die Neue Gesellschaft* 12 (Jan. 28, 1981).

7. Standing apart from the SPD's general line are the Jusos, or Young Socialists, whose militant socialist politics has attracted many students and intellectuals. The problem, however, is that the Jusos have exerted little leftward influence upon the SPD as a whole. See Braunthal, *West German Social Democrats*, ch. 5.

8. Oskar Negt, "The SPD: A Party of Enlightened Crisis Management," *Thesis Eleven* 11 (1984): 55, 57.

9. For an analysis of PSI efforts to situate the party in the space between the DC and the PCI, see Gianfranco Pasquino, "La Strategia del PSI: Tra Vecchie e nuove Forme di Rappresentanza Politica," *Critica Marxista* 21, no. 1 (1983).

10. *La Repubblica*, Nov. 26, 1982.

11. In order to resolve the PSI's "image" predicament, Craxi has sought closer relations with Western European Socialist leaders like Olaf Palme, Willy Brandt, Mário Soares, and Felipe Gonzales—presumably part of an effort to "social-democratize" his party, to transform it into a modernizing agency. See David Hine, "The Italian Socialist Party Under Craxi: Surviving but Not Reviving," in Peter Lange and Sidney Tarrow, eds., *Italy in Transition* (New Haven: Yale University Press, 1979), pp. 139–41.

12. Given this analysis, it would be misleading to include the PSI within the general orbit of a revitalized Eurosocialism, for it neither departs from the traditional social-democratic model nor embraces much in the way of new-movement themes. Thus James Petras' otherwise insightful essay, in subsuming the Italian, Portuguese, French, and Spanish parties under the same Eurosocialist label, overlooks these critical differences. From the standpoint of their relationship to new social movements, the Portuguese Socialists belong in the same category as the PSI, whereas the French, Spanish, and Greek parties are more accurately described as "Eurosocialist." For Petras' analysis, see "The Rise and Decline of Southern European Socialist Parties," *New Left Review* (July–Aug. 1984).

13. The overall growth of working-class power in Western European societies since 1945 can be understood as a function more of sustained economic development than of particular social-democratic policies. See Gosta Esping-Anderson and Roger Friedland, "Class Coalitions in the Making of West European Economies," in Maurice Zeitlin, ed., *Political Power and Social Theory* (Greenwich, Conn.: JAI Press, 1982), p. 34. This point is validated by the Italian case, where strong labor gains (perhaps unparalleled on the continent) occurred in the absence of any social-democratic integration.

14. See Hirsch, "The Fordist Security State and New Social Movements."

15. Robert Skidelsky, "The Decline of Keynesian Politics," in Colin Crouch, ed., *State and Economy in Contemporary Capitalism* (New York: St. Martin's Press, 1979), pp. 71–76. See also the introductory essay by Crouch, "The State, Capital, and Liberal Democracy."

16. Przeworski and Wallerstein suggest that indeed the main functional contribution of Keynesianism was not economic but political insofar as it furnished the ideological basis of "class compromise" within "capitalist democracy." See Adam Przeworski and Michael Wallerstein, "Democratic Capitalism at the Crossroads," *Democracy* (July 1982): 54.

17. On the relationship between the development of new social movements and the French Socialist party, see Arthur Hirsch, *The French New Left* (Boston: South End Press, 1981), pp. 208–14. For a more general discussion of this radicalizing impact of the new movements on Socialist parties in the European context, see Massimo Teodori, "New Lefts in Europe," in Seweryn Bialer and Sophia Sluzar, eds., *Strategies and Impact of Contemporary Radicalism* (Boulder, Colo.: Westview Press, 1977). An attempt to establish a linkage between the May Events and subsequent ideological shifts in both Socialist and Communist parties is Andrew Feenberg's "From May Events to Eurocommunism," in Carl Boggs and David Plotke, eds., *The Politics of Eurocommunism* (Boston: South End Press, 1980). Given the later collapse of the PCF, Feenberg's analysis clearly exaggerated the resiliency and adaptability of the Communists.

18. Byron Criddle, "The French Parti Socialiste," in William E. Paterson and Alastair H. Thomas, eds., *Socialist Democratic Parties in Western Europe* (London: Croom Helm, 1977), pp. 38–39.

19. George A. Codding, Jr., and William Safran, *Ideology and Politics: The Socialist Party of France* (Boulder, Colo.: Westview Press, 1979), pp. 220–27; Hughes Portelli, "The New French Socialist Party and Left Unity," *Telos* 55 (Spring 1983): 58.

20. Mark Kesselman, "Socialism Without the Workers: The Case of France," *Kapitalistate* 10–11 (1983): 17–19.

21. Jonathan Story, "Social Revolution and Democracy in Iberia," in Paterson and Thomas, eds., *Socialist Democratic Parties in Western Europe.*

22. Stanley G. Payne, "Spain's Political Future," *Current History* (Dec. 1982): 19–20. This growing detachment from the Marxist tradition did, of course, create various tensions and divisions within the leadership. See Donald Share, "Two Transitions: Democratization and the Evolution of the Spanish Socialist Left," *West European Politics* 8, no. 1 (1985), for a discussion of ideological change within the PSOE.

23. See "Growing Pains of Spanish Socialism," *Dissent* (Fall 1979), and Payne, "Spain's Political Future."

24. Howard R. Penniman, *Greece at the Polls* (Washington, D.C.: American Enterprise Institute, 1981), pp. 44–46.

25. Ibid., pp. 67–70.

26. On the development of the PS international outlook, see Diana Johnstone, *The Politics of the Euromissiles* (London: Verso, 1984), pp. 81–101.

27. See Raimond Loew, "The Politics of Austro-Marxism," *New Left Review* 118 (Nov.–Dec. 1979). As Loew makes clear, however, Austro-Marxism ultimately followed the pattern of traditional social-democratic politics (p. 50).

28. Henri Weber, "French Employees under Socialism," *New Political Science* 12 (1984): 46–47.

29. For some excellent analyses of this Mediterranean cycle of dependency and stagnation, see Giovanni Arrighi, ed., *Semiperipheral Development: The Politics of Southern Europe in the Twentieth Century* (Beverly Hills, Calif.: Sage Publications, 1985).

30. See Diana Johnstone's account in *In These Times*, May 2–8, 1984, p. 9.

31. As Kesselman notes, it was precisely this (social-democratic) Keynesian dimension of PS economic restructuring that set its austerity program apart from the old-fashioned market approach. See Mark Kesselman, "Capitalist Austerity versus Socialist 'Rigeur': Does it Make a Difference?" *New Political Science* 12 (1984).

32. Daniel Singer, "Letter from Europe," *The Nation*, Feb. 24, 1984. Singer observes that in the Talbot situation and elsewhere, the left government attempted to use the CGT as a "transmission belt" for the purpose of restoring labor peace, but with only mixed success. Where effective, such tactics would have undermined attempts to build a union presence to the left of the CGT. Of course once the PCF departed from the government, the CGT would no longer be available for such deployment.

33. It should be emphasized that the PCF decision to leave the government was not a matter of fundamental differences with the Socialists—they agreed on a program of economic and technological modernization—but involved largely secondary or tactical disagreements over austerity and other issues.

34. Diana Johnstone, "Mitterrand's New Curriculum," *In These Times*, Sept. 26–Oct. 2, 1984, p. 7

35. Mark Kesselman, "Lyrical Illusions or a Socialism of Governance: Whither French Socialism?" *Socialist Register 1985–86* (New York: Monthly Review Press, 1986).

36. Daniel Singer, "Bad News for French Socialists," *The Nation*, Nov. 30, 1985. Singer argues that the PS has evolved in the direction of the American Democratic party. Thus: "To say that the French Socialists have converted to social democracy debases the term."

37. Lucy Komisar, "Democracy First, Then Revolution," *The Nation*, Feb. 11, 1984.

38. Adrian Shubert, "The Socialists and NATO: Bringing Spain Back into Europe," *The Nation*, Dec. 21, 1985.

39. Michalis Sproudalakis, "The Greek Socialists in Action," unpublished manuscript, 1985.

40. Nicholas Xenos, "The Greek Change," *Democracy* (Spring 1983): 83–84.

41. For a report on the 1985 parliamentary elections, see Spyros Draenos, "PASOK's Triumph Is Double-Edged," *In These Times*, June 26–July 9, 1985.

42. See Sharon Zukin, "French Socialists vs. Deindustrialization: The State in the World Economy," *Telos* (Spring 1983): 147.

43. The theme of economic modernization is discussed with reference to the French Socialists by Kesselman in "Socialism Without the Workers," pp. 23–24.

44. Diana Johnstone, *In These Times*, May 2–8, 1984, p. 9.

45. Daniel Singer, "Imagination Has Not Yet Taken Power," *The Nation*, Jan. 29, 1983. Singer points out that the PS chose to resort to Keynesian methods at a time when the crisis of capitalism was undermining the old solutions. One problem is that the Socialists have been unwilling to set forth programs that might be unacceptable to business elites.

46. This perspective is developed by Petras in "The Rise and Decline of Southern European Socialist Parties," esp. pp. 51–52. There is surely a kernel of truth to this generalization, but Petras overlooks two points: first, the Eurosocialist parties do command substantial labor support and, second, the much stronger working-class base of previous Social Democratic and Labor parties failed to generate any real anticapitalist initiatives.

47. Ibid., p. 40.

48. Alain Lipietz, "Which Social Forces Are for Change?" *Telos* (Spring 1983): 29.

49. This democratizing process was of course particularly crucial to Spain and Greece, neither of which had experienced any long period of liberal democratic development. For an analysis of the Spanish case see Christopher Abel and Nissa Torrents, eds., *Spain: Conditional Democracy* (London: Croom Helm, 1984). On the role of the PSOE in democratic transformation see Jose Maria Maravall, *The Transition to Democracy in Spain* (New York: St. Martin's Press, 1982). The PASOK contribution to Greek democratization is examined by Kevin Featherstone, "The Greek Socialists in Power," *West European Politics* 6, no. 3 (1983).

50. Kesselman, "Socialism Without the Workers," p. 35.

51. Roland Cayrol, "The Crisis of the French Socialist Party," *New Political Science* 12 (1984): 9–12.

52. See, for example, Santiago Carrillo's bitter *Memoria de la Transición* (Barcelona: Grijallo, 1983), and Manuel Azcarate's *Crisis del Eurocomunismo* (Barcelona: Argos Vergara, 1982).

53. Nicos Mouzelis, "Capitalism and the Development of the Greek State," in Richard Scase, ed., *The State in Western Europe* (London: Croom Helm, 1980), pp. 260–63.

54. Adamantia Pollis, "Socialist Transformation in Greece," *Telos* 61 (Fall 1984): 107.

55. Alain Touraine, "State and Social Forces in France," *Telos* 55 (Spring 1983): 179–85. Touraine writes that "the Socialist government's reforms meeting some of the social movement's demands has resulted in the cooptation of social militants by the state's institutions. Women's organizations are being financed by the Ministry of Women's Rights, and the administrative reform granted to regional interests much more than regional movements could have gained by their own efforts" (p. 182).

56. Werner J. Feld, *The Foreign Policies of West European Parties* (New York: Praeger, 1978), pp. 68–82.

57. As Diana Johnstone points out, the Mitterrand government, whatever its pretensions toward independence and neutrality, is completely subservient to U.S. global interests. See "How the French Left Learned to Love the Bomb," *New Left Review* (July–Aug. 1984): 36.

58. Daniel Singer, "Mitterrand: Middle of the Journey," *The Nation*, March 10, 1984.

59. Johnstone, *The Politics of the Euromissiles*, p. 133.

60. See, for example, Johnstone's report in *In These Times*, May 23–29, 1984, p. 7.

61. Shubert, "The Socialists and NATO."

62. Johnstone, "A Greek Mystery," *In These Times*, Dec. 19–Jan. 8, 1984, p. 7.

63. John C. Loulis, "Papandreou's Foreign Policy," *Foreign Affairs* (Winter 1984–85): 380–81.

64. Pollis, "Socialist Transformation in Greece," p. 111.

65. A clear and recent statement of the social-democratic outlook, which argues that the "Atlantic Alliance must remain the fulcrum of American foreign policy," is Helmut Schmidt's "Saving the Western Alliance," *New York Review of Books*, May 31, 1984, pp. 25–27.

66. It should be emphasized that the issue is not whether the Mediterranean parties could move immediately toward socialism; this would obviously be a utopian dream. The issue is whether the parties were able to make a significant beginning—whether, that is, they are simply moving in a transformative direction or in some other direction.

67. Petras argues that the Eurosocialist decision to follow the logic of capital was a function of the parties' absence of working-class support. See "The Rise and Decline of Southern European Socialist Parties," p. 51. However, the working-class base of Euro-socialist parties is much broader than Petras suggests.

68. For a parallel interpretation of the modernizing role of the Mediterranean Socialist parties, but one that is much less critical of their direction, see Franco Ferrarotti, "The Modernizing Role of the Working-Class Parties in Southern Europe," in Bogdan Denitch, ed., *Democratic Socialism: The Mass Left in Advanced Industrial Societies* (Totowa, N.J.: Allanheld Osmun, 1981).

69. The similarities of Kautsky and the Eurocommunist theory of structural reforms are further elaborated in my book, *The Impasse of European Communism* (Boulder, Colo.: Westview Press, 1982), ch. 5. As I suggest in that analysis, the seemingly divergent approaches of Bernstein and Kautsky are collapsed into a single framework after the Bolshevik Revolution rendered the agreements on their parliamentarism greater than their differences.

70. The tension between the disruptive logic of popular movements and the stabilizing imperatives of institutional politics analyzed by Piven and Cloward is equally applicable to the West European context, even if the political alignments and the ideological contexts differ. See Frances Fox Piven and Richard Cloward, *Poor People's Movements* (New York: Vintage, 1979), pp. xix–xxiv.

71. Claus Offe, "Political Authority and Class Structures," in Paul Connerton, ed., *Critical Sociology* (New York: Penguin Books, 1976), p. 404.

72. Barry Hindess, *Parliamentary Democracy and Socialist Politics* (London: Routledge & Kegan Paul, 1983), pp. 144–45.

73. On the institutionalization of Eurocommunist-style parties, see my treatment of the PCI in *The Impasse of European Communism*, pp. 84–90.

74. Przeworski, "Social Democracy as a Historical Phenomenon," p. 54.

75. Wilhelm suggests that such a transformative process should go further, to include not only the economy and the political system but also "social relations" in the broadest sense. See Donald Wilhelm, *Creative Alternatives to Communism* (London: Macmillan, 1977), p. 146. This approach represents a decisive break with structural reformism and is consistent with a strategy based in the new social movements.

CHAPTER 4

1. The period since the late 1970s has seen several theoretical efforts in this direction. These include: Martin Carnoy and Derek Shearer, *Economic Democracy* (White

Plains, N.Y.: M. E. Sharpe, 1980), and *The New Social Contract* (New York: Harper & Row, 1983); Tom Hayden, *The American Future: New Visions Beyond Old Frontiers* (Boston: South End Press, 1980); Harry C. Boyte, *The Backyard Revolution: Understanding the New Citizen Movement* (Philadelphia: Temple University Press, 1980), and *Community is Possible: Repairing America's Roots* (New York: Harper & Row, 1984); Mark Kann, *The American Left* (New York: Praeger, 1982). See also the special issue of *Social Policy* (Spring 1983), which is devoted to an assessment of new-populist organizing efforts.

2. For an analysis of right-wing populism see Frances Fox Piven and Richard Cloward, *The New Class War* (New York: Pantheon, 1982), and Kevin Phillips, *Post-Conservative America: Politics and Ideology in a Time of Crisis* (New York: Random House, 1982).

3. As Edelman argues, the state functions less as a medium of decision making than as a mechanism for overcoming tensions and conflicts through its symbolic commitment to future development. See Murray Edelman, "The Future of American Politics," in Mark E. Kann, ed., *The Future of American Democracy: Views from the Left* (Philadelphia: Temple University Press, 1983), pp. 233–38.

4. Here the new-populist model might be seen as an extension of what Kann defines as the tradition of "radical liberalism" in American politics, with its emphasis on democratizing the public sphere. See his *The American Left*. See also the interesting treatment of this problem by C. B. Macpherson in *The Life and Times of Liberal Democracy* (New York: Oxford University Press, 1977), ch. 5. Macpherson distinguishes "participatory democracy," in both its Rousseauian and new-left variants, from three other models of liberal democracy, defining it as an effort to carry the democratic ethic beyond the political system narrowly defined into the community and workplaces.

5. Harry Boyte, "Populism and the Left," *Democracy* (April 1981).

6. Tom Hayden, *The American Future*, p. 181.

7. Kann, *The American Left*, pp. 25–50.

8. These two phenomena—elitism and workerism—can be seen as twin expressions of the same dynamic. As Aronowitz points out, the referents *class* and *class analysis* have often been employed by leftists as rhetorical abstractions largely disconnected from working-class social existence. See Stanley Aronowitz, "Remaking of the American Left," part II, *Socialist Review* 13, no. 3 (May–June 1983): 33.

9. On the limits of left Keynesianism in postwar European Social Democratic parties, see Adam Przeworski, "Social Democracy as an Historical Phenomenon," *New Left Review* (July–Aug. 1980): 51–53.

10. Hayden's critique of the "bureaucratic, impersonal, and expansionistic" character of the Keynesian welfare state in the United States can equally be applied to the social-democratic model. See *The American Future*, pp. 177–78.

11. Carnoy and Shearer, *Economic Democracy*, p. 290.

12. Carnoy and Shearer, *The New Social Contract*, ch. 6.

13. Boyte, "Populism and the Left," pp. 60–63. See also Boyte's "Building the Democratic Movement: Prospects for a Socialist Renaissance," *Socialist Review* (July–Oct. 1978): 17–41.

14. Even though this schema differs from the historical legacy of social democracy, its ideological parallels with a similar American tendency, the DSA, are rather striking. This has allowed for the development of various local alliances between DSA and new-

populist groups. For a concise statement of DSA politics in this context, see Michael Harrington, "A Path for America: Proposals from the Democratic Left," *Dissent* (Fall 1982).

15. See Carnoy and Shearer, *Economic Democracy*, ch. 9, where the authors present a "different view of the seventies."

16. For an excellent overview of such attitudinal changes in the United States and other industrialized societies, see Ronald Inglehart, *The Silent Revolution* (Princeton, N.J.: Princeton University Press, 1977), introduction. See also Daniel Yankelovich, *New Rules* (New York: Random House, 1981), for more recent empirical data in support of this argument for the United States.

17. This point is further developed by Piven and Cloward in *The New Class War*, p. 31. As this statement implies, the authors conclude that the welfare state is not merely functional to the needs of capital accumulation but is also the locus of social conflict.

18. Frances Fox Piven and Richard Cloward, "The American Road to Democratic Socialism," *Democracy* (Summer 1983): 58–61.

19. Not all new-populist theorists share this viewpoint, however. Lawrence Goodwyn, for example, was one of the leading early proponents of the Citizens party, which emerged in 1980 in support of the presidential candidacy of Barry Commoner. Goodwyn served for a brief period on the Citizens party's national executive committee.

20. *Los Angeles Times*, Oct. 2, 1983.

21. More or less the same type of political commitment and organizational cohesion typifies other new-populist formations of the sort described in the next section. I have chosen to emphasize CED in this chapter for two reasons: it is both more ideologically coherent and more electorally advanced than these other organizations.

22. Jeff Lustig, "Community and Social Class," *Democracy* (April 1981): 97.

23. Lawrence Goodwyn, *The Populist Moment* (London: Oxford University Press, 1978), pp. 294–95.

24. Ernesto Laclau, *Politics and Ideology in Marxist Theory* (London: New Left Books, 1977), p. 160.

25. Kann, *The American Left*, p. 186.

26. See, for example, Boyte's discussion in *Backyard Revolution*, ch. 7.

27. Andrew Feenberg, "Paths to Failure: The Dialectics of Organization and Ideology in the New Left," *Humanities and Society* (Summer 1984): 397.

28. It is this particular commitment to democratization, or "empowerment," that links together the various movements that might come under the heading "new populism." See S. M. Miller and Donald Tomaskovic-Dewey, "A Framework for New Progressive Coalitions," *Social Policy* (Spring 1983): 9.

29. John McKnight and John Kretzmann, "Community Organizing in the 80s: Toward a Post-Alinsky Agenda," *Social Policy* (Winter 1984).

30. DARE was created in 1978 by nearly two hundred Detroit activists, including representatives of the black, labor, religious, and neighborhood communities. Begun as part of the campaign to elect Ken Cockrell to the city council, DARE worked to secure community control of housing, schools, and health care. It built a small but militant and independent multiracial grouping in opposition to dominant corporate interests. After a few years of intense political activity, divisions within DARE surfaced over whether to move in the direction of a class-based or community-defined organization— i.e., whether to explicitly embrace a socialist identity—resulting in an impasse that, in

1981, forced DARE to dissolve. See Jim Jacobs, "DARE to Struggle: Organizing in Urban America," *Socialist Review* (May–Aug. 1982): 85–104.

31. On the development of ACORN see Gary Delgado, *Organizing the Movement: The Roots and Growth of ACORN* (Philadelphia: Temple University Press, 1986).

32. Derek Shearer, "How the Progressives Won Santa Monica," *Social Policy* (Winter 1982): 8.

33. Mark E. Kann, *Middle Class Radicalism in Santa Monica* (Philadelphia: Temple University Press, 1986), p. 267.

34. Shearer, "How the Progressives Won Santa Monica," p. 12.

35. The term "ad-hoc radicalism" is Kann's. See his "Radicals in Power: Lessons from Santa Monica," *Socialist Review* (May–June 1983): 86.

36. *Economic Democracy*, p. 403.

37. Ibid., p. 375.

38. Again, the best discussion of this process is contained in Frances Fox Piven and Richard Cloward, *Poor People's Movements* (New York: Vintage, 1979), esp. pp. xi–xxi and 5–36.

39. See, for example, Maurizio Marcelloni, "Urban Movements and Political Struggle in Italy," *International Journal of Urban and Regional Research* (June 1979), and my *The Impasse of European Communism* (Boulder, Colo.: Westview Press, 1982), pp. 84–90.

40. For an excellent discussion of this problem, situated in the European context but applicable elsewhere, see Miliband, *Marxism and Politics* (Oxford: Oxford University Press, 1980), ch. 6. Miliband observes that even "reformist" strategies, if taken seriously and pursued to their logical conclusion, require a fundamental transformation of the state and of pluralist-democratic structures. He further argues that governing leftist parties will not be able to supply what is necessary for this kind of transition—namely, "a flexible and complex network of organs of popular participation operating through civil society and intended not to *replace* the state but to *complement* it" (pp. 188–89; italics in the original).

41. Hayden, *The American Future*, p. 299.

42. On the submergence of left identity within Democratic party politics, see the essay by Andrew Kopkind and Alexander Cockburn, "The Left, the Democrats, and the Future," *The Nation*, July 21–28, 1984.

43. See Stanley Aronowitz, "The Party's Over," *The Progressive* (Feb. 1986): 19–21.

44. James Green, "The Making of Mel King's Rainbow Coalition: Political Changes in Boston 1963–83," *Radical America*, Nov. 1983–Feb. 1984.

45. Robert Brenner, "Can the Left Use the Democratic Party," *Against the Current* (Fall 1984): 7.

46. On this point see Michael Parenti, *Democracy for the Few* (New York: St. Martin's Press, 1977), ch. 11.

47. Sheila Rowbotham, et al., *Beyond the Fragments* (London: Merlin Press, 1979), pp. 132–44. See also Kathy E. Ferguson, *The Feminist Case against Bureaucracy* (Philadelphia: Temple University Press, 1984), pp. 180–82.

48. *Economic Democracy*, ch. 4.

49. Hayden's long interview in *The Executive* (Sept. 1980) is especially revealing on these issues.

50. *The Backyard Revolution*, chs. 4 and 5.

51. Ibid., p. 139.

52. As Lustig notes, Boyte's celebratory approach to virtually all citizens' movements makes it impossible for him to determine which ones are likely to move beyond liberal reform politics and which are not. See "Community and Social Class," p. 109.

53. *Poor People's Movements*, p. xxii.

54. This argument parallels Michels' critique of German Social Democracy with the qualification that the antidemocratic tendencies Michels saw in the SPD were surely more extreme than those that now characterize the new populism—in part because the SPD was a larger and more successful national party with all the bureaucratic trappings.

55. See *The Impasse of European Communism*, pp. 91–100. For a more positive assessment of this experience, see Max Jaggi, et al., *Red Bologna* (London: Writers and Readers, 1977).

56. Isaac Balbus examines the components of such a participatory culture in *Marxism and Domination* (Princeton, N.J.: Princeton University Press, 1982), ch. 10.

57. *Poor People's Movements*, p. xxii.

58. Laurie Lieberman, "The People's Republics of Santa Monica and Red Bologna: Model Democratic Cities?" (unpublished paper, 1984), p. 15.

59. Kann, "Radicals in Power," p. 90.

60. Lieberman, "The People's Republics of Santa Monica and Red Bologna," p. 22.

61. *The American Future*, pp. 33–36.

62. Ibid., pp. 290–92. It is worth noting that Hayden's optimism concerning an American cultural revolution parallels the conclusions of Yankelovich in *New Rules*, discussed in ch. 2.

63. *Economic Democracy*, pp. 26–27.

64. Ibid.

65. Ibid., p. 396.

66. *Backyard Revolution*, pp. 184–86. See also "Populism and the Left," pp. 62–65, where Boyte speaks of the need to "recover our democratic heritage."

67. Boyte, "Beyond 1984," *Social Policy* (Winter 1984): p. 11.

68. See, for example, Boyte's "Populism and the Left."

69. On the theme of linking socialist goals with new-populist-style organizing and campaigning, see Mike Rotkin and Bruce Van Allen, "Community and Electoral Politics," *Socialist Review* (Sept.–Oct. 1979). The need for a coherent strategy of transition, generally downplayed by the American left, is discussed by Michael Albert and Robin Hahnel, *Socialism Today and Tomorrow* (Boston: South End Press, 1981), esp. pp. 280–81.

70. By "instrumentalism" I have in mind the focus of a movement or party on largely power-defined objectives that stress the role of interest-group bargaining and/or institutional engineering over the democratizing goals associated with popular mobilization and direct action. Within the American party system, instrumentalism has historically functioned to narrow political discourse and confine participation within elite-controlled structures. For an analysis of this dynamic, see Brian Murphy and Alan Wolfe, "Democracy in Disarray," *Kapitalistate* 8 (1980): 9–25. See also the analysis of "electoral engineering" in Piven and Cloward, *Poor People's Movements*, introduction.

71. Allan Heskin, *Tenants and the American Dream* (New York: Praeger, 1983),

ch. 1. The Santa Monica rent-control movement drew most of its popular strength from liberal or progressive constituencies that were white, professional, highly educated, and (contrary to common belief) in the lower- to middle-income range.

72. *Backyard Revolution*, pp. 24–26.

73. The "pro-family" tendency achieved its most coherent political expression in the Oakland-based organization "Friends of Family," formed in 1981 by Michael Lerner and Laurie Zoloth. For an excellent discussion and critique of this position, see Barbara Epstein, "Family Politics and the New Left," *Socialist Review* 63–64 (May–Aug. 1982). On the drift toward cultural traditionalism in the American left, see Ellen Willis, "Betty Friedan's 'Second Stage': A Step Backward," *The Nation*, Nov. 14, 1981.

74. In subsequent writings Boyte does modify his perspective somewhat. After identifying two polar views within the American left—the communalism typical of new populism and a cultural radicalism expressed through the "individual liberationist" position—Boyte and Sara Evans argue for a convergence of the two models as the basis of transformative politics. See "Strategies in Search of America: Cultural Radicalism, Populism, and Democratic Culture," *Socialist Review* (May–Aug. 1984): esp. 91–98.

75. "State and Civil Society," in Quintin Hoare and Geoffrey Nowell-Smith, eds., *Selections from the Prison Notebooks of Antonio Gramsci* (New York: International Publishers, 1971), p. 210.

76. This democratizing potential of feminism is stressed by Rowbotham in *Beyond the Fragments* (esp. pp. 71–82) and from a different viewpoint by Zillah Eisenstein, *The Radical Future of Liberal Feminism* (New York: Longman, 1981), and Ferguson, *The Feminist Case against Bureaucracy*, esp. pp. 22–29.

77. Kann, *Middle Class Radicalism in Santa Monica*, pp. 274–75.

78. The possibility that community might be suffocating rather than emancipatory is suggested in John Stuart Mill's "rejoinder" to Rousseau. Mill writes that "when society itself is the tyrant—society collectively over the separate individuals who compose it—its means of tyrannizing are not restricted to the acts which it may do by the hands of its political functionaries. Society can and does execute its own mandates: and if it issues wrong mandates instead of right, or any mandates at all in things with which it ought not to meddle, it practices a social tyranny more formidable than many kinds of political repression, since, though not usually upheld by such extreme penalties, it leaves fewer means of escape, penetrating much more deeply into the details of life, and enslaving the soul itself. Protection, therefore, against the tyranny of the magistrate is not enough: there needs be protection also against the tyranny of the prevailing opinion and feeling; against the tendency of society to impose, by other means than civil penalties, its own ideas and practices as rules of conduct on those who dissent from them. . . ." *On Liberty* (London: J. M. Dent, 1964), p. 68.

79. Jim Green, "Culture, Politics, and Workers' Response to Industrialization in the U.S.," *Radical America* (Jan.–Feb. and March–April 1982): 104.

80. Kann, *Middle Class Radicalism in Santa Monica*, conclusion.

81. Robert Bellah, "Populism and Individualism," *Social Policy* (Fall 1985): 30–31.

82. See Paul Mattick, *Marx and Keynes* (Boston: Porter Sargent, 1969), ch. 21.

83. For a discussion of Santa Monica as a possible model for other new-populist efforts see Dave Moberg, "From Rent Control to Municipal Power: The Santa Monica

Story," *In These Times*, Jan. 12–18, 1983, p. 22, and Kann, *Middle Class Radicalism in Santa Monica*, pp. 269–75.

84. On the conservative drift of CED see Joan Walsh, "The 'New, Improved' Campaign for Economic Democracy," *In These Times*, Aug. 21–Sept. 3, 1985.

85. This critique of the new populism suggests that a crucial problem for the American left is not so much the failure to articulate a compelling vision of the future rooted in a system of collective values—as writers like Alan Wolfe argue—but rather the inability to concretize those values or, put another way, to arrive at a congruence of strategy and vision. For Wolfe's insights see "Toward a New Politics on the Left," *The Nation*, Sept. 22, 1984.

CHAPTER 5

1. Horst Mewes, "The West German Green Party," *New German Critique* 28 (1983): 67.

2. Steve Katz, "The Forest Continues to Beckon Us," *The German Issue* 4, no. 2 (1982): 180–93.

3. Elim Papadakis, *The Green Movement in West Germany* (New York: St. Martin's Press, 1984), p. 114.

4. On the early development of the Greens see ibid., pp. 157–86.

5. For accounts of the 1983 Bundestag election see Rainer Eisfeld, "The West German Elections," *Government and Opposition* 18, no. 3 (Summer 1983), and Andrei S. Markovits, "West Germany's Political Future: The 1983 Bundestag Elections,"*Socialist Review* 70 (Summer 1983).

6. Examples abound of such simplistic descriptions of the Greens in the American press. See, for example, John Vinocur's article in the *New York Times Magazine*, Aug. 8, 1982.

7. This immense complexity of Green politics is enough to suggest that any depiction of the Greens as a "spiritual offspring of the SPD" (Markovits, "West Germany's Political Future," p. 80) is likely to be misleading.

8. Petra Kelly, *Fighting for Hope* (Boston: South End Press, 1984), p. 14.

9. Joaquim Hirsch, "The West German Peace Movement," *Telos* (Spring 1982): 136.

10. Otto Kallscheuer, "Philosophy and Politics in the SPD," *Telos* (Fall 1982): 86. See also Norman Birnbaum, "The Crisis of the Social Democrats," *The Nation*, June 12, 1982.

11. Die Grünen, *Das Bundesprogramm* (Bonn, 1982), p. 5. For the English translation see Die Grünen, *Programme of the German Green Party* (London: Heretic Books, 1983), p. 8.

12. Interview with Petra Kelly, *In These Times*, Feb. 16–22, 1983.

13. For the spirit of this internationalism, see *Das Bundesprogramm*, pp. 17–21 (pp. 23–29 in the English version). This emphasis in Green ideology is conveniently overlooked by critics of the Greens and the West German peace movement, who somehow see only a resurgent nationalism (and romanticism) associated, presumably, with the prospect of a united Germany emerging out of convergent struggles in both the East

and West. Though Green politics is surely open to a number of criticisms, as we shall see, this is not one of them—a fact that even the most cursory glance at the party program will reveal.

14. On the "holistic" dimension of Green thinking, see Fritjof Capra and Charlene Spretnak, *Green Politics* (New York: E. P. Dutton, 1984), pp. 29–56. The authors wish to stress the importance of systems theory, but in relying heavily upon a functionalist interpretation of this framework they wind up eliminating the dynamic element of conflict, which robs Green ideology of its radical thrust.

15. Rudolf Bahro, *From Red to Green* (London: New Left Books, 1984), p. 218.

16. Ibid., p. 183.

17. *Das Bundesprogramm*, p. 5 (p. 9).

18. There is also the hotly debated "imperative mandate," according to which delegates or representatives must endorse policies already determined by Green activists in assemblies, conferences, referenda, and so forth. But this principle has been honored mostly in the breach, and there were indications by late 1984 that the party would formally jettison it, at least in its most rigid formulation.

19. See Kelly, *Fighting for Hope*, p. 22.

20. *Das Bundesprogramm*, p. 29 (pp. 37–38).

21. Ibid., p. 5 (p. 9).

22. Kelly, *Fighting for Hope*, p. 31.

23. Daniel Cohn-Bendit, "The Anti-Nuclear Movement," in *The German Issue* 4, no. 2 (1982): 281.

24. This distinctly radical content of Green ideology, whatever its diverse origins and themes, should be enough to dispel the stereotype that locates the party "beyond left and right." Though it is true that the vast majority of Greens has reacted against Marxism (notably in its orthodox forms), this has in effect broadened rather than closed off space to the left of the SPD. Moreover, the "red-green" tendency within the party has actually been strengthened since 1981, after the more traditional environmentalists decided to leave. The "neither left nor right" interpretation is stressed by Capra and Spretnak in *Green Politics*, p. 3.

25. See, for example, Joaquim Hirsch's excellent analysis of this trend in "Fordist Security State and New Social Movements," in *Kapitalistate* 10–11 (1983).

26. The economic program, entitled "Meaningful Work: Living in Solidarity," was published in *Die Zeit*, Jan. 28, 1983. Formulated in preparation for the March 1983 election, this program was intended to generate further discussion of the issues and therefore was never seen as a final statement. The ideas that came out of the Sindelfingen meeting found their way into the revised Green party program of Nov. 1983 (which is cited in this section).

27. *Das Bundesprogramm*, p. 7 (p. 10).

28. For an extended discussion of this component of Green economics, see Capra and Spretnak, *Green Politics*, ch. 4, and Jonathan Porritt, *Seeing Green: The Politics of Ecology Explained* (Oxford: Basil Blackwell, 1984), ch. 14. Though Porritt's attention is devoted largely to the experience of the British Ecology party, his ideas are clearly shaped by his involvement with the West German Greens. (Porritt wrote the introduction to the English version of the *Bundesprogramm*.)

29. *Das Bundesprogramm*, p. 7 (p. 10).

30. Ibid., p. 7 (p. 11).

31. Ibid., p. 7 (pp. 11–12).

32. Ibid., p. 44 (p. 51).

33. Ibid., p. 20 (p. 28).

34. Ibid., p. 17 (p. 24).

35. Ibid., p. 20 (p. 28).

36. Unfortunately, the concept of social conversion is never explicitly formulated in the party program. It was initially outlined in Petra Kelly's famous letter to Willy Brandt in the fall of 1982 and then developed further in the Sindelfingen report of Jan. 1983. For Kelly's statement, see the *Frankfurter Rundschau*, Nov. 16, 1982.

37. Rudolf Bahro, *Socialism and Survival* (London: Heretic Books, 1982), pp. 125–29.

38. *Das Bundesprogramm*, p. 14 (p. 20).

39. Ibid., p. 23 (p. 30).

40. In this vein Bahro speaks of the need to "reconstruct God" in *From Red to Green* (London: Verso, 1984), p. 194; Kelly urges a shift to a defense system based upon the "spiritual weapons of love and warmth" in *Fighting for Hope*, p. 46; and Porritt argues for the affinity of Green ideology with liberation theology in *Seeing Green*, p. 211. The "spiritualist" outlook also permeates Capra and Spretnak's *Green Politics*. It should be noted, however, that the party program does not explicitly incorporate such a vision, which is, at the same time, held by a sizable minority of Green members and supporters.

41. See Kelly, *Fighting for Hope*, pp. 37–40, where "eco-feminist" principles are seen as a counter to male-centered militarism.

42. The difficulty with most critiques of Green economics is the tendency to focus exclusively on this romanticist element, which is marginal and finds little expression in the party program, while ignoring those more decisive aspects of the developmental model stressed here. For an example of this type of simplistic attack on the Greens, see Michael Barrett Brown, *Models in Political Economy* (New York: Penguin Books, 1984), ch. 7.

43. *New York Times*, March 9, 1983.

44. E. P. Thompson, "Notes on Exterminism: The Last Stage of Civilization," in E. P. Thompson, ed., *Exterminism and the Cold War* (London: New Left Books, 1982), pp. 1–30.

45. Ibid., pp. 20–21.

46. Rudolph Bahro, "The SPD and the Peace Movement," *New Left Review* (Jan.–Feb. 1982): 46.

47. *Das Bundesprogramm*, p. 19 (p. 25).

48. Ibid., p. 18 (p. 25).

49. It should be noted noted here that the CDU electoral victory in 1983 did not constitute a clear go-ahead for missile deployment. Polls at the time of the election showed that a solid majority (as much as 70 percent) of the West German population was opposed to the NATO decision. This apparent contradiction can no doubt be attributed to a greater salience of issues related to the economic crisis during the campaign.

50. *Frankfurter Rundschau*, Nov. 16, 1982.

51. *Das Bundesprogramm*, p. 18 (p. 25).

52. This scenario was discussed by Trampert in an interview in *Die Zeit*, March 4, 1983.

53. For a sense of the differences between the Greens and the SPD, see Bahro, "The SPD and the Peace Movement."

54. Bahro, *From Red to Green*, p. 234.

55. *Das Bundesprogramm*, p. 19 (p. 26).

56. Interview with Bahro conducted by the author in Los Angeles, Sept. 11, 1983.

57. See in particular Sharp's *Making Europe Unconquerable* (London: Taylor and Francis, 1985).

58. The reference under "European Peace Policy" is to a program of "social defense in place of the arms race which is leading to a third world war." *Das Bundesprogramm*, p. 19 (p. 27).

59. Kelly, *Fighting for Hope*, pp. 66–68.

60. *Das Bundesprogramm*, p. 19 (p. 26).

61. Along these lines Bahro argued that the much-advertised question of German reunification was not on the agenda as far as the Greens are concerned. In his words: "If you look at people on both political sides in West Germany I think there is very little interest in reunification. There is some real process of reunification, but not with the idea of some new *state* emerging. Nation-states are an obsolete concept. Nationalism is strongly contradictory to our whole concept of decentralization and with it the abolition of power blocs and large states. Even the state of Bavaria is too big" (interview with Bahro, Sept. 11, 1983).

62. On this point see Timothy Garton Ash, "Which Way Will Germany Go?" *New York Review of Books*, Jan. 31, 1985.

63. For an English-language account of the Greens' role in exposing the Flick scandal see James M. Markham, "Those Troubled Germans," *New York Times Magazine*, Feb. 10, 1985.

64. The urgency of this final priority—the commitment to a unilateralist initiative— was stressed repeatedly by Roland Vogt in an interview that I conducted with him in Bonn on Dec. 1, 1982.

65. For a treatment of these debates in the context of a short-lived "working cooperation" between the Greens and the SPD in the Kreuzberg section of West Berlin, see Jörg R. Mettke, "Das Kreuzberger Modell," in Jörg R. Mettke, ed., *Die Grünen* (Hamburg: Spiegel Buch, 1982), pp. 51–58. The district election of May 1981 gave nineteen seats each to the SPD and CDU, whereas the Alternative List (with 19 percent of the vote) won seven seats and was thereby in a position to determine the makeup of the governing coalition.

66. "Bundesweit dritte Kraft," *Das Parlament*, Dec. 22–29, 1984.

67. On the post-Congress debates regarding the issue of cooperation with the SPD, see "Wir Werden schön Richten!" *Die Zeit*, Dec. 14, 1984.

68. Papadakis, *The Green Movement*, p. 192.

69. Wolf-Dieter Narr, "Andere Politik oder eine neun Form der Politik?" in Mettke, ed., *Die Grünen*, pp. 266–68.

70. Reported in the *Frankfurter Rundschau*, Aug. 12, 1982.

71. Mettke, "Auf beiden Flügeln in die Höhe," in Mettke, ed., *Die Grünen*, p. 24.

72. "Die Grünen vor der Zerreissprobe," *Die Zeit*, May 31, 1985. Fischer suggests that the alternative to full-time cadres may well be political suicide.

73. Wolf-Dieter Hasenclever, "Die Grünen im Lantag von Baden-Wurttemberg," in Mettke, ed., *Die Grünen*, pp. 115–19.

74. Kelly, *Fighting for Hope*, p. 111.

75. This quote is from Capra and Spretnak, *Green Politics*, p. 53. Throughout this book the authors attach a significance to the spiritual dimension beyond what the vast majority of Greens would be willing to accept.

76. By late 1984, in fact, the extreme spiritualist tendency seemed to be on the decline within the party—as reflected, for instance, in Bahro's waning influence and growing marginal status in the organization. The distance between Bahro's antimodernism and the party consensus was most visible in Bahro's "farewell" address to the Hamburg Congress. See "Ein Prophet ohne Jünger," *Die Zeit*, Dec. 14, 1984.

77. For a graphic study of how the Gandhian "revolution" failed to improve the brutal conditions of Indian social existence, see Barrington Moore, Jr., *Social Origins of Dictatorship and Democracy* (Boston: Beacon Press, 1966), ch. 5.

78. For a discussion of this problem in the Green context, see Narr, "Andere Politik," in Mettke, ed., *Die Grünen*, and "Stimmen hören oder Stimmen zählen?" *Die Zeit*, Dec. 14, 1984.

79. Narr, in "Andere Politik," observed the predominance of such adaptive tendencies in the West Berlin Alternative List as early as 1982 (pp. 265–66).

80. This was the theme of a lecture on Green development by Joaquim Hirsch in San Francisco, Calif., in April 1985.

81. Papadakis, *The Green Movement*, pp. 201–22. See also the discussion in "Have West Germany's Greens a Future?" *The Economist*, Aug. 11–17, 1984.

82. Martin Jänicke, "Parlamentarische Entwarmungseffeckte?" in Mettke, ed., *Die Grünen*, pp. 76, 80.

83. To affirm the language of "rupture" in this sense is not the same thing as suggesting that a full transcendence of the system—of the multiple forms of domination— is on the immediate agenda. The pace and timing of radical transformation is yet another issue. On this point see Narr, "Andere Politik," pp. 266–68, and Jänicke, "Parlamentarische," pp. 280–81.

84. Werner Hülsberg, "The Greens at the Crossroads," *New Left Review* (July–Aug. 1985): 11.

85. For a comprehensive statement of the "eco-socialist" position, which explores many of these economic issues, see Thomas Eberman and Rainer Trampert, *Zukunft der Grünen: Ein realistisches Konzept für eine radikale Partei* (Hamburg: Konkret-Verlag, 1984).

86. The Saarland election results in Feb. 1985, in which the Greens received only 2.5 percent of the vote, were particularly painful insofar as the SPD, for the first time, demonstrated that it could undercut the Greens by appealing to new-movement constituencies.

87. The new mood within the Green orbit is examined at length in "Der Spass am Grün-Sein ist 'raus,' " *Die Zeit*, May 10, 1985.

88. Ash, "Which Way Will Germany Go?" p. 40.

89. See Diana Johnstone's account of this meeting in *In These Times*, April 25–May 1, 1984.

90. For an elaborate statement of British Ecology politics, which in fact departs considerably from the West German pattern, see Porritt's *Seeing Green.*

91. This "new age" image of the Greens permeates the Capra and Spretnak analysis in *Green Politics*, which proclaims on its cover, "We are neither left nor right, we are in front."

92. This critique can also be found in Herbert B. Kitschelt's review of the Capra and Spretnak volume in *Theory and Society* (July 1985), and in Wini Breines' review of the same book, in *Socialist Review* (May–June, 1985).

CHAPTER 6

1. Jean Cohen, "Rethinking Social Movements," *Berkeley Journal of Sociology* (1983): 97–98.

2. This is the message of Daniel Yankelovich, *New Rules* (New York: Random House, 1981), and Inglehart, *The Silent Revolution* (Princeton, N.J.: Princeton University Press, 1977). The former is a study of popular consciousness in the United States; the latter focuses mainly upon Western Europe.

3. The political implications of this growing internationalization of capital are discussed at length by the contributors (Samir Amin, et al.) to *The Dynamics of Global Crisis* (New York: Monthly Review Press, 1982).

4. On this point, see Manuel Castells, "Space and Society: Managing the New Historical Relationship," in Michael Peter Smith, ed., *Cities in Transformation: Class, Capital, and the State* (Beverly Hills, Calif.: Sage Publications, 1984), pp. 253–57.

5. George Konrad, *Antipolitics* (London: New Left Books, 1984), pp. 2–6.

6. Ibid., p. 230.

7. As Halliday observes, "the new cold war is a response by the USA and its allies to the failure of detente as a means of waging globalized social conflict to their own advantage." See Fred Halliday, *The Making of the Second Cold War* (London: New Left Books, 1983), p. 293.

8. See, for example, the elaboration of this point by Andrew Kopkind, "The Return of Cold War Liberalism," *The Nation*, April 23, 1983.

9. Once again it is necessary to emphasize that such geopolitical divisions are dramatically reinforced by the advent of nuclear politics. As Konrad writes: "The undisputed hegemony of the state over civil society is manifested in the fact that the state possesses nuclear forces or consents to an alliance that can take the country into nuclear war. It is no exaggeration to say that atomic weapons perform a police function: the opposed blocs mutually intimidate each other's populations." *Antipolitics*, p. 32.

10. Marion Anderson, "The Empty Pork Barrel," in Ronald V. Dellums, ed., *Defense Sense: The Search for a Rational Defense Policy* (Cambridge, Mass.: Ballinger, 1983), p. 184.

11. Marxists tend to stress the functional side of military spending for capitalist development. For an analysis of its disruptive effects (even for capitalist priorities), see Seymour Melman, *The Permanent War Economy: American Capitalism in Decline* (New York: Simon & Schuster, 1974). A more concise statement of Melman's thesis is contained in "Military Spending and Domestic Bankruptcy," in Dellums, ed., *Defense Sense*, pp. 159–61.

12. See Paula Rayman's excellent treatment of this problem in her contribution to Michael Albert and David Dellinger, eds., *Beyond Survival* (Boston: South End Press, 1983).

13. This is the line of argument presented in Raymond Williams, *The Year 2000* (New York: Pantheon, 1983), esp. pp. 165–70. See also Fred Block's contribution to the exchange on "Growth and Employment," *Socialist Review* 75–76 (May–Aug. 1984): 25–27.

14. Suzanne Gordon, "Economic Conversion Activity in Western Europe," in Gordon and David McFadden, eds., *Economic Conversion* (Cambridge, Mass.: Ballinger, 1984), pp. 108–29.

15. It is worth noting that the Campaign for Economic Democracy, one of the largest new-populist groups, has lent its resources to Jobs with Peace.

16. The official Jobs with Peace initiative reads (in part) as follows: "The Los Angeles City Council calls upon the U.S. Congress and the President to make more federal money available for jobs and programs in: education, housing, health and human services, public transportation, the arts, rebuilding the civilian economy, and conversion of military jobs to peacetime production by reducing the amount of our tax dollars spent on nuclear weapons, wasteful military programs, and military aid to undemocratic governments known to violate human rights. These policies will promote a healthy economy, true national security, and jobs with peace."

17. For an extensive treatment of this and other approaches to the state (but which fails to draw out the strategic consequences of the different theories), see Martin Carnoy, *The State and Political Theory* (Princeton, N.J.: Princeton University Press, 1984), ch. 6.

18. Claus Offe, *Contradictions of the Welfare State* (Cambridge: MIT Press, 1984), chs. 8, 11.

19. Ibid., p. 250.

20. Frances Fox Piven and Richard Cloward, *Poor People's Movements* (New York: Vintage, 1979), preface and introduction.

21. Inglehart, *The Silent Revolution*, esp. pp. 363–67.

22. On this point, see Kirkpatrick Sale, *Human Scale* (New York: Doubleday, 1982), pp. 455–65.

23. Richard Worthington argues that ecological theory is vital to the reconstitution of socialist politics along democratic and holistic lines. This view is close to the post-Marxist generalization outlined here, so long as *socialism* is redefined to render it compatible with the radical-democratic strategy outlined in this chapter. See "Socialism and Ecology: An Overview," *New Political Science* (Winter 1984).

24. April Carter, *Direct Action and Liberal Democracy* (London: Routledge & Kegan Paul, 1973), p. 27.

25. Ernesto Laclau and Chantal Mouffe, *Hegemony and Socialist Strategy: Toward a Radical-Democratic Politics* (London: Verso, 1985), p. 180.

26. Ibid., p. 142.

27. Claus Offe, "New Social Movements: Challenging the Boundaries of Institutional Politics," in *Social Research* (Winter 1985): 830–31.

28. Margit Mayer, "Urban Social Movements and Beyond: New Linkages Between Movement Sectors and the State in West Germany and the U.S." (unpublished paper, 1985).

29. See Nigel Young, "Why Do Peace Movements Fail? An Historical and Socio-logical Overview" (Oslo: International Peace Research Institute, Oct. 1983).

30. Raymond Williams, "Toward Many Socialisms," *Socialist Review* 85 (Jan.–Feb. 1986): 46–49.

31. Leo Panitch, "The Impasse of Working-Class Politics," *Socialist Register* (New York: Monthly Review Press, 1986).

32. On the role of direct-action politics in fostering personal empowerment see Barbara Epstein, "The Culture of Direct Action," *Socialist Review* (July–Oct. 1985).

ACRONYMS

ACORN	Association of Community Organizations for Reform Now
AFSCME	American Federation of State, County, and Municipal Employees
BCA	Berkeley Citizens Action
CDU	Christlich-Demokratische Union
	(German) Christian Democratic Union
CED	Campaign for Economic Democracy
CERES	Centre d'Études et Recherches Socialistes
	(French) Center for Socialist Study and Research
CFDT	Confédération Française Démocratique du Travail
	French Democratic Confederation of Labor
CGT	Confédération General du Travail
	(French) General Confederation of Labor
CND	Campaign for Nuclear Disarmament
COPS	Community Organization for Public Safety
DARE	Detroit Alliance for a Rational Economy
DC	Democrazia Christiana
	(Italian) Christian Democracy
DGB	Deutscher Gewerkschaftsbund
	German Trade Union Confederation
DSA	Democratic Socialists of America
EEC	European Economic Community
END	European Nuclear Disarmament
ETA	Euzkadi ta Azkatasuna
	Basque Nation and Liberty
FDP	Freie Demokratische Partei
	(German) Free Democratic Party
KKE	Kommunistiko Komma Elladas
	Greek Communist Party
PASOK	Panellenea Socialistiko Kinema
	Panhellenic Socialist Movement
PCE	Partido Communista Española
	Spanish Communist Party
PCF	Parti Communiste Français
	French Communist Party
PCI	Partito Comunista Italiano
	Italian Communist Party
PS	see PSF
PSF	Parti Socialiste Français
	French Socialist Party

PSI   Partito Socialista Italiano
           Italian Socialist Party
PSOE   Parti Socialista Obrera Española
           Spanish Socialist Workers Party
PSU   Parti Socialiste Unifie
           (French) Unified Socialist Party
SDS   Students for a Democratic Society
SFIO   Section Française de l'Internationale Ouvrière
           French Section of the Worker's International
SI   Socialist International
SMRR   Santa Monicans for Renters' Rights
SPD   Sozialdemokratische Partei Deutschlands
           Social Democratic Party of Germany
UDC   Unión de Centro Democrático
           (Spanish) Union of the Democratic Center
UGT   Unión General de Trabajadores
           (Spanish) General Union of Workers

INDEX